Lives of
The Saints

Lives of
The Saints

by

The Rev. Alban Butler

An illustrated abridged edition with an introduction by

The Rev. Dr. James Bentley

STUDIO

PUBLISHER'S NOTE

For this edition of Butler's *Lives of the Saints*, 235 entries have been chosen from the 535 in the 19th-century illustrated edition and have in some cases been considerably abridged, although every effort has been made to retain the style of the original work. The present selection indicates as far as possible the breadth of Butler's scholarship by including saints from different countries and different historical periods, as well as some of the important festivals of the Christian year. Half of the illustrations have been taken from the 19th-century edition, the others come from the manuscript collections of the British Library in London, and the Bodleian Library in Oxford.

The work of abridging, editing and picture research has been carried out by Christine O'Brien.

*Lives of the Saint*s is an abridged version of
Butler's *Lives of the Saints*, published in a two-volume
edition by J.S. Virtue & Co., Ltd,
London and Dublin, in 1883

This edition first published in 1990 by
Studio, an imprint of Random House UK Ltd,
20 Vauxhall Bridge Road, London SW1V 2SA

Copyright © 1990 Studio

Reprinted 1995, 1997

ISBN 1 85170 273 3

Printed and bound in Slovakia

CONTENTS

LIST OF ILLUSTRATIONS

INTRODUCTION

In 1745 Catholic France seemed for a moment likely to achieve her century-old ambition of transforming her Protestant neighbours, including Britain, into Catholic kingdoms. At Fontenoy in Flanders French troops managed to defeat a force of 15,000 soldiers under the command of the Portestant Duke of Cumberland, leaving 7,000 men on the British side dead or dying.

Alban Butler was at that time teaching at a Catholic college nearby. Though among the most devout Catholic priests of his age and one who certainly shared the French hopes that one day his native England would return to the Catholic fold, he was also a man of deep compassion for his fellow men and women and especially for his fellow Englishmen. When the victorious French brought wounded English prisoners to Douai, Butler instantly set out to comfort them. His exertions so impressed Cumberland that the Duke promised to care especially for Alban Butler should he ever return to his native land. The promise was a generous one. Catholics had once evoked hatred in many English breasts. As Butler well knew, laws penalizing them still lay on the English statute books.

He had been born in Northamptonshire in 1711, the second of three sons of Catholic parents. Simon and Ann Butler decided to have the young Alban educated in Lancashire, long a stronghold of Catholicism. The young boy seen developed a precocious love both for literature and for religious history. When he was barely eight years old his parents agreed to further Alban's education by sending him abroad, to study at Douai in Flanders. There an English college had been set up in 1568 to train learned priests who would later return to their native land as Catholic missionaries.

Both Ann and Simon Butler died shortly after the boy reached Douai. Living up to all his early promise, Alban was ordained priest in 1735. His career blossomed, and soon the English college recognized his qualities by appointing him first as professor of philosophy and then professor of divinity, which post he was holding at the time of the vicious battle of Fontenoy. He began to publish learned and spiritual books. But his chief ambition was to study the lives of the saints, planning to write the superb work which made his name.

Alban Butler adored reading. 'When he was alone, he read,' his nephew remembered; 'when he was in company, he read; at his meals, he read; when he was in his carriage, he read; when he was on horseback, he read; whatever he did, he read.' Since Butler spoke Italian, French and Spanish, and also read Latin and Greek, he searched out both ancient and modern literature in the quest to know more and more about his beloved saints. In 1616 Belgian scholars had begun scouring the great libraries of Europe for information, legends and tales of the saint. They and their successors had published forty-one volumes of these by Butler's time. He knew them all.

Eventually his superiors sent their remarkable professor back to England to serve as a missionary priest. Naturally Alban wished to work near London, where he could find more books about the saints who were the passion of his life. Instead his bishop ordered him to work in Staffordshire, his mother's home county. In distress, Butler begged not to go; the bishop insisted; after half-an-hour's prayer, the humble scholar agreed. Next he was sent as a tutor in the household of the Catholic Duke of Norfolk. Now Cumberland's promise was to be fulfilled. Several large boxes containing Alban's precious books were sent not to the palace of Butler's patron but to that of the hostile Bishop of Norfolk. Realizing that these were the property of one of his religious opponents, the bishop refused to hand them over to their rightful owner. Alban Butler appealed to Cumberland, Cumberland wrote to the bishop insisting on Alban's rights, and the bishop gave way.

After thirty years' labour, Alban Butler felt ready to publish his life's work. The first edition appeared in London anonymously. Even the printer judged it wiser not to add his own name. Under the title *The Lives of the Fathers, Martyrs, and other principal Saints*, two massive volumes appeared in 1756, followed by three more between 1757 and 1759. They would have been even bulkier of Butler had been given his own way, but he was persuaded reluctantly to omit his copious scholarly notes.

The *Lives of the Saints*, as the book has come to be known, included biographies of around 1,600 revered men and women of Christian history whose varied, sometimes dangerous lives had made the church on earth judge them especially worthy of imitation and veneration. It was immediately acclaimed, a twelve-volume edition soon appearing in Dublin and a similar one in Edinburgh. The French translated it. So did the Italians. Since some of these editions included notes Butler was forced to leave out of the first one, we can through them properly appreciate the immense and loving scholarship which he put into his work.

Yet the *Lives of the Saints* is in no way the work of a boring pedant. Alban Butler was both a born teacher, a beautiful writer and a man of translucent faith. For these reasons his work has influenced and delighted generations of Catholics and (as we shall see) non-Catholics alike. In his own words, his aim was to furnish his readers 'with a daily spiritual entertainment'. Butler appreciated what he called 'the most attractive charms of history', and in recounting the histories of the Christian saints he wished to use these charms for the spiritual well-being of his readers.

As Butler's own glittering words expressed it, the saints were 'the greatest personages who have adorned the world, the brightest ornaments of the church militant, the shining stars and suns of the church triumphant, and our future companions in eternal glory'. From their penitential lives and holy maxims he wished to learn how to live a virtuous life. But virtue, as he knew, can appear 'barren and dry'. Her influence, he insisted, must be communicated with pleasure, 'animated and living, arrayed with all her charms, exerting all her powers'. So this saintly man who had loved literature from childhood, used every ounce of literary skill to beguile his readers. It is the product of this skill that has been distilled in the present volume, abridging Alban Butler, but never losing the essence or charm of his own prose.

Would Butler have approved? No doubt remembering his chagrin at having his scholarly notes exercised from the first edition of his work, Butler once wrote with justifiable acerbity that 'Authors who polish the style, or abridge the histories of others, are seldom to be trusted.' The word 'seldom' ought to excuse this abridgment, for two reasons. First it follows his own habit of arranging the saints in accordance with the Christian year (though as set out by the churches today, rather than in the eighteenth century). Secondly, it carefully retains Butler's own entrancing style.

In this second virtue, this abridgment is unique. Others have supposedly abridged Butler while completely destroying his style. Half a century ago, for instance, the Jesuit scholar Fr. Herbert Thurston and the hagiographer Mr. Donald Attwater, collaborated on a twelve-volume edition of Butler which staggeringly retained scarcely anything of the original. Fr. Thurston even confessed to the belief that Butler's style was 'deplorably stilted and verbose', and Mr. Attwater went so far as to dub Butler's manner of writing as 'tiresome'.

The truth is that Bulter's generation produced some of the greatest British prose stylists – Gibbon, Hume, Pope, Johnson, Swift, Walpole, to name a few. Butler has his honoured place amongst them. I have already quoted some of his gems, and readers will relish his skills in the body of this book; but I cannot resist adding a lapidary sentence from his description of St. Elizabeth of Hungary, who though a queen made her own simple clothing and cooked her own meals. 'Whilst her hands were busy,' wrote Butler, 'her heart conversed with God.'

Edward Gibbon, the greatest stylist of the age, and no friend to Catholicism, paid Butler the compliment of describing his *Lives of the Saints* as a work of merit, of sense and of learning. Gibbon added, 'his prejudices are those of his profession.' Even the second remark was an oblique compliment. Of course butler believed in miracles, in the papacy, in the efficacy of the sacraments, in the teachings of the Catholic church. But whenever he considered something manifestly untrue or historically dubious about a saint, he never hesistated to say so.

As later generations delved into his *Lives of the Saints*, they also grew to love a series of beautifully printed illustrations, done in the medieval style to illustrate his text. Today these have taken on a delicious period charm. They embellish this book, and the publishers have sought out more illustrations, this time authentically medieval ones yet similar enough in spirit to the former as not to clash with them.

While recounting the exploits of his heroes, this book also breathes the piety and goodness of Alban Butler himself. Although all Catholics of his generation regarded Protestants as heretics, his *Lives of the Saints* immediately began to speak across denominational divides. One of his earliest admirers was an Anglican clergymen, the Revd. William Cole, Rector of Bletchley and Vicar of Burnham Beeches. Having bought and eagerly read all four volumes of the first edition of the book, Cole determined to call on the author, who was now president of the English college at Saint-Omer in northern France. Butler insisted that his Anglican admirer stay not in an inn but in the college itself, sending for Cole's portmanteau and servant and bidding them sup with him. Cole returned to England overwhelmed with Butler's kindness, grateful to have been shown every part of the college, marvelling that 'it is probable that I was the first priest of the Church of England that ever slept within those walls.' As for Butler, he wrote to his guest, 'I shall always think myself much obliged to your goodness in accepting our humble lodging.'

Alban Butler had seven more years to live. Accepting without vainglory offices from the Bishops of Saint-Omer, Arras, Ypres, and Boulogne-sur-Mer, he could still be seen walking down the street with one book under his nose and a couple more under each arm. On 15 May 1773 he died. Hundreds wept as they lined the streets of the old walled town, watching his body carried in procession and laid to rest close by where he used to hear their confessions. Describing the scene, the English mother of one of his young charges wrote, 'Dear Mr. Butler, he died like a saint and when his speeches failed ye tears of Devotion streamed down his face. With his Eyes Lifted up to Heaven he quitted this miserable World.' In the *Lives of the Saints* he lives on.

James Bentley
October 1989

2 JANUARY

St. Basil

THE GREAT, ARCHBISHOP OF CAESAREA
A.D. 379

St. Basil, doctor of the church, was born in the year 329 at Caesarea, the metropolis of Cappadocia. When he had made himself master of whatever the schools of Caesarea and Constantinople were able to teach him, the thirst after learning carried him to Athens. St. Basil, who had first met St. Gregory Nazianzen at Caesarea, was overjoyed to find so worthy a friend at Athens in 352. They had the same lodging and seemed to have but one will. St. Basil was an adept in all the liberal arts and sciences. He was soon regarded at Athens as an oracle; but he thought it incumbent upon him to serve his own country. Wherefore, leaving St. Gregory some time behind him, he went from Athens in 355 and repaired to Caesarea, where he opened a school of oratory. Seeing himself received with the greatest applause, he felt his heart assaulted by a temptation to vain-glory, and shortly after determined to renounce the world. He gave away the greatest part of his estate and embraced the state of a poor monk.

St. Basil in 357 travelled over Syria, Mesopotamia and Egypt and visited the most celebrated monasteries, instructing himself in all the duties of a monastic life. In 358 he returned to Cappadocia, was ordained reader, and retired into Pontus to the house of his grandmother on the banks of the river Iris. St. Basil established a monastery on the opposite side of the river, which he governed for five years, till in 362 he resigned the abbacy to St. Peter of Sebaste. St. Basil founded several other monasteries, both of men and women, in different parts of Pontus, which he continued to superintend even when he was bishop. The rule of St. Basil is followed to this day by the oriental monks. Nazianzen followed Basil into his retirement in Pontus.

In 362 Basil returned to Caesarea and continued the same manner of life in the city, except that to his other labours he added that of preaching to the people. Eusebius, the bishop, had raised him to the priesthood, but afterwards fell out with him and removed him from his church. The saint withdrew and returned to Pontus, where he recovered again the company of St. Gregory. Returning to Caesarea, after three years, to defend the church against the Arians, he was consecrated archbishop. Reeking with the blood of many martyrs, the Emperor Valens passed through several provinces, blasting them with Arianism, and arrived in Cappadocia. He sent before him the Prefect Modestus who summoned Basil to appear before him. To the angry words of Modestus, Basil replied, 'You may threaten and torment us, but can never overcome us.' And Valens laid aside all further attempts upon him. In 378 peace was restored to the church by the Emperor Gratian. St. Basil fell sick the same year and departed this life on the 1st of January, 379.

PLATE 1. ST. BASIL, 2 JANUARY. BRITISH LIBRARY, EGERTON MS 859, F. 16.

3 JANUARY

St. Genevieve

OR GENOVEFA, CHIEF PATRONESS OF THE CITY
OF PARIS

SIXTH CENTURY

Genevieve's father's name was Severus and her mother's Geron-tia. She was born about 422 at Nanterre, a small village four miles from Paris. When St. Germanus, Bishop of Auxerre, went with St. Lupus into Britain to oppose the Pelagian heresy he lay at Nanterre in his way. The inhabitants flocked about them to receive their blessing and St. Germanus took particular notice of Genevieve, though only seven years of age. After his discourse he inquired for her parents and addressing himself to them foretold their daughter's future sanctity. He then asked Genevieve whether it was not her desire to serve God in a state of perpetual virginity. The virgin answered that this was what she had long desired. The bishop gave her a brass medal on which a cross was engraved to wear always about her neck.

At about fifteen years of age she was presented to the Bishop of Paris to receive the religious veil at his hand. From that time she frequently ate only twice in the week, on Sundays and Thursdays. Her food was barley bread with a few beans. At the age of fifty she mitigated this austerity at the command of certain bishops so far as to allow herself moderate use of fish and milk. Her prayer was almost continual and generally attended with a large flow of tears. After the death of her parents she settled with her grandmother at Paris. God permitted her to meet with some severe trials; for at a certain time all persons seemed to be in a combination against her. Her enemies were fully determined to drown her, when the Archdeacon of Auxerre arrived with blessed bread sent her by St. Germanus, as a testimony of his esteem for her virtues. This converted the prejudices of her calumniators into a singular veneration for her during the rest of her life. The Franks had then possessed themselves of the better part of Gaul, and Childeric, their king, took Paris. During the long blockade of that city the citizens being extremely distressed by famine St Genevieve went out at the head of a company to procure provisions and brought back several boats laden with corn. Nevertheless Childeric, though always a pagan, respected St. Genevieve and upon her interces-sion spared the lives of many prisoners.

Upon the report of the march of Attila with his army of Huns, the Parisians were preparing to abandon their city, but St Genevieve persuaded them to endeavour to avert the scourge by fasting, watching and prayer. Though she was long treated by many as an impostor, the event verified the prediction, that barbarian suddenly changing the course of his march. St. Genevieve died on the 3rd of January 512, being eighty-nine years old. The people raised an oratory of wood over her tomb and this was soon changed into the stately church built under the invocation of SS. Peter and Paul.

5 JANUARY

St. Simeon

STYLITES

A.D. 459

St. Simeon was son to a poor shepherd in Cilicia on the borders of Syria and at first kept his father's sheep. Being only thirteen years of age he was much moved by hearing the beatitudes one day read in church. The youth addressed himself to a certain old man to learn the meaning of these words. He told him that continual prayer, watching, fasting, humiliation and patient suffering were pointed out by those texts as the road to true happiness.

Simeon repaired to a monastery in that neighbourhood and lay prostrate at the gate for several days without eating or drinking, begging to be admitted on the footing of the lowest servant of the house. His petition was granted. Having here spent two years he removed to the monastery of Heliodorus. Here Simeon much increased his mortifications. Judging the rough rope of the well a proper instrument of penance, he tied it close about his naked body, where it remained till such time as it having eaten into his flesh what he had privately done was discovered by the stench proceeding from his wound. On his recovery, the abbot, to prevent the ill consequences such a dangerous singularity might occasion to the prejudice of uni-formity in monastic discipline, dismissed him.

After this he repaired to an hermitage at the foot of Mount Thelanissa, where he came to the resolution of passing the whole forty days of Lent in total abstinence. This was his method of keeping Lent during the remainder of his life. After three years spent in this hermitage, the saint removed to the top of the same mountain where, throwing together some loose stones in the form of a wall, he made for himself an enclosure, but without any roof to protect him from the weather; and to confirm his resolution of pursuing this manner of life, he fastened his right leg to a rock with a great iron chain. Meletius, vicar to the Patriarch of Antioch, told him that a firm will was sufficient without recourse to bodily restraint; hereupon the obedient servant of God sent for a smith and had his chain knocked off.

The mountain began to be thronged and the retreat his soul so much sighted after to be interrupted by the multitudes that flocked to receive his benediction. In 423 he erected a pillar six cubits high and on it dwelt four years; on a second twelve cubits, he lived three years; on a third twenty-two cubits, ten years, and on a fourth forty cubits high, the last twenty-seven years of his life. Thus he lived thirty-seven years on pillars and was called Stylites from the Greek word *stylos* which signifies a pillar. Many were converted by his miracles and discourses which they crowded to hear. In 459, on the 2nd of September, this incomparable penitent, bowing on a pillar as if intent on prayer, gave up the ghost in the sixty-ninth year of his age.

PLATE 2. ST. GENEVIEVE, 3 JANUARY. BUTLER, *LIVES OF THE SAINTS*, TWO-VOLUME ILLUSTRATED 19TH-CENTURY EDITION.

6 JANUARY

THE EPIPHANY OF OUR LORD

Epiphany, which in the original Greek signifies appearance or manifestation, is a festival principally solemnized in honour of the discovery Jesus Christ made of himself to the Magi, or wise men; who, soon after his birth, by a particular inspiration of Almighty God, came to adore him and bring him presents.

Two other manifestations of our Lord are jointly commemorated on this day in the office of the church: that at his baptism, when the Holy Ghost descended on him in the visible form of a dove, and a voice from heaven was heard at the same time: 'This is my beloved Son, in whom I am well pleased.' The third manifestation was that of his divine power at the performance of his first miracle, the changing of water into wine, at the marriage of Cana.

The summons of the Gentiles to Bethlehem to pay homage to the world's Redeemer was obeyed by several whom the Scripture mentions under the name and title of Magi; but is silent as to their number. The general opinion declares for three. The wise men being come by the guidance of the star into Jerusalem, or near it, it there disappears: whereupon they reasonably suppose they are come to their journey's end and that, on entering the royal city, they shall in every street hear the acclamations of a happy people and learn the way to the royal palace made famous by the birth of their king. But to their great surprise the court and city go quietly on. Steady in the resolution of following the divine call they inquire in the city and in the very court of Herod, and quickly learn from the Sanhedrim, or great council of the Jews, that Bethlehem was the place which was to be honoured with the birth of the Messiah.

The Magi, pursuant to the custom of the eastern nations, where great princes are not to be approached without presents, present to Jesus, as a token of homage, gold, as an acknowledgement of his regal power; incense as a confession of his Godhead; and myrrh, as a testimony that he was become man for the redemption of the world. The holy kings, being about to return home, God by a particular intimation diverted them from their purpose of carrying back word to Jerusalem where the child was to be found, and they took another road into their own country.

The ancient author of the imperfect comment on St. Matthew says they were afterwards baptized in Persia, by St. Thomas the apostle, and became themselves preachers of the gospel. Their bodies were said to have been translated to Constantinople under the first Christian emperors. From thence they were conveyed to Milan. The Emperor Barbarossa having taken Milan, caused them to be translated to Cologne in the twelfth century.

PLATE 3. THE ADORATION OF THE MAGI, 6 JANUARY. BRITISH LIBRARY, ADD. MSS 54782, F. 119V.

7 JANUARY (23 JANUARY)

St. Raymund
OF PEÑAFORT
A.D. 1275

Raymund was born in 1175 at Peñafort, a castle in Catalonia. Such was his rapid progress in his studies that at the age of twenty he taught philosophy at Barcelona. He was about thirty when he went to Bologna to perfect himself in the study of canon and civil law. In 1219 Berengarius, Bishop of Barcelona, who had been bishop at Rome, took Raymund home with him and made him archdeacon. In 1221 he took the religious habit of St. Dominic at Barcelona. In a spirit of compunction he begged of his superiors that they would enjoin him in some severe penance. They indeed imposed on him a penance, but not such a one as he expected. It was to write a collection of cases of conscience for the instruction of confessors and moralists. This produced his *Sum*, the first work of that kind.

Pope Gregory IX, having called St. Raymund to Rome in 1230, nominated him his chaplain, made him his own confessarius and in difficult affairs came to no decision but by his advice. The pope ordered the saint to gather into one body all the scattered decrees of popes and councils, since the collection made by Gratian in 1150. Raymund compiled this work in three years, in five books, commonly called the *Decretals*.

For his health he returned to his native country and, being restored to his dear solitude at Barcelona, he continued his former exercises of contemplation, preaching and administering the sacrament of penance. He was employed frequently in important commissions, both by the holy see and by the king. But he was thunderstruck by the arrival of four deputies from the general chapter of his Order in 1238 with the news that he was chosen third general. He wept and entreated but at length acquiesced. He made the visitation of the order on foot and reduced the constitutions into a clearer method, with notes on the doubtful passages. This, his code of rules, was approved in three general chapters. In one held at Paris in 1239 he procured that a voluntary demission of a superior, founded upon just reasons, should be accepted. This he contrived in his own favour; for, to the extreme regret of the Order, he in the year following resigned the generalship, which he had held only two years. He alleged for his reason his age of sixty-five years.

Rejoicing to see himself again a private religious man, he applied himself to the conversion of the Saracens. Having this end in view, he engaged St. Thomas to write his work *Against the Gentiles* and erected convents among the Moors. In 1256 he wrote to his general that ten thousand had received baptism. During his last illness Alphonsus, King of Castile, and his family visited him and received his last benediction. Raymund gave up his soul to God on the 6th of January in the year 1275 and the hundredth of his age.

10 JANUARY (15 JANUARY)

St. Paul
THE FIRST HERMIT
A.D. 342

This saint was a native of the Lower Egypt, and had lost both his parents when he was but fifteen: nevertheless he was a great proficient in the Greek and Egyptian languages and feared God from his earliest youth. The bloody persecution of Decius disturbed the peace of the church in 250; and during these times of danger Paul kept himself concealed in the house of another. But, finding that a brother-in-law was inclined to betray him that he might enjoy his estate, he fled into the desert. He chose for his dwelling a cave near which were a palm tree and a clear spring; the former by its leaves furnished him with raiment, and by its fruit with food; and the latter supplied him with water for his drink.

Paul was twenty-two when he entered the desert. His first intention was to enjoy liberty till the persecution should cease; but relishing the advantages of solitude, he resolved to return no more among men. He lived on his tree till he was forty-three, and from that time till his death he was miraculously fed with bread brought him every day by a raven.

The great St. Antony, who was then ninety, was commanded by God to set out in quest of a perfect servant of his, concealed in the more remote parts of those deserts. After two days and a night spent in the search he discovered the saint's abode, and having long begged admittance at the door, St. Paul at last opened it with a smile. While they were discoursing together, a raven flew towards them and dropped a loaf of bread. Having given thanks to God they sat down by the fountain; but a little contest arose between them who should break the bread; St. Antony alleged St. Paul's greater age, and St. Paul pleaded that St. Antony was the stranger. Both agreed at last to take up their parts together.

The next morning St. Paul told his guest that the time of his death approached, adding 'Go and fetch the cloak given you by St. Athanasius, in which I desire you to wrap my body.' St. Antony hastened to his monastery and, having taken the cloak, returned with it in all haste fearing lest the hermit might be dead. When he came to the cave he found the body kneeling and the hands stretched out. Supposing him yet alive, he knelt down to pray with him, but by his silence soon perceived he was dead. Whilst St Antony stood perplexed how to dig a grave, two lions came up quietly and, tearing up the ground, made a hole large enough for a human body. St. Antony returned home, and always kept as a great treasure, and wore himself on great festivals, the garment of St. Paul of palm-leaves patched together. St. Paul died in 342.

[Editorial note: the cult of St. Paul was suppressed in the Roman church in 1969.]

PLATE 4. ST. PAUL WITH ST. ANTONY, 10 JANUARY. BODLEIAN LIBRARY, MS DOUCE 223, F. 12V.

11 JANUARY

St. Theodosius

THE CENOBIARCH
A.D. 529

St. Theodosius was born in Cappadocia in 423. He was ordained reader, but being moved to quit his country, he set out for Jerusalem, going out of his way to visit the famous St. Simeon Stylites on his pillar. Having visited the holy places he put himself under the directions of a holy man named Longinus, to whom his virtue soon endeared him. A pious lady having built a church on the road to Bethlehem, Longinus could not well refuse her request that his pupil should undertake the charge of it; but Theodosius could not be induced to obey. Absolute commands were necessary to force him to a compliance. Nor did he govern long. He retired into a cave at the top of a neighbouring desert. Many desired to serve God under his direction; he at first determined to admit six or seven, but was soon obliged to receive a greater number and at length came to a resolution never to reject any.

He built a spacious monastery not far from Bethlehem, at a small distance from his cave and it was soon filled with holy monks. To this monastery were annexed three infirmaries, one for the sick, one for the aged and feeble, the other for such as

had lost their senses, and several buildings for the reception of strangers. The monastery was like a city of saints in the midst of a desert. There were four churches belonging to it, one for each of the three nations of which his community was chiefly composed; the fourth for the use of such as were in a state of penance. Sallust, bishop of Jerusalem, appointed St. Sabas superior general of the hermits, and our saint of the Cenobites, or religious men living in community throughout Palestine, whence he was styled the cenobiarch.

The Emperor Anastasius patronized the Eutychian heresy and used all possible means to engage our saint in his party. He sent Theodosius a considerable sum of money. The saint distributed it among the poor. Anastasius now persuading himself that he was as good as gained to his cause, sent him an heretical profession of faith. The saint wrote him an answer in which, besides confuting the Eutychian error, he added that he was ready to lay down his life for the faith of the church. Theodosius went over all Palestine exhorting every one to be firm in the faith of the four general councils. The emperor sent an order for his banishment, which was executed; but dying soon after, Theodosius was recalled by his successor Justin.

Our saint survived his return eleven years. During the last year of his life he was afflicted with a painful distemper, in which he gave proof of an heroic patience. Perceiving the hour of his dissolution at hand, he gave his last exhortations to his disciples. His death happened in the one hundredth and fifth year of his age and of our Lord 529.

12 JANUARY	13 JANUARY (14 JANUARY)

St. Benedict

BISCOP, COMMONLY CALLED BENNET

A.D. 690

St. Hilary

BISHOP

A.D. 368

Benedict was nobly descended and one of the officers of the court of Oswi, the King of the Northumbers. At the age of twenty-five he made a journey to Rome and at his return devoted himself wholly to the studies of the scriptures and other holy exercises. Some time after, our saint travelled thither a second time, and from Rome he went to the great monastery of Lérins and there took the monastic habit. After this he returned to Rome where he received an order to accompany St. Theodorus and St. Adrian to England. St. Bennet stayed about two years in Kent. Then he took a fourth journey to Rome with a view of perfecting himself in the rules of monastic life, for which purpose he made a considerable stay at Rome and other places. He brought home with him a choice library, relics and pictures.

When he returned to Northumberland King Egfrid (who had succeeded Oswi) bestowed on him seventy ploughs of land for building a monastery. This the saint founded on the mouth of the river Wear. When the monastery was built St. Bennet went to France and brought back skilful masons who built the church of stone after the Roman fashion, and glaziers, for the art of making glass was then unknown in Britain. In a fifth journey to Rome he furnished himself with a stock of good books.

His first monastery of Wearmouth was entitled from St. Peter; and such was the edification which it gave that the king added a second donation of lands on which Biscop built another monastery at Jarrow, called St. Paul's. These two monasteries were almost looked upon as one. St. Bennet governed them both, though he placed in each a superior or abbot who continued subject to him.

St. Bennet brought from Rome in his last voyage, John, precentor in St. Peter's church, whom he placed at Wearmouth to instruct his monks in the Gregorian notes and Roman ceremonies for singing the divine office. Being struck with a dead palsy, by which all the lower parts of his body were without life, he lay sick three years, and for a considerable time was entirely confined to his bed. During this long illness, not being able to raise his voice to the usual course of singing the divine office, he sent for some of his monks, and whilst they sung the psalms proper for the day or night, he endeavoured to join his heart with theirs. He earnestly exhorted his monks to a constant observance of the rule he had given them. 'You must not think that the constitutions you have received from me were my own invention; for having in my frequent journeys visited seventeen monasteries I informed myself of all their laws and rules, and picking out the best among them, these I have recommended to you.' The saint expired soon after, on the 12th of January, in 690.

St. Hilary was born at Poitiers and his family was one of the most illustrious in Gaul. He himself testifies that he was brought up in idolatry and gives a particular account of the steps by which God conducted him to the knowledge of his faith. He was married before his conversion, and his wife, by whom he had a daughter, was yet living when he was chosen Bishop of Poitiers about the year 353; but from the time of his ordination he lived in perpetual continency. He omitted no endeavours to escape promotion; but his humility only made the people the more earnest to see him vested with dignity. Soon after he was raised to the episcopal dignity he composed elegant comments on the gospel of St. Matthew. Those on the Psalms he compiled after his banishment. From that time the Arian controversy chiefly employed his pen.

The Emperor Constantine, having laboured for several years to compel the eastern churches to embrace Arianism, came into the west. The Arian council at Milan in 355 required all to sign the condemnation of St. Athanasius. St. Hilary wrote on that occasion his first book to Constantius in which he entreated him to restore peace to the church. But the emperor sent an order for St. Hilary's immediate banishment into Phrygia. He remained in exile upwards of three years, which time he employed in composing several learned works. The principal and most esteemed of these is that *On the Trinity*.

The emperor, by an unjust usurpation in the affairs of the church, assembled a council of Arians at Seleucia to undermine the great council of Nicaea. St. Hilary was invited thither by the Semi-Arians who hoped that he would be useful in crushing the staunch Arians. But he boldly defended the decrees, till tired out with hearing the blasphemies of the heretics, he withdrew to Constantinople.

St. Hilary presented to the emperor his second book to Constantius, begging the liberty of holding a public disputation with Saturninus, the author of his banishment. The Arians, dreading such a trial, persuaded the emperor to rid the east of a man that never ceased to disturb its peace by sending Hilary back to Gaul.

St. Hilary returned through Illyricum and Italy to confirm the weak. He was received at Poitiers with great joy. A synod in Gaul convoked at his instance condemned that of Rimini. Saturninus was excommunicated. Scandals were removed and piety flourished. The death of Constantine put an end to the Arian persecution. Our saint undertook a journey to Milan in 364 against Auxentius, the Arian usurper of that see, and in a public disputation obliged him to confess Christ to be true God, of the same substance and divinity with the Father. Our saint died at Poitiers in the year 368, on the 13th of January or on the 1st of November, for his name occurs in very ancient martyrologies on both these days.

14 JANUARY (13 JANUARY)

St. Kentigern

BISHOP OF GLASCO, SURNAMED MUNGHO
SIXTH CENTURY

This eminent saint of North Britain was of royal blood and born about the year 516. He was placed very young under the discipline of St. Servanus, Abbot of Culross. For his innocence and great virtues, he was beloved by his master and his fellow disciples, for which reason he was called Mungho which signified 'one dearly beloved', and this is the name the Scots usually give him.

When he was grown up he retired to a place called Glasco where he led a solitary life in great abstinence, till the clergy and people earnestly demanded him for their bishop. He was consecrated by an Irish bishop, invited over for that purpose, and fixed his see at Glasco where he assembled a numerous company of religious brethren, who formed their rule of life upon the model of the primitive Christians at Jerusalem. The saint's diocese was of vast extent, reaching from sea to sea, and being wild and uncultivated, afforded continual exercises for his zeal and patience; he travelled always on foot, sparing no pains to spread the light of the gospel amongst the unbelievers, of whom he converted and baptized great numbers. The Pelagian heresy having taken deep root among the Christians in those parts, he so vigorously opposed that evil as entirely to banish it from the church of the Picts. Out of his monks and disciples, he sent many missionaries to preach the faith in the north of Scotland, in the isles of Orkney, in Norway and Iceland.

There happened about that time several revolutions in the monarchy. Rydderch, a religious and deserving prince, was obliged by rebellious subjects under Morcant Mawr to fly into Ireland. In the beginning of the usurpation of Morcant Mawr, St. Kentigern was obliged to fly into Wales, where he stayed some time with St. David, till Cathwallain, a religious prince of part of Denbighshire, bestowed on him the land at the meeting of the rivers Elwy and Cluid, on which he built a famous monastery and school, called Elgwy, where a great number of disciples and scholars soon put themselves under his direction.

After the death of Morcant, Rydderch returned from Ireland, and St. Kentigern went back to Glasco, taking with him several hundreds of his scholars, their number having probably much increased after the death of Daniel, Bishop of Bangor, which happened between 542 and 545. The return of Kentigern is generally placed about 560, nor can it be later, since in 565 he had a conference with St. Columba, when that holy man came to Scotland. King Rydderch powerfully seconded the zeal of our saint in all his undertakings, being his constant friend and protector; as were the two princes who afterwards succeeded him.

St. Kentigern employed his zeal with wonderful success in correcting abuses, reforming the manners of his flock and propagating the faith, and died in 601, aged eighty-five years.

16 JANUARY

St. Honoratus

ARCHBISHOP OF ARLES
FIFTH CENTURY

Honoratus was of a consular Roman family, then settled in Gaul, and was well versed in the liberal arts. In his youth he renounced the worship of idols, and gained his elder brother Venantius to Christ, whom he also inspired with a contempt of the world. They desired to renounce it entirely, but a fond pagan father put continual obstacles in their way; at length they took with them St. Caprais, a holy hermit, for their director, and sailed from Marseilles to Greece, with the design to live there, unknown, in some desert.

Venantius soon died happily at Methone; and Honoratus, being also sick, was obliged to return with his conductor. He first led an eremitical life in the mountains, near Fréjus. Two small islands lie in the sea near that coast; the larger, at a nearer distance from the continent, called Lero, now St Margaret's, the other smaller and more remote, two leagues from Antibes, named Lérins, at present St. Honoré, from our saint, where he settled; and, being followed by others, he there founded the famous monastery of Lérins, about the year 400.

Some he appointed to live in community; others, who seemed more perfect, in separate cells, as anchorites. His rule was chiefly borrowed from that of St. Pachomius. Nothing can be more amiable than the description St. Hilary has given of the excellent virtues of this company of saints, especially of the charity, concord, humility, compunction and devotion which reigned amongst them, under the conduct of our holy abbot.

He was by compulsion consecrated Archbishop of Arles in 426, and died exhausted with austerities and apostolic labours in 429. The style of his letters was clear and affecting; they were penned with admirable delicacy, elegance and sweetness, as St. Hilary assures. The loss of all these precious monuments is much regretted. His tomb is shown empty under the high altar of the church which bears his name at Arles, his body having been translated to Lérins in 1391, where the greatest part remains.

17 JANUARY

St. Antony

ABBOT, PATRIARCH OF MONKS
A.D. 356

St. Antony was born at Coma in Upper Egypt in 251. His parents, who were Christians, to prevent his being tainted by bad example, kept him always at home. By their death he found himself possessed of a considerable estate and charged with the care of a younger sister, before he was twenty. Near six months after, he heard those words of Christ, 'Go sell what thou hast and give it to the poor, and thou shalt have treasure in heaven.' He made over to his neighbours one hundred and twenty acres of good land; the rest of his estate he sold, except what he thought necessary for himself and his sister. Soon after, hearing those other words of Christ 'Be not solicitous for tomorrow', he also distributed in alms the movables he had reserved and

PLATE 5. ST. ANTONY, ABBOT, 17 JANUARY. BODLEIAN LIBRARY, MS. ADD. A 185, F. 64.

placed his sister in a house of virgins, which most take to be the first instance in history of a nunnery. Antony himself retired into a solitude near his village in imitation of a certain old man who led the life of a hermit.

The devil assailed him by various temptations and annoyed him night and day with filthy thoughts till Satan at length confessed himself vanquished. In quest of a more remote solitude Antony hid himself in an old sepulchre, till, resolving to withdraw into the deserts about the year 285, he crossed the Nile and took up his abode on top of the mountains where he lived almost twenty years.

To satisfy the importunities of others, about the year 305, he came down from his mountain and founded his first monastery at Phaium. In 311, when Maximinus renewed his persecution, St. Antony went to Alexandria, served and encouraged the martyrs. In 312, the persecution being abated, he returned to his monastery. Some time after, he built another monastery near the Nile, but chose for the most part to shut himself up in a remote cell upon a mountain of difficult access.

At the request of the bishops about the year 355 he took a journey to Alexandria to confound the Arians. All the people ran to see him, even the pagans, and he converted many. Heathen philosphers often went to dispute with him, and always returned astonished at his wisdom. About the year 337 Constantine the Great and his two sons wrote a joint letter to the saint, recommending themselves to his prayers.

St. Antony visited his monks a little before his death, but no tears could move him to die among them, and he ordered that his body should be buried in the earth on his mountain by his two disciples who had remained with him the last fifteen years. He hastened back to that solitude and, some time after, fell sick. His death happened in the year 356, probably on the 17th of January, on which the most ancient martyrologies name him. He was one hundred and five years old.

19 JANUARY

St. Canutus

KING OF DENMARK
A.D. 1086

St. Canutus, or Knut, was natural son of Swein III, whose great uncle Canutus had reigned in England. Swein, having no lawful issue, took care of his education. The kingdom of Denmark was elective; wherefore when Swein died, many pitched upon our saint, whose virtues best qualified him for the throne; but the majority, fearing his martial spirit, preferred his eldest natural brother Harald, who for his stupidity and vices was commonly called the Slothful. Canutus retired into Sweden, and Harald dying after two years reign, was called to succeed him.

Denmark had received the Christian faith long before, but wanted a zealous hand to put the finishing stroke to that good work. St. Canutus began his reign by a successful war against the troublesome enemies of the state and by planting the faith in the conquered provinces. Amidst the glory of his victories he humbly prostrated himself at the foot of the crucifix, laying there his diadem and offering himself and his kingdom to the King of kings. He then married Alice, daughter of Robert, Earl of Flanders, by whom he had a pious son, St Charles.

His next concern was to reform abuses at home. For this purpose he granted many privileges and immunities to the clergy, showed a royal magnificence in building and adorning churches and gave the crown which he wore to the church of Roskilde, in Zealand, his capital city and the place of his residence, where the kings of Denmark are yet buried. When William the Conqueror had made himself master of England, Canutus sent forces to assist the vanquished but these troops, finding no one willing to join them, were easily defeated in 1069. Some time after, being invited by the conquered English, he raised an army to invade and expel the Normans; but through the treacherous practices of his brother Olas was obliged to wait so long on the coast that his troops deserted him. The king proposed to them either to pay a heavy fine by way of punishment for their desertion, or to submit to the law of tithes for the pastors of the church. Their aversion to the latter made them choose the tax to the great mortification of the king, who ordered it to be levied with vigour. They rebelled and St. Canutus retired for safety into the Isle of Fyn where he went to the church of St Alban. The rebels surrounded the church and threw in bricks and stones, by which they beat down the shrines of certain relics which Canutus had brought from England. The saint, stretching out his arms before the altar, was wounded with a javelin, darted through a window, and fell a victim to Christ. His brother Benedict and seven others were slain with him on the 10th of July, 1086.

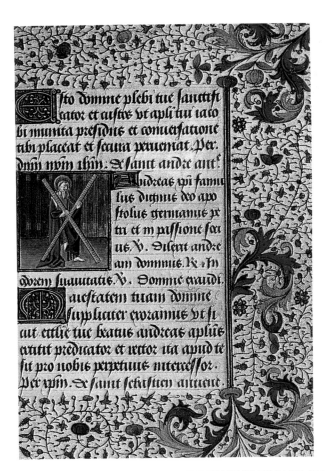

PLATE 6. ST. SEBASTIAN, 20 JANUARY. BODLEIAN LIBRARY, MS. ADD. A 185, F. 60.

20 JANUARY

St. Sebastian

MARTYR
A.D. 288

St. Sebastian was born at Narbonne, in Gaul, but his parents were of Milan and he was brought up in that city. He was a fervent servant of Christ, and though his natural inclinations gave him an aversion to a military life, yet to be better able to assist the confessors and martyrs in their sufferings he went to Rome and entered the army in the year 283.

It happened that the martyrs Marcus and Marcellianus, under sentence of death, appeared in danger of being shaken in their faith. Sebastian stepped in and made them a long exhortation to constancy that strongly affected all his hearers. Zoë, the wife of Nicostratus, having for six years lost the use of speech, fell at his feet and spoke distinctly, by the saint's making the sign of the cross on her mouth. She with her husband were converted; and Nicostratus, who had charge of the prisoners, took them to his own house. The governor or Rome, being informed of this, sent for Sebastian and was baptised with his son. He then enlarged the converted prisoners, made his slaves free and resigned his prefectship.

Diocletian, admiring the courage and virtue of St. Sebastian, who concealed his religion, would fain have him near his person, and created him captain of a company of the praetorian guards. In the year 286, the persecution growing hot, the pope and others concealed themselves in the imperial palace, as a place of the greatest safety in the apartments of one Castulus, a Christian officer of the court. St. Zoë was first apprehended praying at St. Peter's tomb on the feast of the apostles. She was stifled with smoke, being hung by her heels over a fire. Castulus was thrice put on the rack and afterwards buried alive. Marcus and Marcellianus were nailed by the feet to a post and shot to death by arrows.

St. Sebastian, having sent so many martyrs to death before him, was himself impeached before the Emperor Diocletian, who, having grievously reproached him with ingratitude, delivered him over to certain archers of Mauritania, to be shot to death. His body was covered with arrows and he left for dead. Irene, the widow of Castulus, going to bury him, found him still alive and took him to her lodgings where he recovered, but refused to fly, and even placed himself one day where the emperor was to pass, whom he accosted, reproaching him for his cruelties against the Christians. This freedom of speech from a person whom he supposed to have been dead, astonished the emperor; he gave orders for his being seized, and beat to death with cudgels and his body thrown into the common sewer. A pious lady, admonished by the martyr in a vision, got it privately removed and buried it in the catacombs.

21 JANUARY

St. Agnes

A.D. 304 or 305

St. Austin observes that her name signifies chaste in Greek and a lamb in Latin. She has always been looked upon in the church as a special patroness of purity. Rome was the theatre of the triumph of St. Agnes; and Prudentius says that her tomb was shown within sight of that city. She suffered not long after the beginning of the persecution of Diocletian, whose bloody edicts appeared in March in the year of our Lord 303. She was only thirteen years of age at the time of her glorious death. Her riches and beauty excited the young noblemen in Rome to vie with another who should gain her in marriage. Agnes answered them all that she had consecrated her virginity to a heavenly spouse, who could not be beheld by mortal eyes. Her suitors accused her to the governor as a Christian. The judge at first employed the mildest expressions and most inviting promises to which Agnes paid no regard. He then made use of threats but found her soul endowed with a masculine courage. At last terrible fires were made and iron hooks, racks and other instruments of torture displayed before her. The young virgin surveyed them all with an undaunted eye.

The governor seeing his measures ineffectual, said he would send her to a house of prostitution. Agnes answered that Jesus Christ was too jealous of the purity of his spouse to suffer it to be violated in such a manner. The governor was so incensed at this, that he ordered her to be immediately led to the public brothel, with liberty to all persons to abuse her person at pleasure. Many young profligates ran thither but were seized with such awe at the sight of the saint that they durst not approach her – one only excepted, who attempting to be rude to her was that very instant, by a flash, as it were, of lightning from heaven, struck blind and fell trembling to the ground. His companions terrified, took him up, and carried him to Agnes who by prayer restored him to his sight and health.

The governor, highly exasperated to see himself baffled and set at defiance by one of her tender age and sex condemned her to be beheaded. The executioner had secret instructions to use all means to induce her to a compliance, but Agnes always

answered she could never offer so great an injury to her heavenly spouse, and having made a short prayer, bowed down her neck to adore her God and received the stroke of death. The spectators wept to see so beautiful and tender a virgin loaded with fetters, and to behold her fearless under the very sword of the executioner, who with a trembling hand cut off her head at one stroke. Her body was buried at a small distance from Rome near the Nomentan Road. A church was built on the spot in the time of Constantine the Great.

23 JANUARY

St. John

THE ALMONER, PATRIARCH OF ALEXANDRIA
ABOUT A.D. 691

St. John received his name from his profuse almsdeeds; was nobly descended, very rich and a widower at Amathus in Cyprus, where, having buried all his children, he employed the whole income of his estate in the relief of the poor. The reputation of his sanctity raised him to the patriarchal chair of Alexandria about the year 608, at which time he was upwards of fifty years of age.

On his arrival in that city he ordered an exact list to be taken of his masters. Being asked who these were, his answer was, 'The Poor!' Their number amounted to seven thousand five hundred, whom he took under his special protection and furnished with all necessaries. He most rigorously forbade all his officers and servants ever to receive the least presents. Every Wednesday and Friday he sat the whole day on a bench before the church that all might have free access to lay their grievances before him. One of his first actions in Alexandria was to distribute the eighty thousand pieces of gold which he found in the treasury of his church, among hospitals and monasteries. When his stewards complained that he impoverished his church, his answer was that God would provide for them.

When the Persians had plundered the East and sacked Jerusalem, St. John entertained all that fled from their swords into Egypt, and sent to Jerusalem, for the use of the poor there, a large sum of money, one thousand sacks of corn, as many of pulse, one thousand pounds of iron, one thousand loads of fish, one thousand barrels of wine, and one thousand Egyptian workmen to assist in rebuilding the churches. He also sent two bishops and an abbot to ransom captives.

The patriarch lived himself in the greatest austerity and poverty as to diet, apparel and furniture. A person of distinction in the city being informed that our saint had but one blanket on his bed, and this a very sorry one, sent him one of value. He accepted it and put it to the intended use, but only for one night. The next morning he sold it and gave the price to the poor. The friend being informed of it bought it and gave it him a second and a third time, for the saint always disposed of it in the same way, saying 'We shall see who will be tired first.'

Nicetas, the governor, had formed a project of a new tax very prejudicial to the poor. The patriarch modestly spoke in their defence. Nicetas persuaded the saint to accompany him to Constantinople to pay a visit to the emperor. St. John was admonished from heaven whilst he was on his way, at Rhodes, that his death drew near. He therefore sailed for Cyprus, and soon after died at Amanthus, about the year 619.

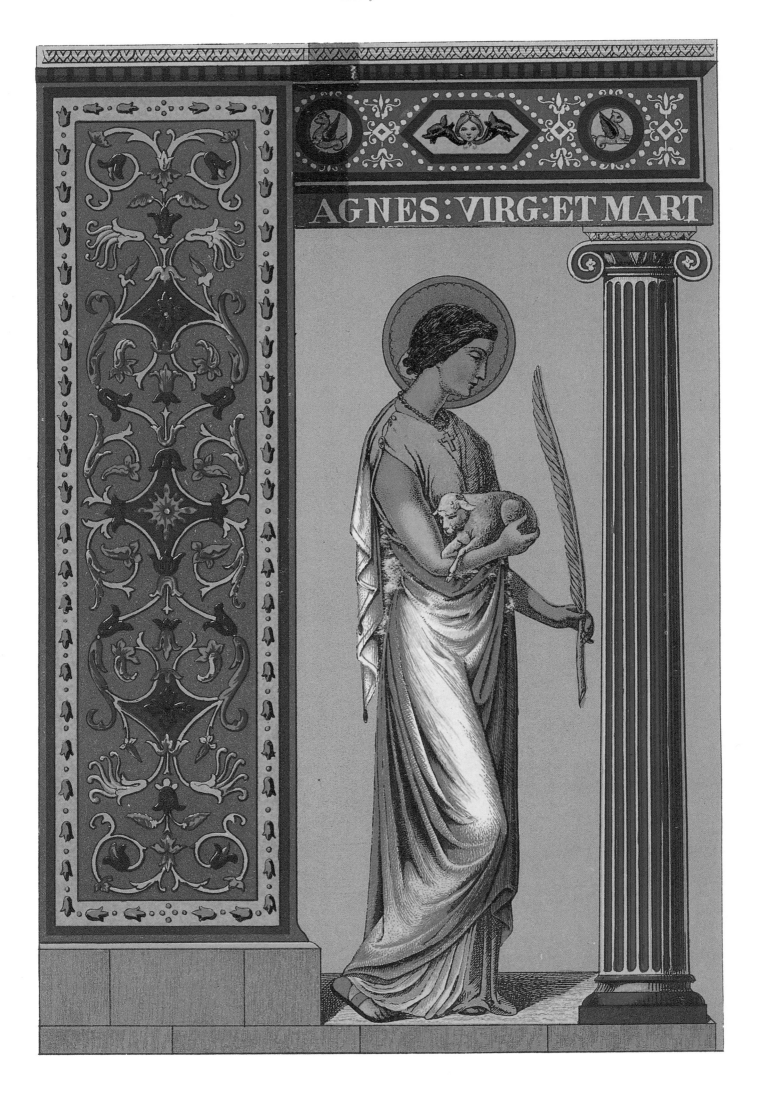

AGNES·VIRG·ET·MART

PLATE 7. ST. AGNES, 21 JANUARY. BUTLER, *LIVES OF THE SAINTS*, TWO-VOLUME ILLUSTRATED 19TH-CENTURY EDITION.

24 JANUARY (29 JANUARY)

St. Francis
OF SALES, BISHOP AND CONFESSOR
A.D. 1662

The saint was born at Sales, three leagues from Annecy. He showed an early inclination for the ecclesiastical state, but was sent to pursue his studies in Paris. He was eighteen when his father recalled him from Paris and sent him to Padua to study the law. Upon his return, his father received him with great joy and obtained patents creating him counsellor of the parliament of Chambéry. Francis firmly refused but durst not propose to his parents his design of receiving holy orders. At last he had recourse to a cousin, Louis of Sales, a priest and canon of Geneva, who obtained their consent, but not without the greatest difficulty.

A short time after, he was promoted to holy orders and employed in preaching. His first sermons gained him an extraordinary reputation, but he was observed to decline whatever might gain him the applause of men, seeking only to please God. He chiefly resorted to cottages and country villages, and made meekness his favourite virtue.

The protestant canon of Bern had seized the republic of Geneva and the duchy of Chablais and there established their heresy. In 1594 the Duke of Savoy, having recovered these territories and resolving to restore the Catholic religion, wrote to the Bishop of Geneva to recommend that work to him. Francis was the only one that offered himself for the work, and was joined by his cousin Louis de Sales. On his arrival at Thonon, the capital of Chablais, he found only seven Catholics. The Calvinists shunned him and some even attempted his life. Nevertheless Francis persevered and in 1598 the public exercise of the Catholic religion was restored all over Chablais.

In 1599 his diocesan, Granier, procured him to be made his coadjutor, but the apprehension of the obligations annexed to episcopy was so strong that it threw him into an illness. On his recovery he set out for Rome to receive his bulls. After the death of Granier he was consecrated bishop in 1602. In his book *The Love of God* he paints his own soul and has been justly admired for it. St. Francis, finding his health decline and his affairs to multiply, chose for his coadjutor his brother John Francis of Sales, but the saint still applied himself to his functions as much as ever. He preached at Grenoble in 1617 and again in 1618, converting many Calvinists. The Bishop of Bellay entreated him at Paris not to preach twice every day, for the sake of his health.

In 1622 he received an order to go to Avignon to wait on Louis XIII. He was obliged to attend the king to Lyons, where he refused all the grand apartments offered him to lodge in the poor chamber of the gardener to the Monastery of the Visitation. After dinner he began to fall into an apoplexy, was put to bed and expired on the 28th of December, 1622.

26 JANUARY (28 JANUARY)

St. Margaret
PRINCESS OF HUNGARY
THIRTEENTH CENTURY

Margaret was daughter to Bala IV, the pious King of Hungary. Her parents consecrated her to God by a vow before her birth, and when but three years and a half old she was placed in the monastery of Dominican nuns at Vesprin, and at ten removed to a new nunnery of that order, founded by her father in an isle of the Danube, near Buda, called from her the isle of St. Margaret. She was professed at twelve. In her tender age she outstripped the most advanced in devotion, and was favoured with extraordinary communications from heaven. It was her delight to serve every body, and to practise every kind of humiliation; she never spoke of herself, as if she was beneath all notice never loved to see her royal parents, or to speak of them, saying it was her misfortune that she was not born of poor parentage. Her mortifications were excessive. She endeavoured to conceal her sicknesses for fear of being dispensed with or shown any indulgence in the rule.

From her infancy she conceived the most ardent devotion towards her crucified Redeemer, and kissed very often, both by day and night, a little cross made of the wood of our Saviour's cross, which she always carried about her. She commonly chose to pray before the altar of the cross. Her affection for the name of Jesus made her have it very frequently in her mouth, which she repeated with incredible inward feeling and sweetness. Her devotion to Christ in the blessed sacrament was most remarkable: she often wept abundantly, or appeared in ecstasies during the mass, and much more when she received the divine spouse of her soul: on the eve she took nothing but bread and water, and watched the night in prayer; on the day itself she remained in prayer and fasting till evening, and then took a small refection. She showed a sensible joy in her countenance when she heard any festival of our Lady announced, through devotion to the mother of God; she performed on them, and during the octaves, one thousand salutations each day, prostrating herself on the ground at each, besides saying the office of our blessed Lady every day.

If anyone seemed offended at her, she fell at their feet and begged their pardon, she was always the first in obedience and was afraid to be excepted if others were enjoined penance for a breach of silence of other fault. Her bed was a coarse skin laid on the bare floor, with a stone for her pillow. She was favoured with the gift of miracles and prophecy. She gave up her pure soul to God, after a short illness, on the 18th of January, in the year 1271, and of her age the twenty-eighth. She is honoured with an office in all the churches of Hungary, especially those of the Dominicans, by virtue of a decree of Pope Pius II.

PLATE 8. ST. FRANCES OF SALES, 24 JANUARY. BUTLER, *LIVES OF THE SAINTS*, TWO-VOLUME ILLUSTRATED 19TH-CENTURY EDITION.

PLATE 9. ST. MARGARET OF HUNGARY, 26 JANUARY. BUTLER, *LIVES OF THE SAINTS*, TWO-VOLUME ILLUSTRATED 19TH-CENTURY EDITION.

28 JANUARY

St. Thomas

AQUINAS, OR OF AQUINO, DOCTOR OF THE
CHURCH
A.D. 1274

The counts of Aquino were allied to the kings of Sicily and Arragon. St. Thomas was born in 1226. The count conducted him to the Abbey of Mount Cassino when he was five to be instructed. He was ten when the abbot told his father that it was time to send him to university, and the count sent him to Naples. The Order of St. Dominic then abounded with men full of the Spirit of God and Thomas conceived a desire to consecrate himself in that Order, and accordingly received the habit in 1243. His mother, being informed of it, set out for Naples to disengage him from that state of life, and two of his brothers so well guarded all the roads that he fell into their hands. They conducted him to the seat of his parents called Rocca-Secca. His constancy was not to be shaken, and his mother ordered him to be confined.

Our saint having suffered this imprisonment upwards of a twelvemonth, his mother began to relent. The Dominicans of Naples hastened to Rocca-Senna where his sister contrived his being let down out of his tower in a basket. He was carried with joy to Naples. The year following he made there his profession. But his mother and brothers renewed their complaints to Pope Innocent IV, who sent for Thomas to Rome and examined him on his vocation, and having received satisfaction on this head approved his choice.

Albertus Magnus teaching then at Cologne, the general, John the Teutonic, took the saint with him from Rome to Paris, and thence to Cologne. Thomas gave all his time to his studies. In 1248 he was appointed to teach at Cologne. He then also began to publish his first works. After four years at Cologne, he went in 1252 to Paris where he consented to be admitted doctor in 1257. The professors of the University of Paris being divided about the question of the accidents remaining really, or only in appearance, in the blessed sacrament of the altar, they agreed in 1258 to consult our saint. The young doctor applied himself to God by prayer, then wrote upon that question the treatise still extant. In 1259 he assisted at the thirty-sixth general chapter of his order, which deputed him to draw up rules for studies which are still extant, and in 1261 Urban IV called him to Rome to teach. The first part of his *Summa theologiae* St. Thomas composed at Bologna; he was called thence to Naples.

From the 6th of December 1273, to the day of his death, he neither dictated nor wrote anything on theological matters. Pope Gregory X had called a general council at Lyons and ordered Thomas to repair thither. Indisposed, he was forced to stop at Fossa-Nuova, a famous abbey of the Cistercians, where he lay ill for near a month. He gave up the ghost on the 7th of March, 1274.

29 JANUARY

St. Gildas

THE WISE, OR BADONICUS, ABBOT
SIXTH CENTURY

Gildas was son to a British lord, who placed him in his infancy in the monastery of St. Iltutus in Glamorganshire. The surname of Badonicus was given him, because, as we learn from his writings, he was born in the year in which the Britons under Aurelius Ambrosius, or according to others King Arthur, gained the famous victory over the Saxons at Mount Badon. Our saint seems therefore to have been born in 494.

Some time after his monastic profession he passed over into Ireland, there to receive the lessons of the admirable masters of a religious life. The author of his Acts compares this excursion to that of the bees in the season of flowers, to gather the juices which they convert into honey.

It was about the year 527 that St. Gildas sailed to Armorica, or Brittany, in France; for he wrote his invective ten years after his arrival there, as is gathered from his life and writings. Here he chose for the place of his retirement the little isle of Houac, so barren as to yield nothing but a small quantity of corn. The saint promised himself that he should live here unknown to men; but certain fishermen who discovered him, were charmed with his heavenly deportment and conversation, and made known on the continent the treasure they had found. The inhabitants flocked from the coast to hear the lessons of divine wisdom which the holy anchorite gave. St. Gildas at length consented to live amongst them, and built a monastery at Rhuis. Then, sighing after closer solitude he withdrew and chose for his habitation a grotto in a rock upon the bank of the river Blavet which he converted into a chapel.

St. Gildas wrote eight canons of discipline and a severe invective against the crimes of the Britons, called *De Excidio Britanniae*, that he might confound those whom he was not able to convert, and whom God delivered first to the plunders of the Picts and Scots, and afterwards to the perfidious Saxons. He reproaches their kings with horrible crimes. He also wrote an invective against the British clergy, whom he accuses of sloth, of seldom sacrificing at the altar, and so on. In his retirement he ceased not to recommend to God the souls of blind sinners, and died in his beloved solitude according to Usher in 570, but according to Ralph of Disse in 581. St. Gildas is the patron of the city of Vannes. His life, compiled from the ancient archives of Rhuis by a monk of that house in the eleventh century, is the best account we have of him, though the author confounds him sometimes with St. Gildas the Albanian.

2 FEBRUARY

St. Bridgit

OR BRIDGET, AND BY CONTRACTION BRIDE,
PATRONESS OF IRELAND

Bridgit was born at Fochard, in Ulster, soon after Ireland had been blessed with the light of faith. She received the religious veil in her youth, from the hands of St. Mel, nephew and disciple of St. Patrick. She built herself a cell under a large oak, thence called Kill-dara, or cell of the oak, living, as her names

PLATE 10. ST. THOMAS AQUINAS, 28 JANUARY. BUTLER, *LIVES OF THE SAINTS*, TWO-VOLUME ILLUSTRATED 19TH-CENTURY EDITION.

implies the bright shining light of that country by her virtues.

Being joined soon after by several of her own sex, they formed themselves into a religious community, which branched out into several other nunneries throughout Ireland, all of which acknowledged her for their mother and foundress, as in effect she was of all in that kingdom.

But a full account of her virtues has not been transmitted down to us, together with the veneration of her name. Her five modern lives mention little else but wonderful miracles. She flourished in the beginning of the sixth century, and is named in the martyrology of Bede, and in all others since that age. Several churches in England and Scotland are dedicated to God under her name, as, among others, that of St. Bride in Fleet Street, London; several also in Germany, and some in France. She is commemorated in the divine office in most churches of Germany, and in that of Paris, till the year 1607, and in many others in France. One of the Hebrides, or western islands which belong to Scotland, near that of Ila, was called, from a famous monastery built there in her honour, Brigidiani. A church of St. Brigit, in the province of Athol, was reputed famous for miracles, and a portion of her relics was kept with great veneration in a monastery of regular canons at Aburnethi, once capital of the kingdom of the Picts. Her body was found with those of SS. Patrick and Columba, in a triple vault in Down-Patrick in 1185, as Giraldus Cambrensis informs us. They were all three translated to the cathedral of the same city; but their monument was destroyed in the reign of Henry VIII.

3 FEBRUARY

St. Blase

(BLAISE), BISHOP AND MARTYR
A.D. 316

Blase was Bishop of Sebaste in Armenia, and was crowned with marytrdom in the persecution of Licinius, in 316, by the command of Agricolaus, governor of Cappadocia and the lesser Armenia. It is mentioned in the acts of St. Eustratius, who received the crown of martyrdom in the reign of Diocletian, and is honoured on the 13th of December, that St. Blase, the Bishop of Sebaste, honourably received his relics and deposited them with those of St. Orestes, and punctually executed every article of the last will and testament of St. Eustratius. His festival is kept a holyday in the Greek church on the 11th of February. He is mentioned in the ancient Western Martyrologies which bear the name of St. Jerome. Ado and Usuard, with several more ancient manuscript Martyrologies, place his name on the 15th.

In the holy wars his relics were dispersed over the west, and his veneration was propagated by many miraculous cures, especially of sore throats. He is the principal patron of the commonwealth of Ragusa. No other reason than the great devotion of the people to this celebrated martyr of the church seems to have given occasion to the woolcombers to choose him

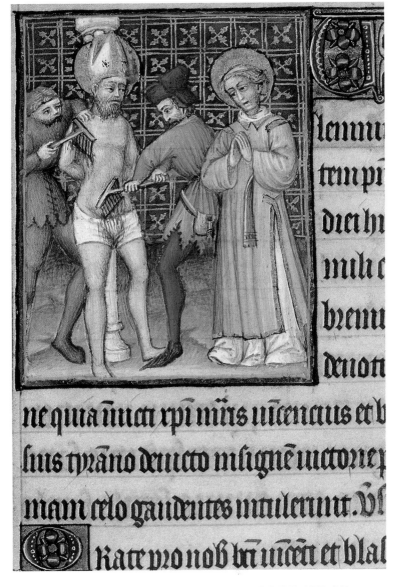

PLATE 11. ST. BLAISE, 3 FEBRUARY. BRITISH LIBRARY, ADD. MS 29433, F. 204.

the titular patron of their profession, on which account his festival is still kept by them with solemn guild at Norwich. Perhaps also his country might in part determine them to this choice, for it seems that the first branch, or at least hint of this manufacture, was borrowed from the remotest known countries of the East, as was that of silk; or the iron combs with which he is said to have been tormented, gave occasion to this choice.

[Editorial note: the blessing of St. Blaise is still in practice today for those afflicted by diseases of the throat.]

4 FEBRUARY

St. Andrew

CORSINI, BISHOP
A.D. 1373

This saint was born in Florence in 1302. The family of the Corsini was then one of the most illustrious, but notwithstanding the care his parents took to instil good principles into him, he spent the first part of his youth in vice and extravagance in the company of such as were as wicked as himself. His devout mother never ceased weeping and praying for his conversion, and one day said to him, 'I see you are the wolf I saw in my sleep', giving him to understand that when with child of him she had dreamed she was brought to bed of a wolf, which running into a church, was turned into a lamb. This discourse made so strong an impression that he went immediately to the church of the Carmelite friars and, having prayed there for some time with great fervour, he took a resolution to return no more to his father's house, but to embrace the religious life professed in that convent. He was readily admitted in the year 1318, and after a novitiate of a year and some months made his solemn profession.

In the year 1328 he was ordained priest; but to prevent the music and feast which his family had prepared, according to custom, for the day on which he was to say his first mass, he privately withdrew to a little convent seven miles out of town where he offered his first fruits to God. After some time employed in preaching at Florence, he was sent to Paris, where he studied three years and took some degress. He prosecuted his studies some time at Avignon with his uncle, Cardinal Corsini, and in 1332, returning to Florence, was chosen prior of that convent.

The Bishop of Fiesole, a town three miles from Florence, being dead, the chapter unanimously chose our saint to fill the vacant see. Being informed of their proceedings, he hid himself, and remained so long concealed that the canons were going to proceed to a second election, when he was discovered by a child. Being consecrated bishop in the beginning of 1360, he redoubled his former austerities. By an excellent talent for composing differences, he never failed to reconcile persons at variance and to appease all seditions.

Urban V, on this account, sent him to Bologna, where the nobility and people were miserably divided. He happily pacified them, and their union continued during the remainder of his life. He was accustomed every Thursday to wash the feet of the poor. In imitation of St. Gregory the Great, he kept a list of all the names of the poor, and furnished them all with allowances. He never dismissed any without alms. He was taken ill whilst he was singing high mass on Christmas night in

the year 1372. His fever increasing, he gave up his soul to God on the 6th of January, 1373, being seventy-one years old.

5 FEBRUARY

St. Agatha

MARTYR
A.D. 251

The cities of Palermo and Catana, in Sicily, dispute the honour of Agatha's birth. It is agreed that she received the crown of martyrdom at Catana, in the persecution of Decius, in the year of our Lord 251. She was of a rich and illustrious family, and having been consecrated to God from her tender years, triumphed over many assaults upon her chastity. Quintianus, a man of consular dignity, bent on gratifying both his lust and avarice, imagined he should easily compass his wicked designs on Agatha's person and estate by means of the emperor's edict against the Christians. He gave orders for her being put into the hands of Aphrodisia, a most wicked woman, who, with six daughters, all prostitutes, kept a common stew. The saint suffered in this infamous place assaults and stratagems against her virtue infinitely most terrible to her than any tortures or death itself. But placing her confidence in God, she never ceased with sighs and most earnest tears to implore his protection, and by it was an overmatch for all their hellish attempts the whole month she was there.

Quintianus, being informed of her constancy ordered her to be brought before him. The virgin told him that to be a servant of Christ was the most illustrious nobility and true liberty. The judge, offended at her resolute answers, commanded her to be buffeted and led to prison. The next day she was arraigned a second time and answered with equal constancy that Jesus Christ was her life and her salvation. Quintianus then ordered her to be stretched on the rack, which torment was usually accompanied with stripes, the tearing of the sides with iron hooks and burning them with torches or matches. The governor, enraged to see her suffer all this with cheerfulness, commanded her breast to be tortured and afterwards to be cut off. At which she made him this reproach – 'Cruel tyrant, do you not blush to torture this part of my body, you that sucked the breasts of a woman yourself?' He remanded her to prison with a severe order that neither salves nor food shall be allowed her. But God would be himself her physician, and the apostle St Peter in a vision, comforted her, healed all her wounds and filled her dungeon with a heavenly light. Quintianus, four days after, not the least moved at the miraculous cure of her wounds, caused her to be rolled naked over live coals mixed with broken potsherds. Being carried back to prison, she made this prayer – 'Lord, my creator, you have ever protected me from the cradle; you have taken me from the love of the world, and given me patience to suffer, receive now my soul.' After which words she sweetly gave up the ghost. Her name is inserted in the canon of the mass in the calendar of Carthage and in all martyrologies of the Latins and Greeks.

PLATE 12. ST. AGATHA, 5 FEBRUARY. BUTLER, *LIVES OF THE SAINTS*, TWO-VOLUME ILLUSTRATED 19TH-CENTURY EDITION.

6 FEBRUARY

THE MARTYRS OF JAPAN

St. Francis Xavier arrived in Japan in 1549, baptized great numbers, and whole provinces received the faith. In 1587 there were in Japan above two hundred thousand Christians, and among these several kings and princes, but in 1588 the haughty emperor commanded all the Jesuits to leave his dominions within six months; however many remained there disguised. In 1592 the persecution was renewed. The emperor was worked up into rage and jealousy by a suspicion suggested by certain European merchants that the view of the missionaries was to facilitate the conquest of the country by the Portuguese or Spaniards.

Three Jesuits and six Franciscans were crucified on a hill near Nagasaki in 1597. The latter had at their head Peter Baptist, a native of Avila in Spain. As to the Jesuits, one was Paul Michi, a noble Japanese and an eminent preacher, at that time thirty-three years old. The other two, John Gotto and James Kisai, were admitted into the Society in prison a little before they suffered.

Several Japanese converts suffered with them. The martyrs were twenty-six in number, among them three boys who used to serve the friars at mass. Of these martyrs, twenty-four had been brought to Meaco, where only a part of their left ears was cut off, by a mitigation of the sentence which had commanded the amputation of their noses and both ears. They were conducted through many towns and public places, their cheeks stained with blood, for a terror to others. When they were arrived at the place of execution, they were allowed to make their confession to two Jesuits, and being fastened to crosses by cords and chains about their arms and legs, and an iron collar about their necks, were raised into the air, the foot of each cross falling into a hole prepared for it in the ground. The crosses were planted in a row, and each martyr had an executioner near him with a spear ready to pierce his side; for such is the Japanese manner of crucifixion. As soon as all the crosses were planted the executioners lifted up their lances, and at a signal, pierced the martyrs almost in the same instant, upon which they expired.

In 1616, Xogun, succeeding his father in the empire, surpassed him in cruelty. The most illustrious of these religious heroes was Charles Spinola, who was conducted from his last prison to Nagasaki, where fifty martyrs suffered together on a hill, twenty-five burned, the rest beheaded. The stakes were fixed all in a row, and the martyrs tied to them. Fire was set to the end of the pile of wood and gradually approached them two hours before it reached them. F. Spinola stood unmoved till he fell into the flames and was consumed, on the 2nd of September, 1622.

8 FEBRUARY (20 JULY)

St. Jerome
AEMILIANI, FOUNDER OF THE CONGREGATION OF REGULAR CLERGY OF SOMASCHA
A.D. 1537

Jerome was born at Venice of a patrician family; and, in the most troublesome times of the republic served in the troops from his childhood. Whilst he was governor of the new castle in the mountains of Tarviso, he was taken prisoner, cast into a dungeon, and loaded with chains. His sufferings he sanctified by penance and prayer; and being delivered by the miraculous protection of the Mother of God, arriving at Tarviso, he hung up his chains before an altar consecrated to God under the invocation of the Blessed Virgin, and, returning to Venice, devoted himself to the exercises of prayer and all virtues.

At that time a famine and a contagious distemper having reduced many families to the greatest distress, he laid himself out in relieving all, but was particularly moved with compassion for abandoned orphans. These he gathered in a house which he hired, clothed and fed them at his own expense, and instructed them himself in the Christian doctrine. By the advice of St. Cajetan and others, he passed to the continent, and erected like hospitals for orphans at Brescia, Bergamo and other places; and others for the reception of penitent women. At Somascha, on the frontiers between Bergamo and Milan, he founded a house which he destined for the exercises of those whom he received into his congregation, and in which he long resided. From this house it took its name.

The instruction of youth and young clergymen became also an object of his foundations and continues still to be in his institute. The brothers, during the life of the founder, were all laymen, and it was only approved as a pious congregation. The holy founder died at Somascha on the 8th of February, 1537, of a contagious distemper which he had caught by attending the sick. Three years after his death, in 1540, his congregation was declared a religious Order by Paul III and confirmed under the rule of St Augustine in 1571 and again in 1586. It has no houses out of Italy and the Catholic Swiss Cantons. It is divided into three provinces of Lombardy, Venice and Rome. The general is chosen every three years, out of each province in its turn.

9 FEBRUARY

St. Apollonia
A.D. 249

A certain poet of Alexandria, who pretended to foretell things to come, stirred up this great city against the Christians on the motive of religion. The first victim of their rage was a venerable old man named Metras, whom they would have compelled to utter impious words against the worship of the true God, which, when he refused to do, they beat him with staffs, thrust splinters of reeds into his eyes, and having dragged him into one of the suburbs, stoned him to death. The next person they seized was a woman called Quinta, whom they carried to one of their temples to pay divine worship to the idol. She loaded the execrable divinity with many reproaches, which so exasperated the people that they dragged her by the heels upon the pavement of sharp pebbles, cruelly scourged her, and put her to the same death. The rioters by this time were in the height of their fury. Alexandria seemed like a city taken by storm. The Christians made no opposition, but betook themselves to flight, and beheld the loss of their goods with joy; for their hearts had no ties on earth.

The admirable Apollonia, whom old age and the state of virginity rendered equally venerable, was seized by them.

Their repeated blows on her jaw beat out all her teeth. At last they made a great fire without the city, and threatened to cast her in it if she did not utter certain impious words. She begged a moment's delay, as if it had been to deliberate on the proposal; but to convince her persecutors that her sacrifice was perfectly voluntary, she no sooner found herself at liberty, than of her own accord, she leaped into the flames.

A civil war among the pagan citizens put an end to their fury this year, but the edict of Decius renewed it in 250. An ancient church in Rome, which is frequented with great devotion, bears the name of St. Apollonia, under whose patronage we meet with churches and altars in most parts of the Western church.

10 FEBRUARY

St. Scholastica

ABOUT THE YEAR 543

This saint was sister to the great St. Benedict. She consecrated herself to God from her earliest youth. Where her first monastery was situated is not mentioned; but after her brother removed to Mount Cassino she chose her retreat at Plombariola in that neighbourhood, where she founded and governed a nunnery about five miles distant to the south from St. Benedict's

PLATE 13. ST. APOLLONIA, 9 FEBRUARY. BODLEIAN LIBRARY, MS. ADD. A 185, F. 26

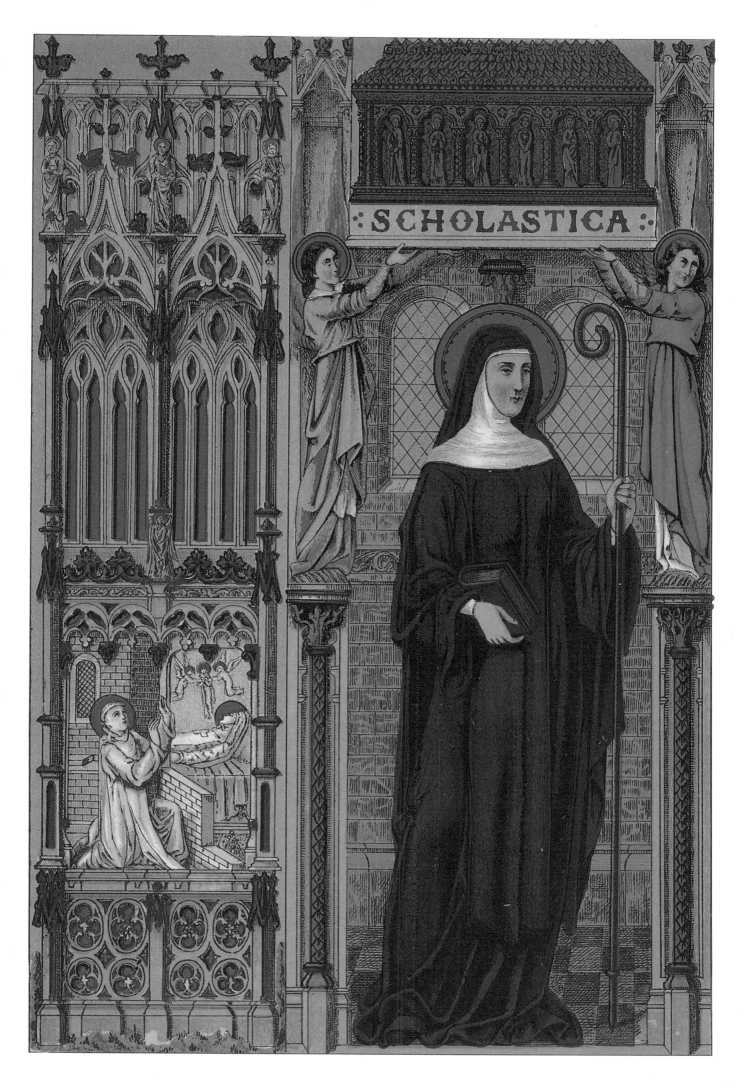

PLATE 14. ST. SCHOLASTICA, 10 FEBRUARY. BUTLER, *LIVES OF THE SAINTS*, TWO-VOLUME ILLUSTRATED 19TH-CENTURY EDITION.

monastery. She instructed in virtue several of her own sex, and whereas St. Benedict governed nuns as well as monks, his sister must have been their abbess under his rule and direction. She visited her holy brother once a year, and as she was not allowed to enter his monastery he went out with some of his monks to meet her at a house at some small distance. They spent these visits in the praises of God, and in conferring together on spiritual matters.

St. Gregory relates a remarkable circumstance of the last of these visits. Scholastica having passed the day as usual in singing psalms and pious discourse, they sat down in the evening to take their refection. After it was over, Scholastica, perhaps foreknowing it would be their last interview in the world, was very urgent with her brother to delay his return till the next day, that they might entertain themselves till morning upon the happiness of the other life. St. Benedict, unwilling to transgress his rule, told her he could not pass a night out of his monastery. Scholastica, finding him resolved on going home, with many tears begged of Almighty God to interpose in her behalf. Her prayer was scarce ended when there happened such a storm of rain, thunder and lightning that neither St. Benedict nor any of his companions could set foot out of doors.

He complained to his sister, saying, 'God forgive you, sister; what have you done?' She answered, 'I asked you a favour and you refused it me: I asked it of Almighty God, and he has granted it me.' St. Benedict was therefore obliged to comply with her request, and they spent the night in conferences on pious subjects, chiefly on the felicity of the blessed, to which both most ardently aspired, and which she was shortly to enjoy.

The next morning they parted, and, three days after, St. Scholastica died in her solitude. St. Benedict was then alone in contemplation on Mount Cassino, and lifting up his eyes to heaven, he saw the soul of his sister ascending thither in the shape of a dove. Filled with joy at her happy passage, he gave thanks for it to God, and declared her death to his brethren, some of whom he sent to bring her corpse to his monastery, where he caused it to be laid in the tomb which he had prepared for himself. She must have died about the year 543. Her relics are said to have been translated into France in the seventh century.

11 FEBRUARY

St. Benedict

OF ANIAN, ABBOT

A.D. 821

Benedict was son of Aigulf, Count of Languedoc, and served King Pepin and his son Charlemagne in quality of cupbearer. At twenty years of age he took a resolution of seeking the kingdom of God with his whole heart. In 774, having narrowly escaped being drowned in the Tesin, near Pavia, in endeavouring to save his brother, he made a vow to quit the world entirely. Returning to Languedoc he was confirmed in his resolution by the pious advice of a hermit called Widmar, and went to the Abbey of St. Seine, five leagues from Dijon, where he became a monk.

He spent two years and a half in wonderful abstinence, and practised all the severest observances prescribed by St. Pachomius and St. Basil. His brethren, upon the abbot's death, were disposed to choose our saint, but he being unwilling to accept of

the charge on account of their known aversion to reformation, left them, and returned to Languedoc in 780, where he built a small hermitage on the brook of the Anian, upon his own estate. Here he lived some years in extreme poverty. Some solitaries, and with them the holy man Widmar, put themselves under his direction. They earned their livelihood by their labour and lived on bread and water, except on Sunday and solemn festivals, on which they added a little wine and milk when it was given in alms. The superior did not exempt himself from working with the rest in the fields; and sometimes he copied good books.

The number of his disciples increasing, he quitted the valley and built a monastery in a more spacious place in that neighbourhood. He had in a short time three hundred religious under his direction, and also exercised a general inspection over all the monasteries of Provence, Languedoc and Gascony. Benedict was become the oracle of the whole kingdom and he established his reformation in many great monasteries. The Emperor Louis Debonnair, who succeeded his father in 814, committed to the saint the inspection of all the abbeys in his kingdom. To have him nearer his own person, the emperor built the monastery of Inde, two leagues from Aix-la-Chapelle. Notwithstanding St. Benedict's constant abode in this monastery he had still a hand in restoring monastic discipline throughout France and Germany. His statutes were adopted by the order and annexed to the rule of St. Benedict, the founder. He wrote the *Code of Rules*, a collection of all the monastic regulations which he found extant. In his *Concord of Rules* he gives that of St. Bennet with those of other patriarchs to show their uniformity in the exercises which they prescribe. This great restorer of the monastic order in the West suffered much from continual sickness the latter years of his life. He died at Inde on the 11th of February, 821, being then about seventy-one years of age.

13 FEBRUARY

St. Catherine

DE RICCI

A.D. 1589

The Ricci are an ancient family, which still subsists in a flourishing condition in Tuscany. The saint was born at Florence in 1522, and called at her baptism Alexandria, but she took the name of Catherine at her religious profession. Having lost her mother in her infancy, when she was between six and seven years old her father placed her in the Convent of Monticelli where her aunt Louisa de Ricci was a nun. This place was to her a paradise; at a distance from the noise and tumult of the world, she served God without impediment or distraction. After some years her father took her home. She continued her usual exercises as much as she was able, but the interruptions and dissipation inseparable from her station gave her so much uneasiness that, with the consent of her father, which she obtained, though with great difficulty, in the year 1535, the fourteenth of her age, she received the religious veil in the convent of Dominicanesses at Prat in Tuscany, to which her uncle Timothy was director.

For two years she suffered inexpressible pains under a complication of violent distempers, which remedies themselves served only to increase. These sufferings she sanctified by the interior dispositions with which she bore them. After the recovery of her health which seemed miraculous, she studied more perfectly to die to her senses, and advance in a penitential life and spirit, in which God had begun to conduct her, by practising the greatest austerities which were compatible with the obedience she had professed. The saint was chosen, very young, first, mistress of the novices, then sub-prioress, and in the twenty-fifth year of her age was appointed perpetual prioress. The reputation of her extraordinary sanctity and prudence draw her many visits from a great number of bishops, princes and cardinals, among others of Cervini, Alexander of Medicis, and Aldobrandini, who all three were afterwards raised to St. Peter's chair under the names of Marcellus II, Clement VIII and Leo XI.

St. Philip Neri and St. Catharine, having some time entertained together a commerce of letters, to satisfy their mutual desire of seeing each other, whilst he was detained at Rome, she appeared to him in a vision, and they conversed together a considerable time, each doubtless being in a rapture. This St Philip, though most circumspect in giving credit to or in publishing visions, declared, saying that Catharine de Ricci, whilst living, had appeared to him in vision, and this was confirmed by the oaths of five witnesses.

Most wonderful were the raptures of St. Catharine in meditating on the passion of Christ, which was her daily exercise, but to which she totally devoted herself every week from Thursday noon to three o'clock in the afternoon on Friday. After a long illness she passed from this mortal life to everlasting bliss on the feast of the Purification of our Lady, the 2nd of February in 1589, the sixty-seventh of her age.

15 FEBRUARY

St. Sigfrid
APOSTLE OF SWEDEN
ABOUT THE YEAR 1002

St. Anscarius had planted the faith in Sweden in 830, but it relapsed soon after into idolatry. King Olas entreated King Edred, who died in 951, to send him missionaries to preach the gospel in his country. Sigfrid, an eminent priest of York, undertook that mission, and on the 21st of June, 950, arrived at Wexiow, in Gothland. He first erected a cross, then built a church of wood, celebrated the divine mysteries and preached to the people. Twelve principle men of the province were converted by him, and one who died was buried after the Christian manner, and a cross placed upon his grave. So great were the numbers in a short time brought to the faith, that the cross of Christ was triumphantly planted in all the twelve tribes into which the inhabitants of South Gothland were divided.

King Olas was much pleased with the accounts he heard of the man of God, and many flocked from remote parts out of mere curiosity to hear his doctrine. St. Sigfrid ordained two bishops, one of East, the other of West Gothland. The see of Wexiow he continued himself to govern so long as he lived. His three nephews, Unaman a priest, and Sunaman and Wiamun, the one a deacon the other a subdeacon, were his chief assistants in his apostolic labours. Having intrusted the administration of his see to Unaman, and left his two brothers to assist and comfort him, the saint himself set out to carry the light of the gospel into the midland and northern provinces. King Olas

received him with great respect, and was baptized by him, with his whole court and his army. St. Sigfrid founded many churches and consecrated a bishop of Upsal and another of Strengues.

During the absence of our saint, a troop of idolatrous rebels plundered the church of Wexiow and barbarously murdered Unaman and his two brothers. Their bodies they buried in the midst of a forest, where they have always remained hid. But the murderers put the heads of the martyrs into a box which they threw into a great pond. But they were afterwards taken out and kept richly enshrined in the church of Wexiow until their relics were removed by the Lutherans.

Upon the news of this massacre St. Sigfrid hastened to Wexiow to repair the ruins of his church. The king resolved to put the murderers to death; but Sigfrid by his earnest entreaties prevailed on him to spare their lives. However, he condemned them to pay a heavy fine, which he would have bestowed on the saint but he refused accepting a single farthing of it, notwithstanding his extreme poverty and the difficulties which he had to struggle with in laying the foundation of that new church. Our saint died about the year 1002 and was buried in his cathedral in Wexiow, where his tomb became famous for miracles. He was honoured by the Swedes as their apostle, till the change of religion among them.

16 FEBRUARY

St. Onesimus
DISCIPLE OF ST PAUL
FIRST CENTURY

St. Onesimus was a Phrygian by birth, slave to Philemon, a person of note in the city of Colossae, converted to the faith by St. Paul. Having robbed his master, and being obliged to fly, he providentially met with St. Paul, then a prisoner for the faith at Rome, who there converted and baptized him, and sent him with his canonical letter of recommendation to Philemon, by whom he was pardoned, set at liberty, and sent back to his spiritual father, whom he afterwards faithfully served. That apostle made him, with Tychicus, the bearer of his epistle to the Colossians, and afterwards, as St. Jerome and other fathers witness, a preacher of the gospel and a bishop. The Greeks say he was crowned with martyrdom under Domitian in the year 95, and keep his festival on the 15th. Bede, Ado, the Roman and other Latin martyrologies mention him on the 16th of February.

Baronius and some others confound him with St. Onesimus, the third bishop of Ephesus, after St Timothy, who was succeeded first by John, then by Caius. This Onesimus showed great respect and charity to St. Ignatius, when on his journey to Rome in 107, and is highly commended by him.

18 FEBRUARY

St. Simeon
BISHOP OF JERUSALEM
A.D. 116

St. Simeon was the son of Cleophas, brother to St. Joseph, and of Mary, sister of the Blessed Virgin. He was therefore cousin to Christ. Simeon and Simon are the same name, and this saint is, according to the best interpreters of the holy scripture, the Simon who was brother to St. James the Lesser. He was eight or nine years older than our Saviour. We cannot doubt but he was an early follower of Christ. Nor does St. Luke leave us any room to doubt but that he received the Holy Ghost on the Day of Pentecost.

St. James, Bishop of Jerusalem, being put to death in the year 62, the apostles and disciples met at Jerusalem to appoint him a successor. They unanimously chose St. Simeon, who had probably before assisted his brother in the government of that church. In the year 66, the civil war began in Judea, by the seditions of the Jews against the Romans. The Christians in Jerusalem were warned by God of the impending destruction of that city and by a divine revelation commanded to leave it. They therefore departed the same year and retired beyond Jordan to a small city called Pella, having St. Simeon at their head. After the taking and burning of Jerusalem they returned thither and settled themselves amidst its ruins.

St. Simeon had the affliction to see two heresies arise, namely those of the Nazareans and the Ebionites. The Nazareans were a sect of men between Jews and Christians, but abhorred by both. They allowed Christ to be the greatest of prophets, but said he was a mere man; they joined all the ceremonies of the old law with the new, and observed both the Jewish Sabbath and the Sunday. Ebion added other errors to these and taught many superstitions, permitted divorces and allowed of the most infamous abominations. The authority of St. Simeon kept the heretics in some awe during his life, which was the longest upon earth of any of our Lord's disciples. But, as Eusebius says, he was no sooner dead than a deluge of heresies broke out, which durst not openly appear during his life.

Vespasian and Domitian had commanded all to be put to death who were of the race of David. St. Simeon had escaped their searches; but Trajan having given the same order, certain heretics and Jews accused him as being both of the race of David and a Christian, to Atticus, the Roman governor in Palestine. The holy bishop was condemned by him to be crucified; after having undergone the usual tortures during several days, which though one hundred and twenty years old, he suffered with so much patience that he drew on him universal admiration, he died in 106, according to Eusebius in his chronicle, but in 116 according to Dodwell, Bishop Loyde and Father Pagi. He must have governed the church of Jerusalem about forty-three years.

21 FEBRUARY

St. Peter

DAMIAN, CARDINAL, BISHOP OF OSTIA
A.D. 1072

Peter, surnamed Damian, was born about the year 988 in Ravenna, of a good family, but reduced. He was the youngest of many children, and losing his father and mother very young, was left in the hands of a brother in whose house he was treated more like a slave; and when grown up, he was sent to keep swine. He had another brother called Damian, who was arch-priest of Ravenna, who, taking pity of him, had the charity to give him an education. He seems from him to have taken the surname Damian. Damian sent Peter to school, first at Faenza, afterwards at Parma. It was not long before he found

himself in a capacity to teach others, which he did with great applause. But he resolved to embrace a monastic life and while his mind was full of these thoughts, two religious of the Order of St. Benedict belonging to Font-Avellano, a desert in Umbria, happened to call at the place of his abode, and being much edified at their disinterestedness, he embraced their institute.

This hermitage was then in the greatest repute. The hermits there remained two and two together in separate cells, occupied chiefly in prayer and reading. Peter gave a considerable time to sacred studies and became well versed in the scriptures. His superior ordered him to make frequent exhortations to the religious and, with the unanimous consent of the hermitage, to take upon him the government of the desert after his death. Wherefore, in 1041 Peter took upon him the direction of that holy family. He also founded five other hermitages in which he placed priors under his inspection. His principal care was to cherish in his disciples the spirit of solitude, charity and humility. He was for twelve years much employed in the service of the church by many zealous bishops and by four popes successively. Stephen IX, in 1057, made him Cardinal-bishop of Ostia. Stephen dying in 1058, Nicholas II was chosen pope and Peter, with great importunity, solicited him for leave to resign his bishopric, but could not obtain it. His successor, Alexander II, out of affection for the holy man, was prevailed upon to allow it in 1062, but not without the reverse of a power to employ him in church matters hereafter. The saint from that time thought himself discharged not only from the burden of his flock, but also from the quality of superior, reducing himself to the condition of simple monk.

In his retirement he laboured by his writings to enforce the observance of discipline and morality. The holy man was obliged to interrupt his solitude in obedience to the pope who sent him as legate into France in 1063 and to Ravenna in 1072. This was his last undertaking for the church. In his return towards Rome he was stopped by a fever at Faenza and died there on the 22nd of February, 1072.

22 FEBRUARY

St. Margaret

OF CORTONA
A.D. 1297

Margaret was a native of Alviano in Tuscany. The harshness of a step-mother and her own indulged propension to vice, cast her headlong into the great disorders. The sight of the carcass of a man, half putrified, who had been her gallant, struck her with so great a fear of the divine judgements, and with so deep a sense of the treachery of this world, that she in a moment became a perfect penitent.

The first thing she did was to throw herself at her father's feet, bathed in tears, to beg his pardon for her contempt of his authority and fatherly admonitions. She spent the days and nights in tears; and to repair the scandal she had given by her crimes, she went to the parish church of Alviano, with a rope about her neck, and there asked public pardon for them.

After this she repaired to Cortona, and made her most penitent confession to a father of the Order of St. Francis, who admired the great sentiments of compunction with which she was filled, and prescribed the austerities and practices suitable to her fervour. Her conversion happened in the year 1274, the twenty-fifth of her age. She was assaulted by violent temptations of various kinds, but courageously overcame them, and after a trial of three years, was admitted to her profession among the penitents of the Third Order of St. Francis in Cortona. The extraordinary austerities with which she punished her criminal flesh soon disfigured her body. To exterior mortification she joined all sorts of humiliations; and the confusion with which she was covered at the sight of her own sins, pushed her on continually to invent many extraordinary means of drawing upon herself all manner of confusion before men.

This model of true penitents, after twenty-three years of severe penance, and twenty of them in the religious habit, being worn out by austerities, and consumed by the fire of divine love, died on the 22nd of February in 1297. After the proof of many miracles Leo X granted an office in her honour to the city of Cortona.

23 FEBRUARY (26 JANUARY)

St. Polycarp
BISHOP OF SMYRNA
A.D. 166

St. Polycarp was one of the most illustrious of the apostolic fathers, who being the immediate disciples of the apostles, received instructions from their mouths. He embraced Christianity very young, about the year 80, was a disciple of St. John the Evangelist and was constituted by him Bishop of Smyrna, probably before his banishment to Patmos in 96. He formed many holy disciples, among whom were St. Irenaeus and Papias. St. Polycarp kissed with respect the chains of St. Ignatius, who passed by Smyrna on the road to his martyrdom and recommended to our saint the care of his church of Antioch, desiring him to write to those churches of Asia to which he had not leisure to write himself. St. Polycarp wrote a letter to the Philippians shortly after, which is still extant.

About the year 158 he undertook a journey to Rome to confer with Pope Anicetus about certain points, especially about the time of keeping Easter. St. Anicetus, to testify his respect, yielded to him the honour of celebrating the Eucharist in his own church.

In the sixth year of Marcus Aurelius, a violent persecution broke out in Asia. The holy man, though fearless, had been prevailed upon by his friends to withdraw and conceal himself in a neighbouring village. When the persecutors were in quest of him he changed his retreat, but was betrayed by a boy, who was threatened with the rack unless he discovered him. Herod, the keeper of the peace, sent horsemen by night to beset his lodgings. The saint went down, met them at the door, ordered them supper, and desired only some time for prayer before he went with them. He was led to the tribunal of the proconsul who exhorted him to swear by the genius of Caesar and blaspheme Christ. Polycarp replied, 'I have served him these fourscore and six years, and he never did me harm, but much good, and how can I blaspheme my King and my Saviour?' Whilst he said this and many other things he appeared in a transport of joy and confidence, that the proconsul himself was struck with admiration. However, he ordered a crier to make public proclamation, 'Polycarp hath confessed himself a Christian.' The whole multitude demanded that he should be burnt alive.

Wood and other combustibles were heaped all round him, and fire was set to the pile. But the flames forming themselves into an arch gently encircled the body of the martyr, which stood in the middle resembling purified gold or silver. The infidels ordered a spearman to pierce him through, and such a quantity of blood issued out of his left side as to quench the fire. The centurion, seeing a contest raised by the Jews, placed the body in the middle and burnt it to ashes.

24 FEBRUARY

St. Pretextatus
OR PRIX, ARCHBISHOP OF ROUEN
SIXTH CENTURY

Pretextatus was chosen Archbishop of Rouen in 549, and in 557 assisted at the third council of Paris, held to abolish incestuous marriages, and remove other crying abuses; also at the second council of Tours in 566. By his zeal in reproving Fredegonda for her injustices and cruelties, he had incurred her indignation. King Clotaire I in 562 had left the French monarchy divided among his four sons, Charibert, Gontran, Sigebert and Chilperic. Sigebert married Brunehault, daughter of the King of the Visigoths in Spain, and Chilperic her elder sister Galsvinda; but after her death he took to wife Fredegonda, who had been his mistress and was strongly suspected to have contrived the death of the queen by poison. Hence Brunehault stirred up Sigebert against her and her husband. But Fredegonda contrived the assassination of Sigebert in 575 and Chilperic secured Brunehault, her three daughters and her son Childebert. This latter soon made his escape and fled to Metz where he was crowned King of Austrasia.

Chilperic sent Meroveus, his son by his first wife, to reduce the country about Poitiers, which belonged to Childebert. But Meroveus at Rouen, fell in love with his aunt Brunehault, then a prisoner in that city; and Bishop Pretextatus, in order to prevent a grievous scandal, judging circumstances to be sufficiently cogent to require a dispensation, married them, for which he was accused of high treason by Chilperic before a council in Paris in 577. Pretextatus confessed the marriage, but denied that he had been privy to the prince's revolt, but was afterwards prevailed upon through the persuasion of certain emissaries of Chilperic, to plead guilty, and confess that out of affection he had been drawn in to favour the young prince, who was his godson. Whereupon he was condemned by the council and banished into a small island near Coutances. The rage and clamour with which his enemies spread their slanders to beat down his reputation staggered many of his friends, but St Gregory of Tours never forsook him.

Meroveus was assassinated by an order of his stepmother Fredegonda, who was also suspected to have contrived the death of her husband Chilperic in 584. She had three years before procured Clovis, his younger son, to be assassinated, so that the crown devolved upon her own son; but for his and her own protection she had recourse to Gontran, the King of Orleans and Burgundy. By his order Pretextatus after a banishment of six years was restored to his see. He assisted at the council of Macon in 585 and continued his pastoral labours in the care of his flock. Fredegonda grew daily more and more hardened in iniquity, and by her secret order St Pretextatus was assassinated while he assisted at matins in his church in the midst of his clergy on Sunday, the 25th of February.

25 FEBRUARY

St. Ethelbert

FIRST CHRISTIAN KING AMONG THE ENGLISH
A.D. 616

Ethelbert was King of Kent, the fifth descendant from Hengist, who first settled the English Saxons in Britain in 448. He married Bertha, only daughter of Charibert, King of Paris, and cousin to Clotaire of Soissons and Childebert of Austrasia. Ethelbert succeeded his father in 560. The kingdom of Kent having enjoyed a continued peace for about a hundred years, was arrived at a degree of power and riches which gave it a pre-eminence in the Saxon heptarchy in Britain, and so great a superiority over the rest that Ethelbert is said by Bede to have ruled as far as the Humber, and is often styled King of the English.

His queen, Bertha, was a very zealous and pious Christian and by the articles of her marriage had free liberty to exercise her religion, for which purpose she was attended by a venerable French prelate named Luidhard. He officiated constantly in an old church dedicated to St. Martin, lying a little out of the walls of Canterbury. The exemplary life of this prelate, and his frequent discourses on religion, disposed several pagans about the court to embrace the faith. Divine Providence by this means mercifully prepared the heart of a great king to entertain a favourable opinion of our holy religion when St. Augustine landed in his dominions. From that time he appeared quite changed into another man, it being for the remaining twenty years of his life his only ambition and endeavour to establish the perfect reign of Christ both in his own soul and in the hearts of all his subjects.

In the government of his kingdom his thoughts were altogether turned on the means of best promoting the welfare of his people. He enacted most wholesome laws, which were held in high esteem in succeeding ages; he abolished the worship of idols throughout his kingdom, and shut up their temples, or turned them into churches.

His royal palace at Canterbury he gave for the use of the Archbishop St. Augustine; he founded in that city the cathedral called Christchurch, and built without the walls the abbey and church of SS. Peter and Paul, afterwards called St. Austin's. The foundation of St. Andrew's at Rochester, St. Paul's at London, and many other churches affords standing proofs of his munificence to the church. He was instrumental in bringing over to the faith of Christ Sebert, King of the East Saxons, with his people, and Redwald, King of the East Angles, though the latter afterwards relapsing, pretended to join the worship of idols with that of Christ. King Ethelbert, after having reigned fifty-six years, died in 616.

26 FEBRUARY

St. Porphyrius

BISHOP OF GAZA
A.D. 420

Porphyrius, a native of Thessalonica in Macedonia, was of a noble and wealthy family. The desire of renouncing the world made him leave his country at twenty-five years of age, in 378, to pass into Egypt, where he consecrated himself to God in a famous monastery in the desert of Scete. After five years there he went into Palestine to visit the holy places of Jerusalem. After this he took up his abode in a cave near the Jordan, where he passed another five years in great austerity, till he fell sick, when a complication of disorders obliged him to return to Jerusalem.

There he never failed daily to visit all the holy places, leaning on a staff, for he was too weak to stand upright. It happened about the same time that Mark, an Asiatic, came to Jerusalem with the same intent. He was much edified at the devotion of Porphyrius and ran to offer him assistance, which Porphyrius refused, saying, 'It is not just that I, who am come hither to beg pardon for my sins, should be eased by any one.' His confidence always supported him. The only thing which afflicted him was that his fortune had not been sold for the use of the poor. This he commissioned Mark to do for him, who accordingly set out for Thessalonica, and in three months' time returned to Jerusalem. Porphyrius was now so well recovered that Mark scarce knew him to be the same person. As to the money which Mark had brought he distributed all among the necessitous so that he reduced himself to labouring for his daily food. He therefore learned to make shoes and dress leather. He led this life till he was forty years of age, when the Bishop of Jerusalem ordained him priest in 393 and he was elected Bishop of Gaza in 396.

There happened that year a very great drought, which the pagans ascribed to the coming of the new Christian bishop. As no rain fell the first two months after St. Porphyrius's arrival, the idolaters assembled to make supplications to Marnas, whom they called the lord of rains. The Christians, by the order of their bishop, went out in procession to St Timothy's church. But at their return to the city they found the gates shut against them. In this situation the Christians, and St. Porphyrius above the rest, addressed Almighty God with redoubled fervour; when in a short time there fell such a quantity of rain that the heathens opened their gates and accompanied the Christians to church.

The good bishop spent the rest of his life in pastoral duties; and though he lived to see the city clear for the most part of the remains of paganism, he had always enough to suffer from such as continued obstinate in their errors. He died in 420, being about sixty years of age, on the 26th of February.

28 FEBRUARY

St. Oswald

BISHOP OF WORCESTER AND ARCHBISHOP OF YORK

A.D. 992

St. Oswald was nephew to St. Odo, Archbishop of Canterbury, and to Oskitell, Bishop first of Dorchester, afterwards of York. He was educated by St. Odo, and made Dean of Winchester; but, passing into France, took the monastic habit at Fleury. Being recalled to serve the church, he succeeded St. Dunstan in the see of Worcester about the year 959. He shone as a bright star in this dignity, and established a monastery of monks at Westberry, a village in his diocese. He was employed by Duke Aylwin in superintending his foundation of the great monastery of Ramsey, in an island formed by marshes and the river Ouse in Huntingdonshire in 972.

St. Oswald was made Archbishop of York in 974, and he dedicated the church of Ramsey under the names of the Blessed Virgin, St. Benedict and all holy virgins. Nothing of this rich abbey remains standing except an old gate-house, and a neglected statue of the founder Aylwin, with keys and a ragged staff in his hand to denote his office; for he was cousin to the glorious King Edgar, the valiant general of his armies, and the chief judge and magistrate of the kingdom, with the title of alderman of England, and half king, as the historian of Ramsey usually styles him.

St. Oswald was almost always occupied in visiting his diocese, preaching without intermission, and reforming abuses. He was a great encourager of learning and learned men. St. Dunstan obliged him to retain the see of Worcester with that of York. Whatever intermission his function allowed him he spent it at St. Mary's, church and monastery of Benedictins, which he had built at Worcester, where he joined with the monks in their monastic exercises. This church from that time became the cathedral. The saint, to nourish in his heart the sentiments of humility and charity, had everywhere twelve poor persons at his table, whom he served, and also washed and kissed their feet.

After having sat thirty-three years he fell sick at St. Mary's in Worcester, and having received the extreme unction, continued in prayer, repeating 'Glory be to God the Father', with which words he expired amidst his monks, on the 29th of February.

1 MARCH

St. David

ARCHBISHOP, PATRON OF WALES

A.D. 544

St. David, in Welsh Dewid, was son of Xantus, Prince of Cardiganshire. He was brought up in the service of God, and being ordained priest, retired into the Isle of Wight and embraced an ascetic life. He studied a long time to prepare himself for the functions of the holy ministry. At length, coming out of his solitude, he preached the word of eternal life to the Britons. He built a chapel at Glastonbury, a place which had been consecrated to the divine worship by the first apostles

of this island. He founded twelve monasteries, the principal of which was in the vale of Ross, where he formed many great pastors and eminent servants of God. By his rule he obliged all his monks to assiduous manual labour: he allowed them the use of no cattle to ease them at their work in tilling the ground. They were never suffered to speak but on occasions of absolute necessity, and they never ceased to pray, at least mentally, during their labour. Their food was only bread and vegetables with a little salt. Their habit was of the skins of beasts. All the monks discovered their most secret thoughts and temptations to their abbot.

The Pelegian heresy springing forth a second time in Britain, the bishops, in order to suppress it, held a synod at Brevy in Cardiganshire in 512 or 519. St. David, being invited to it, went thither, and in that venerable assembly confuted and silenced the infernal monster by his eloquence, learning and miracles. On the spot where this council was held, a church was afterwards built called Llan-Devi Brevi, or the church of St. David near the river Brevi. At the close of the synod, St. Dubritius, the Archbishop of Caerleon, resigned his see to St. David, whose tears and opposition were only to be overcome by the absolute command of the synod; which, however, allowed him, at his request, the liberty to transfer his see from Caerleon, then a populous city, to Menevia, now called St. David's, a retired place, formed by nature for solitude, being as it were almost cut off from the rest of the island. Soon after the former synod, another was assembled by St. David at a place called Victoria, in which the acts of the first were confirmed, and several canons added relating to discipline; and these two synods were the rule and standard of the British churches.

As for St. David, he continued in his last see many years; and having founded several monasteries, and been the spiritual father of many saints, both British and Irish, died about the year 544, in a very advanced age. He was buried in his church of St. Andrew, which has since taken his name, with the town and the whole diocese. Near the church stand several chapels; the principal is that of St. Nun, mother of St. David.

2 MARCH

St. Ceada

OR CHAD

SEVENTH CENTURY

Ceada was brother to St. Cedd, Bishop of London, and the two holy priests Celin and Cymbel, and had his education in the monastery of Lindisfarne, under St. Aidan. For his greater improvement in sacred letters and divine contemplation he passed into Ireland and spent a considerable time in the company of St. Egbert, till he was called back by St. Cedd to assist in settling the monastery of Lestingay which he had founded in the Wolds of Yorkshire. St. Cedd being made Bishop of London left to him the entire government of this house.

Oswi having yielded up the northern part of his kingdom to his son Alefrid, this prince sent St. Wilfrid into France that he might be consecrated to the bishopric of York; but he stayed so long abroad that Oswi himself nominated St. Chad to that dignity, who was ordained by Wini, Bishop of Winchester in 666. Bede assures us that he zealously devoted himself to all the functions of his charge, preaching the gospel, and seeking out the poorest persons to instruct and comfort. When St. Theodorus, Archbishop of Canterbury, arrived in England he adjudged the see of York to St. Wilfrid. St. Chad made him this answer, 'If you judge that I have not duly received the episcopal ordination, I willingly resign this charge, having never thought myself worthy of it; but which, however unworthy, I submitted to undertake in obedience.' The archbishop was charmed with his candour and humility, would not admit his abdication but supplied certain rites which he judged defective in his ordination.

St. Chad, leaving the see of York, retired to his monastery of Lestingay, but was not suffered to bury himself long in that solitude. Jaruman Bishop of the Mercians dying, St. Chad was called upon to take upon him the charge of that most extensive diocese. He was the fifth bishop of the Mercians, and first fixed that see at Lichfield, so called from a great number of martyrs slain and buried there, the name signifying the field of carcases. St. Theodorus, considering Chad's old age and the great extent of his diocese, absolutely forbade him to make his visitations on foot, as he used to do at York.

When the laborious duties of his charge allowed him to retire, he enjoyed God in solitude with seven or eight monks, whom he had settled in a place near his cathedral. Here he gained new strength for the discharge of his functions. By the bounty of King Wulfere he founded a monastery at a place called Barrow (in the northern part of Lincolnshire).

St. Chad governed his diocese of Lichfield two and a half years, and died in the great pestilence on the 2nd March in 673. He was buried in the Church of St Mary in Lichfield, but his relics were translated into the great church built in 1148, which is now the cathedral.

3 MARCH

St. Cunegundes
EMPRESS
A.D. 1040

St. Cunegundes was the daughter of Sigefride, the first Count of Luxemburg, and his pious wife. They instilled into her from the cradle the most tender sentiments of piety, and married her to St. Henry, Duke of Bavaria, who was chosen King of the Romans and crowned on the 6th of June, 1002. In the year 1014 she went with her husband to Rome, and received the imperial crown with him from the hands of Pope Benedict VIII. She had, by St. Henry's consent before her marriage, made a vow of virginity. Calumniators afterwards accused her to him of freedoms with other men. The holy empress, to remove the scandal of such a slander, walked over red hot plough-shares without being hurt. The emperor condemned his fears and made her ample amends. They lived from that time in the strictest union of hearts.

Going once to make a retreat in Hesse, she fell dangerously ill, and made a vow to found a monastery if she recovered in a place then called Capungen, now Kaffungen, near Cassel, which she executed in a stately manner, and gave it to nuns of the order of St. Benedict. Before it was finished St. Henry died, in 1024. She earnestly recommended his soul to the prayers of others, especially to her dear nuns. She had already exhausted her treasures and her patrimony in founding bishop-

rics and monasteries, and in relieving the poor. She had, therefore, little left to give. But still thirsting to embrace perfect poverty, on the anniversary day of her husband's death, 1025, she assembled a great number of prelates to the dedication of her church of Kaffungen; and after the gospel was sung at mass, put off her imperial robes and clothed herself with a poor habit; her hair was cut off, and the bishop put on her a veil, and a ring as the pledge of her fidelity to her heavenly spouse. After she was consecrated to God she seemed entirely to forget that she had been empress, and behaved as the last in the house, being persuaded that she was so before God. Thus she passed the last fifteen years of her life. Her mortification at length reduced her to a very weak condition and brought on her last sickness. Her monastery and the whole city of Cassel were grievously afflicted at the thought of their approaching loss. She alone appeared without concern, lying on a coarse haircloth, ready to give up the ghost, whilst the prayers of the agonising were read by her side. Perceiving they were preparing a cloth fringed with gold to cover her corpse after her death, she ordered it to be taken away, nor could she be at rest till she was promised she should be buried as a poor religious in her habit. She died on the 3rd of March, 1040. Her body was carried to Bamberg and buried near that of her husband.

4 MARCH

St. Casimir
PRINCE OF POLAND
A.D. 1433

St. Casimir was the third among the thirteen children of Casimir III, King of Poland, and Elizabeth of Austria. He was born in 1458 on the 5th of October. From his childhood he was remarkable pious and devout. His preceptor was John Dugloss, called Longinus, Canon of Cracow, a man of extraordinary learning who constantly refused all bishoprics and other dignities which were pressed upon him. Casimir and the other princes were so affectionately attached to the holy man that they could not bear to be separated from him. But Casimir profited most by his pious maxims and example. He consecrated the flower of his age to the exercises of devotion and had a horror of that softness and magnificence which reigns in courts. His bed was frequently the ground and he spent a considerable part of the night in prayer and meditation. He often went out in the night to pray before the church doors. He respected the least ceremonies of the church.

His love for Jesus Christ showed itself in his regard for the poor, to whose relief he applied whatever he had, and employed his credit with his father, and his brother Vladislas, King of Bohemia, to procure them succour. The Palatines and other nobles of Hungary dissatisfied with Matthias Corvin, their king, begged the King of Poland to allow them to place Casimir on the throne. The saint, not then quite fifteen years of age, was very unwilling to consent, but in compliance with his father's will he went, at the head of an army of twenty thousand men, to the frontiers in 1471. There, hearing that Matthias had formed an army to defend him, and that all differences were accommodated between him and his people, Casimir joyfully returned. However, as his dropping this project was disagreeable to his father, he did not go directly to Cracow, but retired to the castle of Dobzki three miles from that city where he continued three months in the practice of penance. Having learned the injustice of the attempt against the King of Hungary in which obedience to his father's command prevailed upon him to embark, he could never be engaged to resume it by the iterated orders and entreaties of his father.

The twelve years he lived after this he spent in sanctifying himself in the same manner as he had done before. He observed to the last an untainted chastity, notwithstanding the advice of physicians who excited him to marry, imagining this to be a means necessary to preserve his life. Being wasted with a lingering consumption he foretold his last hour and made a happy end at Vilna, the capital of Lithuania, on the 4th of March, 1482, being twenty-three years old. He was buried in the church of St. Stanislaus. St. Casimir is the patron of Poland and several other places, and is proposed to youth as a particular pattern of purity.

6 MARCH

St. Colette

VIRGIN AND ABBESS
A.D. 1447

Colette Boilet, a carpenter's daughter, was born at Corbie in Picardy in 1380. Her parents, out of devotion to St. Nicholas, gave her the name of Colette, the diminutive of Nicholas. She was brought up in the love of humiliations and austerities. Her desire to preserve her purity without the least blemish made her avoid all company, even of persons of her own sex. She served the poor and the sick with an affection that charmed and comforted them. She lived in strict solitude in a small poor abandoned apartment in her father's house, and spent her time in manual labour and prayer. Her parents, who though poor were virtuous, seeing her directed by the Spirit of God, allowed her full liberty in her devotions.

After their death she distributed the little they left her among the poor, and retired among the Beguines, devout societies of women established in several parts of Flanders, Picardy and Lorraine, who maintained themselves by the work of their hands but made no solemn vows. Not finding this way of life austere enough, she took the habit of the Penitents, and three years after that of the mitigated Clares, with the view of reforming that Order and reducing it to its primitive austerity.

Having obtained of the Abbot of Corbie a small hermitage, she spent in it three years. After this she went to the convent at Amiens and from thence to several others. To succeed in her undertaking it was necessary that she should be vested with proper authority; to procure which she made a journey to Nice to wait on Peter de Luna who in the great schism was acknowledged pope by the French. He constituted her superioress-general of the whole Order of St. Clare, with full power to establish in it whatever regulations she thought conducive to God's honour and the salvation of others. She attempted to revive the spirit of St. Francis in the convents of Paris, Beauvais, Noyon and Amiens, but met with the most violent opposition and was treated as a fanatic. Some time after she met with a more favourable reception in Savoy and her reformation began to take root there and passed thence into Burgundy, France, Flanders and Spain. Many ancient houses received it, and she lived to erect seventeen new ones. Several houses of Franciscan friars received the same. But Leo X, in

1517, united all the different reformations of the Franciscans, and thus the distinction of Colettines is extinct.

So great was her love for poverty that she never put on so much as sandals. Her habit was of most coarse stuff, made of above a hundred patches sewed together. She continually inculcated to her nuns the denial of their own wills in all things. Being seized with her last sickness in her convent at Ghent, she received the sacraments of the church and happily expired in her sixty-seventh year, on the 6th of March in 1447.

8 MARCH

St. John

OF GOD, FOUNDER OF THE ORDER OF CHARITY
A.D. 1550

St. John, surnamed of God, was born in Portugal in 1495. His parents were of the lowest rank, but devout. John spent a considerable part of his youth in service, and in 1522 he served in the wars between the French and Spaniards, as he did afterwards in Hungary against the Turks. The troop which he belonged to being disbanded, he went into Andalusia in 1536, where he entered the service of a rich lady near Seville, in quality of shepherd. Being now about forty years of age, stung with remorse for his past misconduct, he began to entertain serious thoughts of a change of life.

His compassion for the distressed moved him to take a resolution of passing into Africa. At Gibraltar his piety suggested to him to turn pedlar and sell little pictures and books of devotion. His stock increasing, he settled in Granada, where he opened a shop in 1538. The great preacher John d'Avila preached that year at Granada. John, having heard his sermon, was so affected that he ran about the streets like a distracted person. He then gave away all he had in the world and began again to counterfeit the madman, till some had the charity to take him to John d'Avila, covered with dirt and blood. The holy man gave him advice and promised his assistance. John was taken up and put in a madhouse. D'Avila came to visit him and found him reduced almost to the grave by weakness, but his soul was still vigorous. D'Avila advised him to employ himself in something more conducive to the public good, and John grew instantly calm and sedate. He continued some time in the hospital, serving the sick, but left it entirely in 1539. He began by selling wood in the market-place to feed some poor by his labour. Soon after, he hired a house to harbour poor sick persons in. The Bishop of Tuy, having invited the holy man to dinner gave him the name John of God and prescribed him a kind of habit, though St. John never thought of founding a religious order; the rules which bear his name were only drawn six years after his death.

Worn out at last by ten years' hard service in his hospital, he fell sick. He at first concealed his sickness that he might not be obliged to diminish his labours but in the mean time he carefully revised the inventories of all things belonging to his hospital. His illness increasing, the news of it was spread abroad. The lady Anne Ossorio was no sooner informed than she came to see him, and caused him to be taken up and carried to her own house. At last he gave the city his dying benediction. The archbishop said mass in his chamber. The saint expired on his knees, before the altar, on the 8th of March, in 1550, being exactly fifty-five years old.

9 MARCH

St. Frances
WIDOW
A.D. 1440

St. Frances was born at Rome in 1384. Her parents were both of illustrious families. She had always an aversion to the amusements of children, and loved solitude and prayer. At eleven years of age, she desired to enter a monastery, but in obedience to her parents, was married to a rich young Roman nobleman, named Laurence Ponzani, in 1396. All her delight was in prayer, meditation, and visiting churches. Above all, her obedience and condescension to her husband was inimitable, which engaged such a return of affection that for forty years which they lived together, there never happened the least disagreement. She treated her domestics not as servants, but as future co-heirs in heaven. Her mortifications were extraordinary, especially when some years before her husband's death she was permitted by him to inflict on her body what hardships she pleased. Her ordinary diet was hard and mouldy bread. Her garments were of coarse serge. Her example was of such edification that many Roman ladies, having renounced a life of idleness, pomp, and softness, joined her in pious exercises, and put themselves under the direction of the Benedictine monks of Monte-Oliveto, without leaving the world, making vows or wearing any particular habit.

It pleased God for her sanctification to make trial of her virtue by many afflictions. During the trouble which ensued upon the invasion of Rome by Ladislas, King of Naples, and the great schism in 1413 her husband was banished Rome, his estate confiscated, his house pulled down and his eldest son detained a hostage. The schism being extinguished her husband recovered his dignity and estate. Some time after, moved by her eminent virtue he permitted her to found a monastery of nuns, called Oblates, for the reception of such of her own sex as were disposed to embrace a religious life. The foundation of this house was in 1425. She gave them the rule of St. Benedict, adding some particular constitutions of her own, and she enlarged it in 1433, from which year the founding of the order is dated. St. Frances could not yet join her new family; but, as soon as she had settled her domestic affairs, after the death of her husband, she went barefoot with a cord about her neck to the monastery which she had founded and begged to be admitted. She accordingly took the habit in 1437. She continued the same humiliations and the same universal poverty, though soon after chosen superioress of her congregation. She was particularly devout to St. John the Evangelist, and above all to our lady, under whose singular protection she put her order.

Going out to see her son John Baptist, who was dangerously sick, she felt so ill herself that she could not return to her monastery that night. After having foretold her death, and received the sacraments, she expired on the 9th of March in the year 1440, and of her age the fifty-sixth.

10 MARCH

The Forty Martyrs
OF SEBASTE
A.D. 320

These holy martyrs suffered at Sebaste in the Lesser Armenia, under the Emperor Licinius. They were of different countries, but enrolled in the same troop. This was the twelfth legion, then quartered in Armenia. Lysias was general of the forces, and Agricola the governor of the province. The latter having signified to the army the orders of the emperor for all to sacrifice, these forty went boldly up to him and said they were Christians, and that no torments should make them abandon their religion.

The judge first endeavoured to gain them by mild usage; finding these methods ineffectual he had recourse to threats, but all in vain. After some day Lysias, their general, coming to Sebaste, they were re-examined and no less generously rejected the promises made them than they despised the torments they were threatened with. The governor, highly offended at their courage devised a kind of death, which being slow and severe he hoped would shake their constancy.

The cold in Armenia is very sharp, especially towards the end of winter when the wind is north, as it then was. Under the walls of the town stood a pond, which was frozen so hard that it would bear walling upon with safety. The judge ordered the saints to be exposed quite naked on the ice; and in order to tempt them the more powerfully to renounce their faith, a warm bath was prepared at a small distance from the pond for any of this company to go to. The martyrs, on hearing their sentence, ran to the place and, without waiting to be stripped, undressed themselves. Though it is not easy to form a just idea of the pain they must have undergone, of the whole number only one, losing courage, went off from the pond, but no sooner had he entered the warm water but he expired. A sentinel warming himself near the bath had a vision of blessed spirits descending on the martyrs and was converted by it. He threw off his clothes and placed himself among the thirty-nine martyrs.

In the morning the judge ordered both those that were dead and those that were still alive to be cast into a fire. When the rest were thrown into a waggon to be carried to the pile, the youngest (whom the acts call Melito) was found alive; and the executioners, hoping he would change his resolution when he came to himself, left him behind. His mother, a woman of mean condition but rich in faith, reproached the executioners, took him up, and put him with her own hands into the waggon with the rest of the martyrs.

Their bodies were burned and their ashes thrown into the river; but the Christians secretly carried off, or purchased part of them with money. Some of these relics were kept at Caesarea and they were honoured by miracles.

12 MARCH

St. Theophanes
ABBOT
A.D. 818

The father of Theophanes, who was governor of the isles of the Archipelago, died when he was only three years old, and left him heir to a very great estate, under the guardianship of the Iconoclast Emperor Constantine Copronymus. Being arrived at man's estate, he was compelled by his friends to take a wife; but on the day of his marriage he spoke in so moving a manner to his consort on the shortness and uncertainty of this life, that they made a mutual vow of perpetual chastity. She afterwards became a nun, and he built two monasteries in Mysia, one of which he governed himself.

In 787 he assisted at the second council of Nicaea, where all admired to see one whom they had formerly known in so much worldly grandeur, now so meanly clad and so full of self-contempt as he appeared to be. He never laid aside his hair shirt; his bed was a mat and his pillow a stone. At fifty years of age he began to be grievously afflicted with the stone and nephritic colic; but bore with cheerfulness the most excruciating pains.

The Emperor Leo, the Armenian, in 814 renewed the persecution against the church and abolished the use of holy images. Knowing the great reputation of Theophanes, he endeavoured to gain him by civilities and crafty letters. The saint discovered the hook concealed under his alluring baits, which did not, however, hinder him from obeying the emperor's summons to Constantinople. The emperor sent him this message, 'From your mild and obliging disposition I flatter myself you are come to confirm my sentiments. It is the readiest way for obtaining my favour. But if you refuse to comply with my desires, you will incur my highest displeasure.' The holy man returned for answer, 'If you think to frighten me into a compliance by your treats, as a child is awed by the rod, you only lose your labour.' The emperor employed several persons to endeavour to overcome his resolution, but in vain; so seeing himself vanquished, he confined him two years in a close stinking dungeon where he suffered much. He was also cruelly scourged, having received three hundred stripes. In 818 he was removed out of his dungeon and banished into the isle of Samothracia, where he died seventeen days after his arrival on the 12th of March. He has left us his *Chronographia*, or short history from the year 284 to the year 813. His imprisonment did not allow him leisure to polish the style.

13 MARCH

St. Euphrasia
VIRGIN
A.D. 410

Antigonus, the father of this saint, was a nobleman of the first rank in the court of Theodosius the Younger, nearly allied in blood to that emperor. He was married to Euphrasia, by whom he had one only daughter and heiress, called also Euphrasia. Antigonus died within a year, and the holy widow, to shun the importunate addresses of young suitors and the distraction of friends, not long after withdrew with her little daughter into Egypt, where she was possessed of a very large estate.

In that country she fixed her abode near a holy monastery of one hundred and thirty nuns, who never used any other food than herbs and pulses, which they took only after sunset. The devout mother frequently visited these servants of God, and entreated them to accept a considerable annual revenue, with an obligation that they should always be bound to pray for the soul of her deceased husband. But the abbess refused the estate, and could only be prevailed upon to accept a small matter to supply the church lamp with oil, and for incense to be burned on the altar.

The young Euphrasia, at seven years of age, made it her earnest request to her mother that she might permitted to serve God in this monastery. The mother, hearing this, wept for joy and not long after presented her to the abbess. Turning to her daughter she said, 'May God who laid the foundations of the mountains, strengthen you always in his holy fear.' And leaving her in the hands of the abbess, she went out of the monastery. Some time after this she fell sick and soon slept in peace.

Upon the news of her death, the Emperor Theodosius sent for the noble virgin to court, having promised her in marriage to a favourite young senator. But the virgin wrote him with her own hand the following answer, 'Invincible emperor, having consecrated myself to Christ, I cannot marry a mortal man. For the sake of my parents, be pleased to distribute their estates among the poor, the orphans and the church. Set all my slaves at liberty and discharge my servants, giving them whatever is their due.' The emperor punctually executed all she desired a little before his death, in 395.

St. Euphrasia was a perfect pattern of humility, meekness and charity. If she found herself assaulted by any temptation, she immediately discovered it to the abbess, who often enjoined her, on such occasions, some humbling and painful penitential labour, as sometimes to carry great stones from one place to another; which employment she once continued thirty days together till the devil left her in peace. She cleaned out the chambers of the other nuns and cheerfully employed herself in the meanest drudgery. She was favoured with miracles both before and after her death, which happened in the year 410, and the thirtieth of her age.

14 MARCH

St. Maud

OR MATHILDIS, QUEEN OF GERMANY

A.D. 968

This princess was the daughter of Theodoric, a powerful Saxon count. Her parents, being sensible that piety is the only true greatness, placed her very young in the monastery of Erford, of which her grandmother Maud was then abbess. She remained in that house till her parents married her to Henry, son of Otho, Duke of Saxony, in 913. Her husband, surnamed the Fowler, from his fondness for hawking, became Duke of Saxony in 916 and in 919 was chosen King of Germany. Whilst he, by his arms, checked the insolence of the Hungarians and Danes and enlarged his dominions, Maud gained domestic victories over her spiritual enemies. It was her delight to visit, comfort and exhort the sick, to serve and instruct the poor, teaching them the advantages of their state, from the example of Christ; and to afford her charitable succours to prisoners, procuring them their liberty where motives of justice would permit it, or at least easing the weight of their chains by liberal alms; but her chief aims was to make them shake off their sins, by sincere repentance. Her husband, edified by her example, concurred with her in every pious undertaking.

After twenty-three years' marriage, God was pleased to call the king to himself by an apoplectic fit in 936. Maud, during his sickness, went to the church to pour forth her soul in prayer for him. As soon as she understood, by the tears of the people, that he had expired she cut off the jewels which she wore and gave them to the priest, as a pledge that she renounced from that moment the pomp of the world.

She had three sons: Otho, afterwards emperor; Henry Duke of Bavaria; and St. Bruno, Archbishop of Cologne. Maud, in the contest between her two elder sons for the crown which was elective, favoured Henry, who was the younger. These two sons conspired to strip her of her dowry on the unjust pretence that she had squandered away the revenues of the state on the poor. This persecution was long and cruel, coming from all that was most dear to her in this world. The unnatural princes at length repented of their injustice, and restored all that had been taken from her. She then became more liberal in her alms than ever, and founded many churches, with five monasteries; of which the principal were that of Polden, in the duchy of Brunswick, in which she maintained three thousand monks, and that of Quedlinbourg in the duchy of Saxony.

In her last sickness she made her confession to her grandson William, the Archbishop of Mentz, who yet died twelve days before her, on his road home. She again made a public confession before the priests and monks of the place, received a second time the last sacraments, and lying on a sackcloth with ashes on her head, died on the 14th of March in 968.

16 MARCH

St. Abraham

HERMIT, AND HIS NIECE, ST MARY, A PENITENT

ABOUT THE YEAR 360

St. Abraham was born at Chidana in Mesopotamia of wealthy and noble parents, who, after giving him a most virtuous education, were desirous of engaging him in the married state. In compliance with their inclinations, Abraham took to wife a pious virgin; but as soon as the marriage ceremony and feast were over, he secretly withdrew to a cell two miles from the city Edessa, where his friends found him at prayer after a search of seventeen days. After their departure he walled up the door of his cell, leaving only a little window, through which he received what was necessary for his subsistence. For fifty years he was never wearied with his austere penance. Ten years after he had left the world, by the demise of his parents, he inherited their great estates, but commissioned a virtuous friend to distribute the revenues in alms.

A large country town in the diocese remained addicted to idolatry and its inhabitants had loaded with injuries all the holy monks and others who had attempted to preach the gospel to them. The bishop at length cast his eye on Abraham, ordained him priest, though much against his will, and sent him to preach the faith to those obstinate infidels. Although the citizens resolutely determined not to hear him speak, he continued to pray and weep among them without intermission and though he was often beaten and ill-treated and thrice banished by them he always returned with the same zeal. After three years, the infidels were overcome by his meakness and patience and all demanded baptism. He stayed one year longer with them and went back to his cell.

His brother dying soon after, left an only daughter called Mary, whom the saint undertook to train up in a religious life. For this purpose he placed her in a cell near his own. At the end of twenty years she was unhappily seduced by a wicked monk and falling into despair, went to a distant town, where she gave herself up to the most criminal disorders. The saint ceased not for two years to pray for her. Being then informed where she dwelt he dressed himself like a citizen of that town, and going to the inn where she lived desired her company with him at supper. When he saw her alone, he took off his cap which disguised him. Seeing her filled with horror he tenderly encouraged her, set her on his horse and conducted her back to his desert. There she spent the remaining fifteen years of her life. St. Abraham died five years before her: at the news of whose sickness almost the whole city and country flocked to receive his benediction. When he had expired, every one strove to procure some part of his clothes and St. Ephrem relates that many sick were cured by the touch of these relics.

PLATE 15. ST. MATHILDIS, 14 MARCH. BUTLER, *LIVES OF THE SAINTS*, TWO-VOLUME ILLUSTRATED 19TH-CENTURY EDITION.

PLATE 16. ST. PATRICK, 17 MARCH. BUTLER, *LIVES OF THE SAINTS*, TWO-VOLUME ILLUSTRATED 19TH-CENTURY EDITION.

17 MARCH

St. Patrick

APOSTLE OF IRELAND

A.D. 464

St. Patrick was born in the decline of the fourth century in Scotland, between Dunbriton and Glasgow. He calls himself both a Briton and a Roman and says his father was of a good family. At fifteen years of age he committed a fault, which appears not to have been a great crime, yet was to him a subject of tears during the remainder of his life. In his sixteenth year he was carried into captivity by certain barbarians. They carried him into Ireland, where he was obliged to keep cattle on the mountains and in the forests, in hunger and nakedness. His afflictions were to him a source of heavenly benedictions, because he carried his cross with patience, resignation and holy joy. St. Patrick after six months spent in slavery was admonished by God in a dream to return to his own country and informed that a ship was then ready to sail thither. He repaired immediately to the sea coast but could not obtain his passage, probably for want of money. The sailors, though pagans, took him on board.

When he was at home with his parents, God manifested to him by divers visions that he destined him to the great work of the conversion of Ireland. Some think he travelled into Gaul before he undertook his mission. But it seems from his Confession that he was ordained deacon, priest and bishop in his own country. Great opposition was made against his episcopal consecration and mission, but he persevered in his resolution. He forsook his family, sold his birthright and dignity and consecrated his soul to God. In this disposition he passed into Ireland to preach the gospel where the worship of idols still generally reigned. Such was the fruit of his preachings and sufferings that he consecrated to God by baptism an infinite number of people, ordained everywhere clergymen and instituted monks. The happy success of his labours cost him many persecutions.

St. Patrick held several councils to settle the discipline of the church which he had planted. He fixed his metropolitan see at Armagh. In the first year of his mission he attempted to preach Christ in the general assembly of the kings and states of all Ireland held yearly at Taraghe, the principal seat of the Druids and their paganish rites. The son of Neill, the chief monarch, declared himself against the preacher: however he converted several, and afterwards baptized the Kings of Dublin and Munster, and the seven sons of the King of Connaught, and before his death almost the whole island. He founded a monastery at Armagh, another called Domnach-Padraig, or Patrick's church; also a third, named Sabhal-Padraig, and filled the country with churches and schools of piety and learning, the reputation of which for the three succeeding centuries, drew many foreigners into Ireland. He died and was buried at Down, in Ulster.

17 MARCH

St. Joseph

OF ARIMATHEA

FIRST CENTURY

St. Joseph was a member of the Jewish Sanhedrim, but a faithful disciple of Jesus. It was no small proof of his great piety, that though he had riches and honours to lose, he feared not the malice of men, but at a time when the apostles trembled, boldly declared himself a follower of Jesus who was crucified; and with the greatest devotion embalmed and buried his sacred body.

This saint was the patron of Glastenbury [Glastonbury] where a church and hermitage, very famous in the times of the ancient Britons, were built by the first apostles of this island, among whom some moderns have placed St Joseph himself.

[Editorial note: the legends associating Joseph of Arimathea with Glastonbury also suggest that he brought to England the Holy Grail, a cup allegedly containing the blood of Christ shed at Calvary, and a staff of thorn-wood which he planted at Glastonbury and which grew into the Holy Thorn still to be found there. There were claims in the Middle Ages that Joseph had been buried at Glastonbury, although his body was never found, and further claims from the abbey of Moyenmoutier in France that his relics were held there.]

18 MARCH

St. Cyril

ARCHBISHOP OF JERUSALEM

A.D. 386

Cyril was born at or near the city of Jerusalem about the year 315. He read diligently both the Fathers and the pagan philosophers. Maximus, Bishop of Jerusalem, ordained him priest about the year 345, and soon after appointed him his preacher to the people, likewise his catechist to instruct and prepare for baptism; thus committing to his care the two principal functions of his own pastoral charge. This office St. Cyril performed for several years. He succeeded Maximus in the see of Jerusalem about the end of the year 350.

The beginning of his episcopy was remarkable for a prodigy. St. Cyril, an eye-witness, wrote to the Emperor Constantius an account of his miraculous phenomenon, as follows: 'On the nines (or 7th) of May, about the third hour a vast luminous body in the form of a cross appeared in the heavens, just over the holy Golgotha, reaching as far as the holy Mount of Olivet, seen not by one or two persons, but clearly and evidently by the whole city.'

Some time after this memorable event a difference happened between our saint and Acacius, Archbishop of Caesarea, first a Semi-Arian, afterwards a thorough Arian. Acacius in a council of Arian bishops convened by him, declared St. Cyril deposed for not appearing, after two years' warning, to answer to the crimes alleged against him. St. Cyril appealed to higher powers but withdrew to Antioch and thence removed to Tarsus. Upon the death of Constantius in 361, Julian the Apostate, partly in hopes to see the Christian sects and the orthodox more at variance, suffered all the banished bishops to return to their churches. Thus did God make use of the malice of his enemy to restore St. Cyril to his see.

Emperor Julian affected a show of great moderation; but he sought to undermine the faith. This he attempted to do by a project of rebuilding the Jewish temple. The Jews were so elated that flocking from all parts to Jerusalem they began to scorn and triumph over the Christians. All things were in readiness, workmen were assembled; stone, brick and timber laid in. But the good bishop Cyril, lately returned from exile, beheld all these preparations without any concern. They began to dig the new foundations, but what they had thrown up in the day was by repeated earthquakes the night following cast back again into the trench. Lastly there appeared over Jerusalem a lucid cross, as large as that in the reign of Constantine.

St. Cyril was again driven from his see in 367, but recovered it in 378. He found his flock miserably divided by heresies and schisms; but he continued his labours among them. In 381 he assisted at the general council of Constantinople, in which he condemned the Semi-Arians and Macedonians, whose heresy he had always opposed. He had governed his church eight years in peace when in 386 he passed to a glorious immortality.

19 MARCH

St. Joseph
FIRST CENTURY

St. Joseph was lineally descended from the great kings of the tribes of Judah; but his true glory consisted in his humility and virtue. God entrusted him with the education of his divine Son. In this view he was espoused to the Virgin Mary. He was given her to be the protector of her chastity, to secure her from calumnies in the birth of the Son of God, and to assist her in her journeys, fatigues and persecutions. This holy man seems to have been unacquainted that the great mystery of the Incarnation had been wrought by the Holy Ghost. Conscious, therefore, of his own chaste behaviour towards her, it could not but raise a concern in his breast to find that she was with child. But being a just man he was determined to leave her privately without condemning or accusing her. These dispositions were so acceptable to God that he sent an angel from heaven to dissipate all his doubts.

We should be ungrateful to this great saint if we did not remember that it is to him that we are indebted for the preservation of the infant Jesus from Herod's jealousy. An angel appearing to him in his sleep bade him arise, take the child Jesus, and fly with him into Egypt. After the death of Herod, God ordered him to return with the child and his mother into the land of Israel, which our saint readily obeyed, and retired into Galilee, to his former habitation in Nazareth.

St. Joseph being a strict observer of the Mosaic law, annually repaired to Jerusalem to celebrate the passover. Our Saviour being advanced to the twelfth year of his age accompanied his parents thither; who, having performed the usual ceremonies were now returning with many of their neighbours towards Galilee, never doubting but that Jesus had joined himself with some of the company. When night came and they could hear no tidings of him they returned with the utmost speed to Jerusalem, where, after an anxious search of three days, they found

him sitting in the temple, sitting among the learned doctors of the law asking such questions and made them astonished. When his mother said to him, 'Son, why hast thou thus dealt with us? Behold, thy father and I sought thee in great affliction of mind', she received for answer that he must be about his Father's business and therefore it was most likely for them to find him in his Father's house.

As no further mention is made of St. Joseph, he must have died before the marriage of Cana, and the beginning of our divine Saviour's ministry. We cannot doubt but that he had the happiness of Jesus and Mary attending at his death, praying by him, assisting and comforting him in his last moments; whence he is particularly invoked for the great grace of a happy death and the spiritual presence of Jesus in that hour.

20 MARCH

St. Cuthbert
A.D. 687

When the Northumbrians had embraced the Christian faith, St. Aidan founded two monasteries, that of Melrose (Mailros), on the Tweed, and another in the island of Lindisfarne. St. Cuthbert was born not very far from Melrose and in his youth was much edified by the devout department of the holy inhabitants of that house whose fervour he endeavoured to imitate on the mountains where he kept his father's sheep. It happened one night that whilst he was watching in prayer near his flock he saw the soul of St. Aidan carried up to heaven by angels at the very instant that he departed this life in the isle of Lindisfarne. The young man repaired without delay to Melrose where he put on the monastic habit, whilst Eata was abbot, and St. Boisil prior.

Eata being called to govern the new monastery of Rippon, he took with him St. Cuthbert and committed him to the care of entertaining strangers. When St. Wilfrid was made Abbot of Rippon, Cuthbert returned to Melrose, and St. Boisil dying of the great pestilence in 774, he was chosen prior in his place. In this station he laboured assiduously among the people to bring them off from severe heathenish customs and superstitious practices which still obtained among them. He chiefly visited those villages at a distance which, being among high and craggy mountains, were the less frequented by other teachers. After St. Cuthbert had lived many years at Melrose, St. Eata, abbot also of Lindisfarne, appointed him prior of that larger monastery. The saint had governed Lindisfarne several years when, earnestly aspiring to a closer union with God, he retired, with his abbot's consent, into the little isle of Farne, nine miles from Lindisfarne, there to lead an eremetical life. The place was uninhabited and afforded neither water, tree nor corn. Cuthbert built himself a hut and by his prayers obtained a well of fresh water in his cell. Although the brethren came to see him, he gave spiritual advice only through a window, without ever stirring out of his cell.

In a synod of bishops held at Twiford in Northumberland, it was resolved that Cuthbert should be raised to the episcopal see of Lindisfarne. But as neither letters nor messengers were of force to obtained his consent, King Egfrid sailed over to the island and conjured him not to refuse. Their remonstrances were so pressing that he received consecration at York the Easter following. In this new dignity the saint continued his

IOSEPH

PLATE 17. ST. JOSEPH, 19 MARCH. BUTLER, *LIVES OF THE SAINTS*, TWO-VOLUME ILLUSTRATED 19TH-CENTURY EDITION.

former austerities but, remembering what he owed to his neighbour, he went about preaching and instructing.

St. Cuthbert, foreseeing his death approach, resigned his bishopric which had held two years, and retired to his solitude in Farne Island. Two months after, he fell sick and permitted Herefrid, the Abbot of Lindisfarne, who came to visit him, to leave two of his monks to attend him. He died on the 20th of March, 687.

22 MARCH

St. Basil

OF ANCYRA, PRIEST
A.D. 362

St. Basil was a priest of Ancrya under the Bishop Marcellus, and a man of most holy life who preached the word of God with great assiduity. He was forbidden by the Arian bishops in 360 to hold ecclesiastical assemblies; but he despised the unjust order and defended the Catholic faith before Constantius himself. When Julian the Apostate re-established idolatry Basil ran through the whole city, exhorting the Christians to continue steadfast and not pollute themselves with the sacrifices of the heathens. The heathens laid violent hands on him and dragged him before the proconsul, accusing him of sedition; that he stirred up the people against the gods and had spoken irreverently of the emperor. The proconsul commanded him to be tortured on the rack, remanded him to prison, and informed his master, Julian, of what he had done. The emperor approved of his proceedings and dispatched two apostate courtiers to assist the proconsul in the trial of the prisoner. Basil did not cease to praise and glorify God in his dungeon.

In the mean time Julian set out for Constantinople to Antioch in order to prepare for his Persian expedition. When he arrived at Ancyra, St. Basil was presented before him, and the crafty emperor, putting on an air of compassion, said to him, 'I myself am well skilled in your mysteries; and I can inform you that Christ remains among the dead.' The martyr answered, 'You are deceived; you have renounced Christ at a time when he conferred on you the empire. But he will deprive you of it, together with your life.' Julian replied, 'I designed to dismiss thee; but thy impudent manner of rejecting my advice force me to use thee ill. It is therefore my command, that every day thy skin be torn off in seven different places, till thou hast no more left.'

The saint, having suffered with wonderful patience the first incisions, desired to speak to the emperor. Not doubting but Basil intended to comply and offer sacrifice Julian instantly ordered that the confessor should meet him in the temple of Esculapius. But the martyr replied that he could never adore blind and deaf idols, and taking a piece of his flesh which still hung to his body by a bit of skin, he threw it upon Julian. The emperor went out in great indignation and the torments of the martyr were redoubled. So deep were the incisions made in his flesh that his bowels were exposed to view and the spectators wept for compassion. The martyr prayed aloud all the time, and at evening was carried back to prison. Next morning Julian set out for Antioch. The saint was laid on his belly and his back pierced with red-hot iron spikes. The martyr expired under these torments on the 29th of June, in 362; but his name is honoured, both by the Latins and Greeks, on the 22nd of March.

23 MARCH

St. Alphonsus

TURIBIUS, ARCHBISHOP OF LIMA
A.D. 1606

St. Toribio, or Turibius Alphonsus Mogrobejo, was born in the kingdom of Leon on the 16th of November, 1538. He began his higher studies at Vallodolid, but completed them at Salamanca. He was introduced early to the notice of King Philip II, honoured by him with several dignities, and made chief judge at Granada. This office he discharged during five years with so much integrity, prudence and virtue, that, the archbishopric of Lima falling vacant, Turibius was unanimously judged the person of all others the best qualified to be an apostle of so large a country, and to remedy the scandals which obstructed the conversion of the infidels. The king readily nominated him to that dignity. Turibius was thunderstruck at the news and wrote the most urgent letters to the king's council, in which he pleaded his incapacity and laid green stress of the canons which forbid laymen to be promoted to such dignities in the church.

Being compelled by obedience to acquiesce, after suitable preparation he received the four minor orders on four successive Sundays; and after passing through the other orders, he was consecrated bishop. Immediately after which he set out for Peru, and landed at Lima in 1581. That diocese is extended one hundred and thirty leagues along the coast and over two ridges of the mountains of the Andes, esteemed the highest and the most rugged in the world. Civil wars and dissensions were the misfortune of that country, and covetousness, cruelty and debauchery seemed triumphant. The good pastor, upon his arrival, immediately began a visitation of his vast diocese, an undertaking attended with many dangers. To settle and maintain discipline he appointed diocesan synods to be held every two years and was severe in chastising the least scandal in the clergy. Many of the first conquerors of Peru were men who sacrificed everything to their passions. From some of these the saint suffered persecutions and was often thwarted by them in the discharge of his duty. But he overcame all affronts and injuries and extirpated the most inveterate abuses. He filled the country with seminaries, churches and many hospitals; but would never suffer his own name to be recorded in any of his munificent charities or foundations.

He spent seven years in performing his first visitation, his second employed him four years, but the third was shorter. He preached and catechized, having for this purpose learned all the various languages of the nations of the country. Even on his journeys he said mass every day and usually went to confession every morning. St. Turibius, in 1606, fell sick at Santa, a town one hundred and ten leagues distant from Lima. By his last will he ordered what he had about him to be distributed among his servants and whatever else he possessed to be given to the poor. He received extreme unction in his sick bed and died on the 23rd of March.

25 MARCH

The Annunciation of the Blessed Virgin Mary

This great festival takes it name from the happy tidings brought by the angel Gabriel to the Blessed Virgin Mary, concerning the incarnation of the Son of God. It commemorates the most important embassy that was ever known: an embassy sent by the King of kings, performed by one of the chief princes of his heavenly court; directed not to the kings or emperors of the earth, but to a poor, unknown, retired virgin.

This is not the first time that angels appeared to women; but we find not that they were ever treated with that respect which the angel Gabriel shows to Mary. Sarah and Agar were visited by these celestial spirits, but not with an honour like that wherewithal the angel on this occasion addresses the Blessed Virgin, saying 'Hail! full of grace,' and concludes his address with these words, 'Blessed art thou among women.' Mary, guarded by her modesty, is in confusion at expressions of this sort, and dreads the least appearance of deluding flattery. Such high commendations make her cautious how she answers, till in silence she has more fully considered the matter. Ah, what numbers of innocent souls have been corrupted for want of using the like precautions! Mary is retired, but how seldom now-a-days are young virgins content to stay at home!

A second cause why Mary was disturbed at the words of the angel was because they contained her praises. Humble souls always tremble and sink with confusion in their own minds when they hear themselves commended; because they are deeply penetrated with a sense of their own weakness and insufficiency.

The angel, to calm her disquiets, says to her, 'Fear not Mary, for thou hast found favour before God.' He then informs her that she is to conceive and bring forth and son whose name shall be Jesus, who shall be the son of the Most High. In submission to God's will, without any further inquiries, she expresses her assent in these humble but powerful words: 'Behold the handmaid of the Lord, be it done to me according to thy word.' That moment the Word of God is for ever united to humanity, this being the principal point in all the wonderful revelations of God made to his church since the fall of Adam in paradise.

St. Austin says that, according to an ancient tradition, this mystery was completed on the 25th of March. Both eastern and western churches celebrate it on this day, and have done so at least ever since the fifth century.

PLATE 18. THE ANNUNCIATION, 25 MARCH. BRITISH LIBRARY, KINGS MS 9, F. 66V.

26 MARCH

St. Ludger
BISHOP OF MUNSTER, APOSTLE OF SAXONY
A.D. 809

St. Ludger was born in Friseland about the year 743. His father committed him very young to the care of St. Gregory of the see of Utrecht. Gregory educated him in his monastery and gave him the clerical tonsure. Ludger, desirous of further improvement, passed over into England, and spent four years and a half under Alcuin, rector of a famous school at York. In 773 he returned home and, St. Gregory dying in 776, his successor Alberic compelled our saint to receive the order of priesthood and employed him for several years in preaching in Frieseland, where he converted great numbers, founded several monasteries and built many churches.

When the pagan Saxons, ravaging the country, obliged him to leave Friseland, he travelled to Rome to consult Pope Adrian II what course to take. He then retired for three years and a half to Mount Cassino, where he wore the habit and conformed to the rule, but made no religious vows. In 787 Charlemagne overcame the Saxons and conquered Friseland and the coast as far as Denmark. Ludger, hearing that the mission was again opened, returned into East Friseland where converted the Saxons, as he did also Westphalia. He founded the monastery of Werden twenty-nine miles from Cologne.

In 802 Hildebald, Archbishop of Cologne, not regarding his strenuous resistance, ordained him Bishop of Mimigardeford, a city which afterwards changed its name to Munster, from the great monastery of regular canons which St. Ludger built there to serve for his cathedral. He joined to his diocese five cantons of Friseland, which he had converted, and also founded the monastery of Helmstad, afterwards called Ludger-Clooster, in the duchy of Brunswick.

He was very learned in the holy scriptures and read daily lectures thereon to his disciples. Except what was absolutely necessary for his subsistence, he employed the revenues of his own estates, and that of the bishopric in charities. St. Ludger required so devout an attention at divine service that being at prayers one night with his clergy, and one of them stooping down to mend the fire and hinder it from smoking, the saint after prayer severely rebuked him for it.

His last sickness, though violent, did not hinder him from continuing his functions to the very last day of his life, which was Passion Sunday, on which day he preached very early in the morning, said mass towards nine, and preached again before night, foretelling withal to those that were about him that he would die the following night, and fixing upon a place, in his monastery of Werden, where he chose to be interred. He died, accordingly, on the 26th of March, at midnight. His relics are still kept at Werden.

30 MARCH

St. John
CLIMACUS, ABBOT
A.D. 605

St. John, generally distinguished by the appellation of Climacus, from his excellent book entitled *Climax*, or *The Ladder to Perfection*, was born about 525, probably in Palestine. At sixteen years of age he renounced all the advantages which the world promised him to dedicate himself to God. He retired to Mount Sinai, which from the time of the disciples of St. Antony, had been peopled by holy men. Our novice chose not to live in the great monastery on the summit, but in an hermitage on the descent of the mountain, under the discipline of Martyrius, an ancient anchoret. By silence he curbed the itch of talking about everything, an ordinary vice in learned men. By perfect humility and obedience he banished self-complacency in his actions.

In the year 560, the thirty-fifth of his age, he lost Martyrius by death. By the advice of a director, he then embraced an eremitical life in a plain called Thole, near the foot of Mount Sinai. His cell was five miles from the church. Thither he went every Saturday and Sunday to assist with all the other monks of that desert at the holy office. He assiduously read the holy scriptures and fathers, and was one of the most learned doctors of the church, but concealed his talents. As if this cell had not been sufficiently remote, St. John frequently retired into a cavern which he made in the rock where no one could come to disturb his devotions.

St. John was seventy-five years old, and had spent forty of them in his hermitage, when in 600 he was chosen Abbot of Mount Sinai. That posterity might receive some share in the benefit of his instructions, the Abbot of Raithu, a monastery situated towards the Red Sea, entreated him that he would draw up the rules by which fervent souls might arrive at Christian perfection. Wherefore he took up his pen and set himself to draw some outlines. This produced the excellent work which he called *The Ladder of Religious Perfection*. John, Abbot of Raithu, explained this book by judicious comments, which are also extant. We have likewise a letter of St. John Climacus to the same person, concerning the duties of a pastor.

St. John sighed continually under the weight of his dignity during the four years that he governed the monks of Mount Sinai; and as he had taken upon him that burden with reluctance he found means to resign the same a little before his death. He died in his hermitage on the 30th day of March in 605, being fourscore years old.

1 APRIL

St. Hugh

CONFESSOR, BISHOP OF GRENOBLE
A.D. 1132

Hugh was born at Chateauneuf in Dauphiné in 1053. His father, Odilo, served his country in the army, and by the advice of his son became a Carthusian monk when he was upwards of fourscore years old, and lived eighteen years in great humility under St. Bruno in the Great Chartreuse, where he died one hundred years old, having received extreme unction from his son. Our saint likewise assisted in her last moments his mother, who had for many years served God in her own house.

Hugh from the cradle appeared to be a child of benediction. Having chosen to serve God in an ecclesiastical state, he accepted a canonry in the cathedral of Valence. He was tall and comely but naturally bashful, and such was his modesty that for some time he found means to conceal his learning and eloquence.

Hugh, then Bishop of Die, but soon after cardinal legate of the holy see was so charmed at first sight of the saint when he happened to come to Valence that he would not be contented until he had taken the good man into his household. He employed him in extirpating simony, and in many other affairs of importance. In 1081 the Legate Hugh held a synod at Avignon in which he took under consideration the desolate condition into which the church of Grenoble was sunk. The eyes of the whole council were fixed on St. Hugh as the person best qualified to reform the abuses, but his reluctance and fears were not to be overcome till he was compelled by the repeated commands of the legate.

St. Hugh, after his ordination, hastened to his flock, but was exceedingly afflicted when he found the people plunged in vice and immorality. Many lands belonging to the church were usurped by laymen; and the revenues of the bishopric were dissipated so that the saint found nothing either to assist the poor or to supply his own necessities. He set himself in earnest to reform abuses and had to comfort to see the face of his diocese in a short time exceedingly changed.

After two years he privately resigned his bishopric and entered the austere abbey of Chaise-Dieu in Auvergne. St. Bruno and his six companions addressed themselves to him for advice in their design of forsaking the world and he appointed them a desert which was in his diocese, whither he conducted them in 1084. It is called the Chartreuse, or Carthusian Mountains, which place gave name to the order St. Bruno founded there. The meek and pious behaviour of these servants of God took deep root in the heart of our holy pastor. Sometimes the charms of contemplation detained him so long in this hermitage that St. Bruno was obliged to order him to go to his flock. He closed his penitential course on the 1st of April, in 1132, wanting only two months of being eighty years old.

PLATE 19. ST. HUGH, 1 APRIL. BRITISH LIBRARY, KINGS MS 9, F. 51V.

2 APRIL

St. Francis

OF PAULA, FOUNDER OF THE ORDER OF MINIMS
A.D. 1508

This saint was born about the year 1416 at Paula, a small city in Calabria. His parents were very poor. Having lived together several years without issue, they earnestly begged of God a son who might faithful serve him. A son some time after this was born, whom they named after their patron, St. Francis.

In the thirteenth year of his age his father placed him in the convent of Franciscan friars at St. Mark's where he learned to read and laid the foundation of the austere life which he ever after led. Having spent one year here, he performed with his parents a pilgrimage to Assisi and Rome. When he returned to Paula, he chose a remote retreat in the corner of a rock upon the sea-coast. He was scarce fifteen years old. Before he was quite twenty, two other devoutly inclined persons joined him. The neighbours built them three cells and a chapel. This is reputed the foundation of his religious order in 1436.

Near seventeen years after, their number being much increased, a large church and monastery were built for them in the same place. Penance, charity and humility he laid down for the basis of his rule. He obliged his followers to observe a perpetual Lent, and always to abstain from all white meats, food made of milk, and eggs. In order more effectually to enforce obedience to this injunction, he prescribed a fourth vow, and to show his value for humility as the ground of all virtues he gave them a name Minims, to signify that they were the least in the house of God. The Archbishop of Cosenza approved the rule and order in 1471. Pope Sixtus IV confirmed it by bull dated 1474.

Louis XI, King of France, after an apoplectic fit, fell into a lingering decay. Never had any man a greater dread of death. He ordered prayers, processions and pilgrimages for his health. His distemper still increasing, he sent to our holy hermit in Calabria begging he would come to restore his health. Hearing that Francis would not be prevailed on to comply, he desired the pope to interpose. Sixtus commanded Francis to repair to the king. Hereupon the obedient saint set out and arrived on the 24th of April, 1482. The king went out to meet him and conjured him to obtain of God the prolongation of his life. St. Francis told him no wise man ought to entertain such a desire. By his prayers and exhortation he effected a perfect change in the king's heart who died in his arms, perfectly resigned, in 1483.

St. Francis spent the three last months of his life within his cell, denying himself all communication with mankind that nothing might divert his thoughts from eternity. He fell sick of a fever on Palm Sunday, in 1506. He died on the 2nd of April, in 1508, being ninety-one years old.

3 APRIL

St. Richard

A.D. 1253

St. Richard was born at the manor of Wiche, famous for its salt wells, four miles from Worcester, being second son to Richard and Alice de Wiche. In order to keep faithfully his baptismal vows, he from his infancy ever held in contempt all worldly pomp; instead of which his attention was wholly employed in establishing a solid foundation of virtue and learning. The unfortunate situation of his eldest brother's affairs gave him an occasion of exercising his benevolent disposition. Richard condescended to become his servant and by his industry effectually retrieved his brother before distressed circumstances. Having completed this good work, he resumed at Paris those studies he had begun at Oxford, leading with two select companions a life of piety and mortification.

Upon his return to England he proceeded master of arts at Oxford from whence he went to Bologna. After having taught there a short time he returned to Oxford and, on account of his merit, was soon promoted to the dignity of chancellor in that university. St. Edmund, Archbishop of Canterbury, appointed him his chancellor. He accompanied this holy prelate in his banishment into France and after his death retired into a convent of Dominican friars in Orleans. Having in that solitude received the order of priesthood he returned to England to serve a private curacy in the diocese of Cantery. Boniface, who had succeeded Edmund in that see, compelled him to resume his office of chancellor. Ralph Nevil, Bishop of Chichester dying in 1244, King Henry III recommended to that see an unworthy court favourite called Robert Passelaw; the archbishop declared the person not qualified and preferred Richard to that dignity. He was consecrated in 1245. But the king seized his temporalities and the saint suffered many hardships from him during two years till he recovered his revenues, but much impaired. And as, after having pleaded his cause at Rome before Pope Innocent IV against the king, he had permitted no persecution to excuse him for the omission of any part of his duty to his flock; so now, the chief obstacles being removed he redoubled his fervour and attention. When his steward complained that his alms exceeded his income. 'Then', said he, 'sell my plate and my horse.' The affronts he always repaid with favours. In maintaining discipline he was inflexible, especially in chastising crimes in the clergy, yet penitent sinners he received with inexpressible tenderness and charity.

Whilst he was employed in preaching a holy war against the Saracens, being commissioned thereto by the pope, he fell sick of a fever. He died in an hospital at Dover, called God's House, on the 3rd of April, in the year 1253, of his episcopal dignity the ninth, of his age the fifty-sixth. His body was conveyed to Chichester and interred before the altar which he himself had consecrated in his cathedral to the memory of St. Edmund.

4 APRIL

St. Isidore

BISHOP OF SEVILLE
A.D. 606

The city of Carthagena was the place of Isidore's birth, which his parents, Severian and Theodora, persons of the first quality in the kingdom, edified by the example of their extraordinary piety. His two brothers, Leander and Fulgentius, bishops, and his sister Florentina, are also honoured among the saints. Isidore, having qualified himself in his youth for the service of the church, assisted his brother Leander, Archbishop of Seville, in the conversion of the Visigoths from the Arian heresy. Upon the decease of Leander, in 600 or 601, he succeeded him in the see of Seville.

In 610, the bishops of Spain, in a council held at Toledo, agreed to declare the archbishop of that city Primate of all Spain. Yet we find that in the fourth council of Toledo, in 633, St. Isidore presided, not by the privilege of his see, but on the bare consideration of his extraordinary merit.

St. Isidore, to extend to posterity the advantages which his labours had procured to the church, compiled many useful works, in which he takes in the whole circle of the sciences, and discovers a most extensive reading and a general acquaintance with the ancient writers, both sacred and profane. The saint was well versed in the Latin, Greek and Hebrew languages.

When he was almost fourscore years old, though age and fatigues had undermined and broken into his health, he never interrupted his usual exercises and labours. During the last six months of his life, he increased his charities with such profusion that the poor of the whole country crowded his house from morning till night. Perceiving his end to draw near, he entreated two bishops to come to see him. With them he went to church, where one of them covered him with sackcloth, the other put ashes on his head. Clothed with the habit of penance, he stretched his hands towards heaven, prayed with great eagerness and begged aloud the pardon of his sins. He then received from the hands of the bishops the body and blood of our Lord, recommended himself to the prayers of all that were present, remitted the bonds of his debtors, exhorted the people to charity, and caused all the money which he had not as yet disposed of to be distributed among the poor. This done, he returned to his own house, and calmly departed this life on the fourth day after, which was the 4th of April, in the year 636, as is testified by his disciple, who was present at his death. His body was interred in his cathedral between those of his brother St. Leander and his sister St. Florentina. Ferdinand, King of Castile and Leon, recovered his relics from the Moors and placed them in the church of St. John Baptist at Leon, where they still remain.

5 APRIL

St. Vincent

FERRER
A.D. 1419

St. Vincent Ferrer was born at Valencia in Spain on the 23rd of January, 1357. His father having proposed to him the choice of a religious or a secular state, Vincent without hesitation said it was his earnest desire to consecrate himself to the service of God in the Order of St. Dominic, and he put on the habit in 1374, in the beginning of his eighteenth year. He made surprisingly rapid progress in the paths of perfection, and published a treatise on Dialectic Suppositions, being not quite twenty-four. He was sent to Barcelona, and from thence to Lerida. At the earnest importunities of the bishop, clergy and people of Valencia he was recalled to his own country, and pursued there both his lectures and his preaching.

St. Vincent had lived thus six years when Cardinal Peter de Luna, legate in Spain, was appointed to go from thence in the same capacity to Charles VI, King of France, and obliged the saint to accompany him. Clement VII, dying at Avignon in 1394, during the great schism, Peter de Luna was chosen pope by the French and Spaniards and took the name of Benedict XIII. He commanded Vincent to repair to Avignon and made him master of the Palace. The saint laboured to persuade Benedict to put an end to the schism, but obtained only promises, and after eighteen months entreated to be appointed apostolic missionary.

Before the end of 1398 St. Vincent set out from Avignon. He preached in every town with wonderful efficacy; and the people having heard him in one place followed him in crowds to others. He visited every province in Spain in this manner, except Galicia. He returned to France and went thence into Italy, part of Germany and through Flanders, England, Scotland, and Ireland. He laboured thus nearly twenty years, till 1417. He preached to the Mahometans the gospel with great success at Granada and converted many. He cured innumerable sick every where.

Falling at last into a perfect decay, his companions persuaded him to return to his own country. Accordingly he set out with that view, riding on an ass, as was his ordinary manner of travelling in long journeys. But after they were gone a considerable distances, they found themselves near the city of Vannes. Wherefore the saint perceiving his illness increase determined to return into the town, saying that God had chosen that city for the place of his burial. His fever increasing he prepared himself for death by devoutly receiving the sacraments. On the tenth day of his illness he caused the passion of our saviour to be read to him. It was on Wednesday in Passion Week, the 5th of April that he slept in the Lord, in the year 1419, having lived sixty-two years. Joan of France, Duchess of Brittany, washed his corpse with her own hands. The duke and the bishop appointed the cathedral for the place of his burial.

PLATE 20. ST. ST. ISIDORE OF SEVILLE, 4 APRIL. BUTLER, *LIVES OF THE SAINTS*, TWO-VOLUME ILLUSTRATED 19TH-CENTURY EDITION.

9 APRIL (ALSO 2 APRIL)

St. Mary
OF EGYPT
Fifth age

In the reign of Theodosius the Younger, there lived in Palestine a monk named Zosimus famed for his sanctity. About the year 430 the holy man passed over the Jordan in hopes of meeting with some hermit of greater perfection than he had hitherto conversed with. Having advanced thus for twenty days, as he stopped at noon to rest he saw the figure of a human body that appeared naked, extremely sunburnt and with short white hair who fled from him. He drew nearer by degrees and when he was within hearing he cried out to the person to stop, who answered, 'Abbot Zosimus I am a woman; throw me your mantle to cover me.'

He, surprised to hear her call him by name, complied. Having covered herself, she approached him and they entered into conversation. She said, 'I ought to die with shame in telling you what I am. My country is Egypt. When my father and mother were still living, at twelve years of age, I went without their consent to Alexandria.' She then described how she lived a public prostitute seventeen years. She added, 'I continued my wicked course till the twenty-ninth year of my age, when perceiving several persons making towards the sea I was told they were about the Exaltation. I embarked with them, looking only for fresh opportunities to continue my debauches. On the day appointed for the festival, all going to church, I found myself withheld from entering the place by some invisible force. This happened to me three or four times I began to consider that my criminal life might be the cause. I arose and went to the picture of the Mother of God and addressed my prayers to her, begging her intercession. I seemed to hear this voice "If thou goest beyond the Jordan, thou shalt there find rest and comfort." After these words I went out in haste, passed the Jordan, and from that time I have carefully shunned the meeting of any human creature, as near as I can judge, forty-seven years.' Zosimus taking notice that she made use of scripture phrases asked her if she had ever applied herself to the study of the sacred books. Her answer was that she could not even read, neither had she seen any human creature since she came into the desert. She concluded with desiring him to bring with him on Maundy Thursday the body and blood of our Lord and wait for her on the banks of the river. The year following, on Maundy Thursday he went to the Jordan. At night she appeared, walking upon the surface of the water. She begged Zosimus to return to the following Lent. But on his arrival at the place he had first seen her, he found her corpse stretched out on the ground. Zosimus buried her.

11 APRIL

St. Stanislas
MARTYR, BISHOP OF CRACOW
A.D. 1079

Stanislas was born on the 26th of July, 1030, at Sezepanow in the diocese of Cracow. His parents had passed thirty years together without issue when this son was given them after they had lost all hopes of children. They received him with thanksgiving to God and devoted him from his birth to the divine service.

When grown up he was sent to pursue his studies at Gnesna, the first university in the kingdom, and thence to Paris. After seven years he returned home, and upon the demise of his parents disposed of his fortune in favour of the poor. He received the order of priesthood from Lambert Zula, Bishop of Cracow, and was by him made his preacher and vicar-general. Upon the death of Lampert, he was consecrated bishop in 1072.

Boleslas II was then King of Poland. This prince sullied the glory of his victories by his unbridled lust and by horrid acts of tyranny which procured for him the surname of the Cruel. Though married, he was not ashamed to offer violence to several ladies of quality. Stanislas boldly laid before him the enormity of his conduct and the king made some show of repentance. But it soon wore off, and the king began to express his aversion against the good bishop. He carried off and kept by violence the wife of a gentleman in the palatinate of Sirad, and had by her several children. The Archbishop of Fnesna and others of the episcopal order were solicited by the nobility to lay before him the enormity of his crime; but the fear of offending their sovereign stopped their mouths. Stanislas was the only person that had the courage to discharge this duty. He went to court and once more conjured the king to put an end to his scandalous disorders, telling him he ran the risk of being cut off from the communion of the faithful by excommunication.

Seeing no remedy applied to the evils he deplored, and finding all measures ineffectual Stanislas at last excommunicated him. And, having left orders to break off the church office in case the king should attempt to enter the church while the service was performing, he left the city and retired to St. Michael's, a small chapel a little distance from Cracow. Thither the king followed him with his guards, whom he ordered to massacre him on the spot, but they were struck with such respect and dread that they durst not attempt it, till the king himself rushed forward and dispatched him with his own hand. Then his guards cut the martyr's body into pieces which they scattered about the fields. But eagles are said to have defended them till the canons of his cathedral gathered them together and buried them before the door of the chapel in which he was martyred Ten years after, the body was translated into the cathedral at Cracow in 1088.

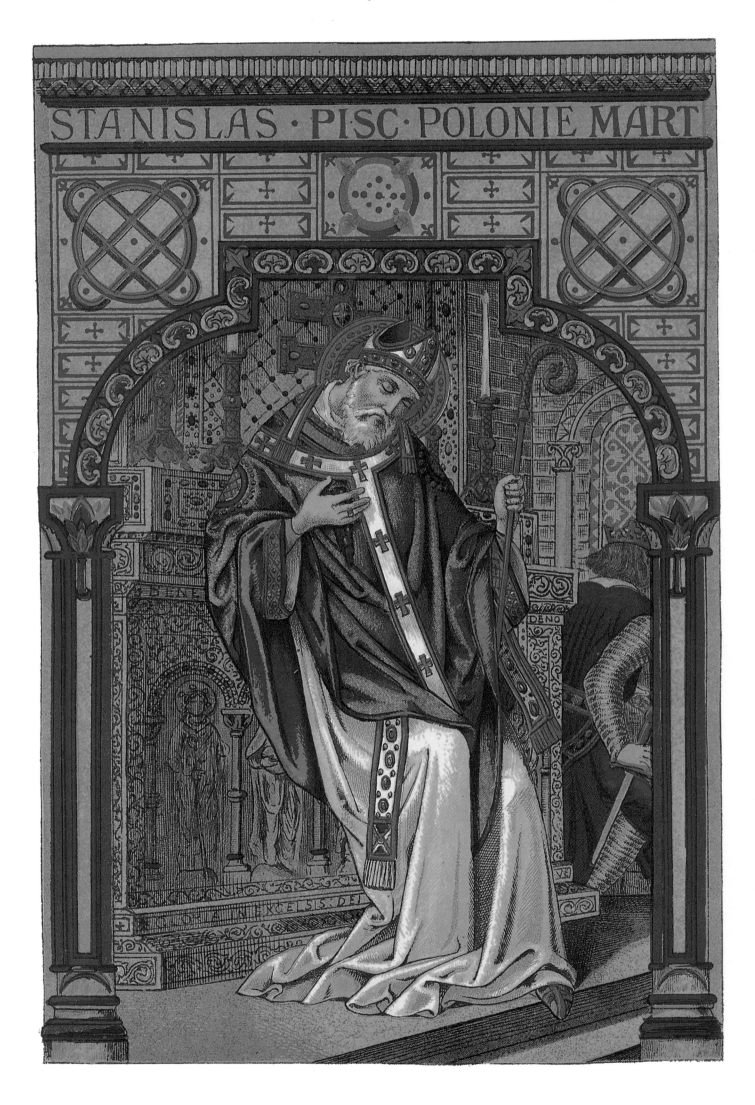

PLATE 21. ST. STANISLAUS, 11 APRIL. BUTLER, *LIVES OF THE SAINTS*, TWO-VOLUME ILLUSTRATED 19TH-CENTURY EDITION.

12 APRIL

St. Zeno
BISHOP OF VERONA
A.D. 380

This holy prelate is styled a martyr by St. Gregory the Great, and in several martyrologies; but was honoured only with the title of confessor in the ancient missal of Verona and it appears that he did not die by the sword. Living in the days of Constantius, Julian and Valens, he might deserve the title martyr by sharing in the persecutions carried on by those princes. Hence in some calendars he is styled martyr, in others confessor. Some pretend from his name that he was a Grecian; but the Ballerini show that he was by birth, or at least by education, a Latin, and an African.

Our saint seems to have been made Bishop of Verona in 362. We learn from several of his sermons that he baptized every year a great number of idolaters, and that he exerted himself with great success against the Arians, whose party had been exceedingly strengthened in those parts by the artifices of the ringleaders of that sect. He also opposed himself against the errors of the Pelagians. His flock being grown exceeding numerous, he found it necessary to build a great church. By his precepts and example the people were so liberal in their alms that their houses were always open to poor strangers and none of their own country had occasion even to ask for relief. After the battle of Adrianople in 378, the Goths made an incredible number of captives. It seems to have been on this occasion that the charities of the inhabitants of Verona were dispersed like fruitful seeds through the remotest provinces, and by them many were ransomed from slavery, many rescued from cruel deaths, many freed from hard labour.

St. Zeno himself lived in great poverty. He makes frequent mention of the clergy which he trained and the priests his fellow labourers. He speaks of the ordinations which he performed at Easter; also the solemn reconciliation of penitents which was another function of that holy time. St. Ambrose mentions, at Verona, virgins consecrated to God by St. Zeno, who wore the sacred veil and lived in their own houses in the city; and others who lived in a monastery, of which he seems to have been both the founder and director. Love-feasts, or agapes, were originally established on the festivals of martyrs in their cemeteries, which by the degeneracy of manners were at length converted into occasions of intemperance and vanity. St. Zeno inveighed warmly against the abuse.

St. Zeno extended his charity to the faithful departed and condemned severely the intemperate grief of those who interrupted by their lamentation the divine sacrifices and public office of the church for their deceased friends. He received the crown of his labours by a happy death in 380, on the 12th of April.

13 APRIL

St. Hermenegild
A.D. 186

Levigild the Goth, King of Spain, had two sons by his first wife Theodosia, namely Hermenegild and Recared. These he educated in the Arian heresy, which he himself professed, but married Hermenegild to Ingondes, a zealous Catholic. The grandees had hitherto disposed of their crown by election, but Levigild associated his two sons with him in his sovereignty, and allotted to each a portion of his dominions, Seville falling to the lot of Hermenegild.

Ingondes had much to suffer from Gosvint, a bigoted Arian, whom Levigild had married after the death of Theodosia; but in spite of all her cruel treatment she adhered strictly to the Catholic faith. And such was the force of her example that the prince became a convert, abjured his heresy, and was received into the church by the imposition of hands and the unction of chrism on the forehead. Levigild in a transport of rage divested him of the title of king and resolved to deprive him of his possessions, his princess, and even his life, unless he returned to his former sentiments. Hermenegild resolved to stand upon his defence, and was supported by all the Catholics in Spain; but they were by much too weak to defend him against the Arians.

The prince therefore sent St. Leander to Constantinople to solicit Tiberius for succours. But he dying soon after, and his successor being obliged to employ all his forces to defend his own dominions against the Persians, no succours were to be obtained. Hermenegild implored next the assistance of the Roman generals in that part of Spain. They engaged to protect him, and received his wife and infant son as hostages but, being corrupted by Leveilgild's money they basely betrayed him. The prince sought refuge in a church; and the Arian king, not presuming to violate that sacred place, permitted his second son Recared to go to him and promise him pardon. Hermenegild believed his father sincere, and going out threw himself at his feet. Levigild loaded him with chains and conducted him prisoner to the tower of Seville.

The solemnity of Easter being come, the perfidious father sent to him an Arian bishop in the night, offering to take him into favour if he received the communion from the hand of that prelate, but Hermenegild rejected the proposal with indignation. The furious father, seeing the faith of his son proof against all his endeavours to pervert him, sent soldiers to dispatch him. They found the saint ready to receive the stroke of death, which they instantly inflicted on him, cleaving his head with an axe. This saint received the crown of martyrdom on Easter Eve, the 13th of April.

17 APRIL

St. Stephen

CONFESSOR, ABBOT OF CÎTEAUX
A.D. 1134

St. Stephen Harding was an Englishman of an honourable family. He had his education in the monastery of Sherbourne in Dorsetshire. Out of a desire of learning the means of Christian perfection he travelled into Scotland, and afterwards to Paris and Rome. Stephen heard at Lyons of the great austerity and sanctity of the Benedictine monastery of Molesme, lately founded by St. Robert. Charmed with this house he made choice of it to accomplish there the sacrifice of himself to God.

Such was the extreme poverty of this place that the monks were often obliged to live on wild herbs. The compassion of the neighbourhood at length supplied their wants, but with plenty a spirit of relaxation crept in and drew many from their duty. St. Robert, Alberic his prior, Stephen, and other fervent monks, being twenty-one in number, with the permission of Hugh Archbishop of Lyons, retired to Cîteaux, a marshy wilderness five leagues from Dijon. The monks with their own hands cut down trees and built themselves a monastery, and in it made a profession of the rule of St. Bennet on St. Bennet's day, 1098, which is regarded as the date of the foundation of the Cistercian Order. After a year Robert was recalled to Molesme and Alberic chosen the second abbot of Cîteaux. Alberic finished his course on the 26 of January, 1109, and St Stephen was chosen the third abbot.

The order seemed then in great danger of failing: it was the astonishment of the universe, but had appeared so austere that scarce any had the courage to embrace that institute. St. Stephen carried its rule to the highest perfection. The frequent visits of strangers were prevented, and only the Duke of Burgundy permitted to enter. He was also entreated not to keep his court in the monastery on holy days. The duke and his court were much offended and withdrew their charities and protection. This trial was succeed by another. In 1111 and 1112, sickness swept away the greater part of this small community. St. Stephen feared he should leave no successors to his poverty, and many presumed to infer that their institute was too severe. St. Stephen had the consolation to receive at once into his community St. Bernard with thirty gentlemen, whose example was followed by many others. St. Stephen then lived to found himself thirteen abbeys and to see above a hundred founded by monks of his Order under his direction. He published several statutes, called the *Charte of Charity*, and caused a collection of ceremonies and customs to be drawn up under the name the *Usages of Cîteaux*. The saint, having assembled the chapter of his order in 1133, alleging his great age and incapacity, begged to be discharged from his office that the might have leisure to prepare himself to appear at the judgement seat. He passed to immortal glory on the 28th of March 1134.

19 APRIL

St. Elphege

MARTYR, ARCHBISHOP OF CANTERBURY
A.D. 1012

St. Elphege was born of noble and virtuous parents who gave him a good education. He served God first in the monastery of Derherste in Gloucestershire. After some years he built himself a cell in a desert place of the abbey of Bath where he shut himself up. His virtue shone to men the brighter through the veils of his humility and he was at length obliged to take upon him the direction of the great abbey of Bath.

St. Ethelwold, Bishop of Winchester, dying in 984, St. Dunstan obliged our holy abbot to accept episcopal consecration, though he was no more than thirty years of age. He was no less remarkable for charity to his neighbour than severity to himself. During his time there were no beggars in the whole diocese of Winchester. The holy prelate had governed the see twenty-two years when in 1006 he was translated to that of Canterbury, being fifty-two years of age.

The Danes at that time made the most dreadful havoc in England. They landed where they pleased and not only plundered the country, but committed excessive barbarities on the natives, with little or no opposition from the weak king Ethelred. Their army being joined by the traitorous Earl Edric they marched out of the West and sat down before Canterbury. The English nobility desired the archbishop then in the city to provide for his security by flight, which he refused to do. Canterbury was taken by storm. The infidels made a dreadful slaughter of all that came in their way. The holy prelate pressed his way through the Danish troops and made his way to the place of slaughter. Turning to the enemy he desired them to forbear the massacre of his people. The archbishop was immediately seized, laid in irons and confined several months in a filthy dungeon.

Being afflicted with an epidemical mortal colic in their army and attributing this scourge to their cruel usage of the saint, they drew him out of prison and the calamity ceased. Their chiefs deliberated about setting him at liberty, but covetousness prevailing they exacted for his ransom three thousand marks of gold. He said that the patrimony of the poor was not to be squandered. He was therefore bound again and on Easter Sunday was brought before the commanders of their fleet, which then lay at Greenwich, and threatened with torments and death unless he paid the ransom. He answered that he had no other gold to offer than that of true wisdom. The barbarians, enraged at this answer, knocked him down with the backs of their battle axes and then stoned him. A Dane that had been lately baptized by the saint, grieved to see him suffer in so slow and painful a manner, clove his head and gave the finishing stroke to his martyrdom. Thus died St. Elphege in the fifty-ninth year of his age.

20 APRIL

St. Agnes

OF MONTEPULCIANO, VIRGIN AND ABBESS
A.D. 1317

This holy virgin was a native of Monte Pulciano, in Tuscany. She had scarce attained to the use of reason, when she conceived an extraordinary relish and ardour for prayer, and in her infancy often spent whole hours in reciting the Our Father and Hail Mary, on her knees, in some private corner of a chamber. At nine years of age she was placed by her parents in a convent of Sackins, of the Order of St Francis, so called from their habit, or at least their scapular, being made of sackcloth. Agnes, in so tender an age, was a model of all virtues to this austere community; and she renounced the world, though of a plentiful fortune, being sensible of its dangers before she knew what it was to enjoy it. At fifteen years of age she was removed to a new foundation of the Order of St. Dominic, at Proceno, in the county of Orvieto, and appointed abbess by Pope Nicholas IV.

She slept on the ground, with a stone under her head in lieu of a pillow, and for fifteen years she fasted always on bread and water, till she was obliged by her directors, on account of sickness, to mitigate her austerities. Her townsmen, earnestly desiring to be possessed of her again, demolished a lewd house, and erected upon the spot a nunnery, which they bestowed on her. This prevailed on her to return, and she established in this house nuns of the Order of St. Dominic, which rule she herself professed. The gifts of miracles and prophecy rendered her famous among men, though humility, charity, and patience under her long sicknesses were the graces which recommended her to God. She died at Monte Pulciano, on the 20th of April, 1317, being forty-three years old. Her body was removed to the Dominicans' church of Orvieto in 1435, where it remains.

21 APRIL

St. Anselm

ARCHBISHOP OF CANTERBURY
A.D. 1109

St. Anselm was born of noble parents in Piedmont about the year 1033. At the age of fifteen, he petitioned an abbot to admit him into his house, but was refused out of apprehension of his father's displeasure. The ill-usage he met with from his father, induced him, after his mother's death, to leave his own country, and after a diligent application to his studies for three years in Burgandy, invited by the great fame of Lanfranc, prior of Bec in Normandy, he went thither and became his scholar, and a member of that house at the age of twenty-seven, in 1060. Three years after, Lanfranc was made Abbot of St. Stephen's at Caen and Anselm Prior of Bec.

St. Anselm applied himself diligently to the study of every part of theology. In 1078 he was chosen Abbot of Bec, being forty-five years old. The abbey being possessed at that time of some lands in England this obliged the abbot to make his appearance there in person. He was received with great honour by all ranks of people. In the year 1092 Hugh, Earl of Chester, entreated Anselm to come to England. The metropolitan see of Canterbury had been vacant ever since the death of Lanfranc in 1089. The sacrilegious King William Rufus had usurped the revenues of vacant benefices, but seized with a violent sickness, which in a few days brought him to extremity, he nominated Anselm to the see of Canterbury, being convinced that he should lose his soul if he died before the archbishopric was filled. Anselm declined the charge, till the king had promised him the restitution of all lands and was consecrated on the 4th of December, 1093.

Finding the king always seeking occasions to oppress his church the saint set out from Canterbury in 1097 towards Rome. The pope having heard his cause, assured him of his protection. Anselm retired to the monastery of St. Saviour in Calabria where he finished his work *Why God was made Man*. He entreated the pope to discharge him of his bishopric,

believing he might be more serviceable to the world in a private station, but the pope would by no means consent.

King William Rufus being snatched away by sudden death in 1100 St Anselm made haste to England, whither he was invited by King Henry I. But this harmony was of no long continuance. Anselm persisted to refuse to ordain bishops named by the king, without a canonical election. The contest became every day more serious. At last the king persuaded Anselm to go in person and consult the pope about the matter. Pope Pascal II condemned the king and excommunicated those who should receive church dignities from him. After further disagreement with the king, Anselm finally returned to England in 1106. The last years of his life his health was entirely broken and he expired at Canterbury on the 26th of April, 1109.

23 APRIL

St. George

MARTYR
About the year 303

The extraordinary devotion of all Christendom to this saint is an authentic proof how glorious his triumph and name have always been in the church. According to the account given us by Metaphrastes, he was born in Cappadocia, of noble Christian parents. After the death of his father, he went with his mother into Palestine, she being a native of that country, and having there a considerable estate, which fell to her son George. He was strong and robust in body, and having embraced the profession of a soldier, was made a tribune, or colonel in the army. By his courage and conduct he was soon preferred to higher stations by the Emperor Diocletian.

When that prince waged war against the Christian religion, St George laid aside the marks of his dignity, threw up his commissions and posts, and complained to the emperor himself of his severities and bloody edicts. He was immediately cast into prison, and tried, first by promises, afterwards put to the question, and tortured with great cruelty; but nothing could shake his constancy. The next day he was led through the city and beheaded.

Some think him to have been the same illustrious young man who tore down the edicts when they were first fixed up at Nicomedia. The reason why St. George has been regarded as the patron of military men, is partly upon the score of his profession, and partly upon the credit of a revelation of his appearing to the Christian army in the holy war, before the battle of Antioch. The success of this battle proving fortunate to the Christians, under Godfrey of Bouillon, made the name of St. George more famous in Europe, and disposed the military men to implore more particularly his intercession. This devotion was confirmed, as it is said, by an apparition of St. George to King Richard I in his expedition against the Saracens; which vision being declared to the troops, was to them a great encouragement and they soon after defeated the enemy.

St. George is usually painted on horseback, and tilting at a dragon, under his feet; but this representation is no more than an emblematical figure, purporting that, by his faith and Christian fortitude, he conquered the devil, called the dragon in the Apocalypse.

PLATE 22. ST. GEORGE, 23 APRIL. BUTLER, *LIVES OF THE SAINTS*, TWO-VOLUME ILLUSTRATED 19TH-CENTURY EDITION.

St. Fidelis

OF SIGMARENGEN, MARTYR

A.D. 1622

Fidelis was born in 1577 at Sigmarengen, a town in Germany. The name of his father was John Rey. The saint was christened Mark, performed his studies in the university of Fribourg in Switzerland, and whilst he taught philosophy, commenced doctor of laws. He at that time never drank wine and wore a hair shirt. In 1604 he accompanied three young gentlemen of that country on their travels through the principal parts of Europe during six years. After this he practised law at Colmar in Alsace with great reputation. Justice and religion directed all his actions. His charity produced him the surname of advocate for the poor, but the injustices of a colleague gave him a disgust of a profession which was to many an occasion of sin, and determined him to enter among the Capuchin friars. On the feast day of St. Francis in 1612 he consecrated himself to God by taking the habit.

He had no sooner finished his course of theology than he was employed in preaching and in hearing confessions. The congregation De Propaganda Fide sent to Father Fidelis a commission to go and preach among the Grisons, and he was the first missionary that was sent into those parts after that people had embraced Calvinism. The Calvinists, being incensed, loudly threatened his life, and he prepared himself for martyrdom. On the 24th of April 1622 he made his confession to his companion with great compunction, said mass, and then preached at Gruch, a considerable borough. At the end of his sermon, which he delivered with more than ordinary fire, he stood silence on a sudden, foretold his death to several persons and subscribed his last letters in this manner: 'brother Fidelis, who will be shortly the food of worms'. From Gruch he went to preach at Sevis where he exhorted the Catholics to constancy in the faith. A Calvinist having discharged his musket at him in the church, the Catholics entreated him to leave. On the road back to Gruch he met twenty Calvinist soldiers with a minister at their head. They called him false prophet and urged him to embrace their sect. He answered, 'I am sent to you to confute, not to embrace your heresy.' One of them beat him to the ground by a stroke on his head with his backsword. The martyr rose again on his knees and said with a feeble voice, 'Pardon my enemies O Lord blinded by passion they know not what they do.' Another stroke clove his skull and he fell to the ground. The soldiers, not content with this, left many stabs in his body and hacked his left leg to punish him for his many journeys into those parts to preach to them. He died in 1622, the forty-fifth year of his age. He was buried by the Catholics the next day. The minister was converted by this circumstance and made a public abjuration of his heresy.

St. Mark

EVANGELIST

First century

St. Mark was of Jewish extraction. By his office of interpreter to St. Peter, some understood that St. Mark was the author of the style of his epistles; others that he was employed as a translator into Greek or Latin of what the apostle had written in his own tongue, as occasion might require it. St. Jerome and some others take him to be the same with that John, surnamed Mark, son to the sister of St. Barnabas; and that the latter was with St. Paul in the East. According to Papias and St. Clement of Alexandria, he wrote his gospel at the request of the Romans; who, as they relate, desired to have that committed to writing which St Peter had taught them by word of mouth. St. Peter having revised the work, approved of it, and authorized it to be read in the assemblies of the faithful.

This evangelist is concise in his narrations, and writes with a most pleasing simplicity and elegance. He wrote his gospel in Italy, and in all appearances before the year of Christ 49. He was sent by St. Peter into Egypt and was by him appointed Bishop of Alexandria. We are told that St. Mark landed at Cyrene, a part of Lybia bordering on Egypt, and by innumerable miracles brought many over to the faith. He likewise carried the gospel into other provinces of Lybia and other parts of Egypt before he entered Alexandria, where he soon assembled a very numerous church of which it is thought that the Jewish converts made up the greatest part.

The prodigious progress of the faith in Alexandria stirred up the heathen. The apostle therefore left the city and returned to Pentapolis where he preached two years. On his return to Alexandria the heathens called him a magician on account of his miracles and resolved upon his death. God, however, concealed him long from them. At last, on the pagan feast of the idol Serapis, some there employed to discover the holy man found him offering to God the prayer of the mass. They seized him, tied his feet with cords and dragged him about the streets. The saint was thus dragged the whole day, staining the stones with his blood and leaving the ground strewd with pieces of his flesh. At night he was thrown into prison in which God comforted him by two visions. The next day the infidels dragged him as before till he happily expired on the 25th of April, on which day the churches kept his festival. The Christians gathered up the remains of his mangled body and buried them at Bucoles. His body is said to have been conveyed by stealth to Venice in 815. It is said to be deposited in the Doge's stately chapel of St. Mark in a secret place under one of the great pillars. This saint is honoured by this republic with extraordinary devotion as principal patron.

in illo tempore. Recumbenti
bus vndecim discipulis ap
paruit illis ihus et exprobra
uit incredulitatem illorum et duri

PLATE 23. ST. MARK, 25 APRIL. BODLEIAN LIBRARY, MS. ADD. A 185, F. 18.

27 APRIL

St. Zita

VIRGIN
A.D. 1272

Zita was born in the beginning of the thirteenth century at a village near Lucca in Italy. She was brought up with the greatest care by her poor mother who reduced all her instructions to two short heads, and never had occasion to use any further remonstrance to enforce her lessons than to say 'This is most pleasing to God; this is the divine will,' or 'That would displease God.' The sweetness of the young child charmed every one. She spoke little and was most assiduous at her work; but her business never seemed to interrupt her prayers.

At twelve years of age she was put to service in the family of a citizen of Lucca, called Fatinelli, whose house was contiguous to the church. Zita considered her work as an employment assigned her by God; and obeyed her master and mistress in all things. She always rose several hours before the rest of the family, and employed in prayer a considerable part of the time which others gave to sleep. She took care to hear mass every morning. Who would not imagine that such a person should have been esteemed and beloved by all who knew her? Nevertheless it fell out quite otherwise, and for several years she suffered the harshest trials. Her modesty was called by her fellow servants simplicity and want of sense; and her diligence was judged to have no spring other than affectation and pride. Her mistress was extremely prepossessed against her, and her master could not bear her in his sight without transports of rage. The saint never repined nor lost her patience, and at length her master and mistress discovered the treasure which their family possessed and the other servants gave due praise to her virtue.

Being made housekeeper, she was most careful in point of economy, and though head servant she never allowed herself the least privilege or exemption in her work on that account. She kept fast the whole year, and often on bread and water; and took her rest on the bare floor, or on a board. She never kept anything for herself but the poor garments which she wore, everything else she gave to the poor. Her master, seeing his goods multiply in her hands, gave her leave to bestow liberal alms on the poor. She happily expired on the 27th of April, in 1272, being sixty years old.

29 APRIL

St. Catharine

OF SIENA

A.D. 1380

St. Catharine was born at Siena in 1347. Her father, a dyer, was solicitous to leave to his children a solid inheritance of virtue. Her mother, Lapa, had a particular affection for her. Catharine withdrew very young to a solitude a little way out of the town to imitate the lives of the fathers of the desert. Returning after some time to her father's house, she continued to be guided by the same spirit. In her childhood she consecrated her virginity to God by a private vow.

At twelve years of age her parents thought of engaging her in a married state. Catharine found them deaf to her entreaties that she might live single, and therefore redoubled her prayers, watching and austerities. Her parents endeavoured to divert her from her solitude and laid on her the drudgery of all the house as if she had been a person hired into the family for that purpose. Her father, edified at her patience, at length approved and seconded her devotion and in 1365 she received the habit of the Third Order of St. Dominic. From that time her cell became her paradise, prayer her element, and her mortifications had no longer any restraint. For three years she never spoke to any one but to God and her confessor. Her days and nights were employed in contemplation; the fruits wereof were supernatural lights.

A pestilence laying waste the country in 1374, Catharine devoted herself to serve the infected and obtained the cure of several. Thousands flocked to hear or only to see her, and were brought over by her words to true repentance. Whilst she was at Pisa in 1374, the people of Florence and Perugia, with a great part of Tuscany entered into a league against the holy see. Pope Gregory XI, residing at Avignon, sent his legate with an army and laid the diocese of Florence under an interdict. The magistrates of Florence sent to Siena to beg St. Catharine would become their mediatrix. The saint arrived at Avignon in 1376 and was received by the pope with great marks of distinction. The conclusion of this work was deferred until 1378, when a memorable reconciliation was effected, and Catharine hastened to her solitary abode at Siena. What above all pierced her heart was the great schism which followed the death of Gregory XI, when Urban VI was chosen at Rome. Our saint wrote to Urban, exhorting him to mollify that rigidness which had driven the world from him. The pope listened to her and sent for her to Rome.

We pass over the ecstasies and other wonderful favours this virgin received from heaven. She has left us, besides the example of her life, six treatises, a discourse on the Annunciation, and three hundred and sixty-four letters. Whilst she was labouring to extend the obedience of Urban VI, her infirmities and pains increasing, she died at Rome on the 29th of April, 1380.

PLATE 24. ST. CATHERINE OF SIENA, 29 APRIL. BRITISH LIBRARY, YATES THOMPSON MS 29, F. 36.

30 APRIL (5 MAY)

St. Puis

V, POPE

A.D. 1572

Michael Ghisleri, known afterwards by the name of Pius V, was born at Bosco, a little town in the diocese of Tortona, in 1504. He studied grammar under the Dominican friars and took the habit of that Order when he was only fifteen. Having prepared himself by a long retreat he was ordained priest at Genoa in 1528. He taught philosophy and divinity sixteen years and was long employed in instructing the novices and governing different houses of his Order. Pope Paul IV in 1556 promoted him to the united bishoprics of Nepi and Sutri. In 1557 he was created cardinal by the same pope. His dignities served to render his humility more conspicuous, but produced no alteration in his furniture, table, fasts or devotions. Pope Paul IV dying in 1559, he was succeeded by Pius IV, who translated our cardinal to the bishopric of Mondovi in Piedmont, a church reduced by wars to a deplorable condition. The saint re-established peace, reformed abuses and restored the splendour of that church. But an order of his holiness recalled him to Rome.

Pope Pius IV, after a tedious illness, expired in the arms of St. Charles Borromeo in December, 1565. St. Charles united the conclave in favour of our saint who gave his consent on the 7th of January, 1556, and took the name of Pius. The largesses usually bestowed by the popes at their coronation he distributed among the poor. He forbade the public exhibition of the sights of wild beasts, as savouring too much of inhumanity, and by rigorous edicts banished numbers of lewd women. His charities are not to be expressed. His rigorous fasts and abstemiousness he would scarce mitigate, even on account of sickness. He generously assisted the knights of Malta when they were besieged by the Turks. In the time of a famine in Rome he imported corn at his own expense from Sicily and France. He was a great encourager of learning and he wrote to Queen Mary Stuart in 1570 to comfort her during her imprisonment.

Selimus, Emperor of the Turks, proposed to overrun all Christendom. Alarmed at the danger, St. Pius entered into a league with Philip II of Spain and the Venetians in order to check the progress of the Mahometans. The pope was declared chief of the league, was appointed Mark Antony Colonna general of his galleys and Don John of Austria generalissimo of all the forces. In the battle of Lepanto, the infidels lost thirty thousand men, with their general. In consequence of this miraculous victory, the pope caused a triumph to be decreed to Don John and bestowed honours on other generals. The year followed he died of the stone on the 1st of May, 1572, having governed the church six years.

2 MAY

St. Athanasius

PATRIARCH OF ALEXANDRIA,
DOCTOR OF THE CHURCH

A.D. 373

St. Athanasius was a native of Alexandria and seems to have been born about the year 296. St. Alexander took upon himself the direction of his studies and employed him as his secretary. The desire of grounding himself in the most perfect practice of virtue drew St. Athanasius into the desert to the great St. Antony, about the year 315. When he had prepared himself for the ministry he returned to the city and was ordained deacon about 319. St. Alexander in 325 took the holy deacon with him to the Council of Nicaea and he had a great share in the disputations and decisions of that venerable assembly. Five months after this council, St. Alexander, lying on his deathbed, recommended the choice of Athanasius for his successor.

Allegations were laid against Athanasius, charging him with the murder of Arsenius, a Meletian bishop and with other crimes. Constantine sent an order to Athanasius to clear himself in a council at Tyre in August 335, consisting chiefly of Arians. The truth was Arsenius had fallen into some irregularity and absconded. The saint therefore made him appear before the whole assembly. The Arians called the saint a magician and would have torn him to pieces had not the governor rescued him and sent him on board a ship that sailed the same night.

Having thus escaped he went for Constantinople. Constantine, who had refused to see or give audience to our saint, whom he looked up on as justly condemned, requested that his pretended judges might be obliged to confront him. But only six obeyed the summons. These agreed to attack Athanasius with a fresh accusation, which was believed by Constantine, who banished him in consequence to Triers, then the chief city of Belgic Gaul. The year after, Constantine departed this life. Constantine's three sons divided the empire and Constantius, the second son restored Athanasius to his see.

The Arians accused St. Athanasius afresh for sedition and other crimes. He repaired to Rome to Pope Julius, who acquitted him and confirmed him in his see; but he was obliged to continue at Rome three years. The Arians placed Gregory in the see of Alexandria in 341. A general council of the East and West met in 347, and St. Athanasius was acquitted. The Arians never ceased to prepossess the emperor against Athanasius, and the saint was obliged to leave Alexandria for above six years. In 359 the council of Rimini had the weakness to omit in the creed the word consubstantial. St Athanasius in 362 assembled a council at Alexandria which condemned those who denied the divinity of the Holy Ghost, and this decision was approved at Rome. After innumerable combats and as many great victories, this glorious saint was called to a life exempt from suffering on the 2nd of May, 373.

3 MAY

St. Philip

AND ST. JAMES THE LESS, APOSTLES

First century

St. Philip was of Bethsaida in Galilee, and called by our Saviour to follow him the after after St. Peter and St. Andrew. He was at that time a married man, and had several daughters, but forsook all to follow him. Philip no sooner discovered the Messiah than he was desirous to make his friend Nathanael a sharer in his happiness, saying, 'We have found him of whom Moses in the law and the prophets did write.' Nathanael was not so ready to give his assent to this assertion. Philip therefore desired him to come himself to Jesus and see. Nathanael complied.

When our Lord formed the college of the apostles, Philip was appointed one of that number, and from several passages of the gospel he appears to have been particularly dear to his divine Master. A little before our Saviour's passion, certain Gentiles, desirous to see Christ, made their first address to St. Philip, and by him and St. Andrew obtained that favour.

After our Lord's Ascension the gospel was to be preached to the whole world. That this might be accomplished, it was necessary that the disciples should quickly disperse themselves.

St. Philip accordingly preached in the two Phrygias, as Theodoret and Eusebius assure us. St. Polycarp, who was only converted in the year 80, enjoyed his conversation for some time, consequently St. Philip must have lived to a very advanced age.

St. James, to distinguish him from the other apostle of the same name, the son of Zebedee, was called the Less: which appellation is supposed to have taken its rise either from his having been called later to the apostleship, or from the lowness of his stature, or from his youth. He was the son of Alpheus and Mary, the sister of the Blessed Virgin, and seems to have been born some years before our Lord. James and his brother Jude were called to the Apostleship in the second year of Christ's preaching in 31. He was favoured with an extraordinary apparition of his Master, after his resurrection.

In the year 51 he assisted at the council of the apostles held at Jerusalem. This apostle, being bishop of a church which then chiefly consisted of Jewish converts, tolerated the use of the legal ceremonies. He is the author of a canonical epistle which he wrote in Greek, some time after those of St. Paul to the Galatians in 55 and to the Romans in 58.

Josephus, the Jewish historian, says that St. James was accused of violating the laws and delivered to the people to be stoned to death. This happened on the festival of Pasch, the 10th of April, in the year 62. He was buried near the temple, in the place in which he was martyred, where a small column was erected.

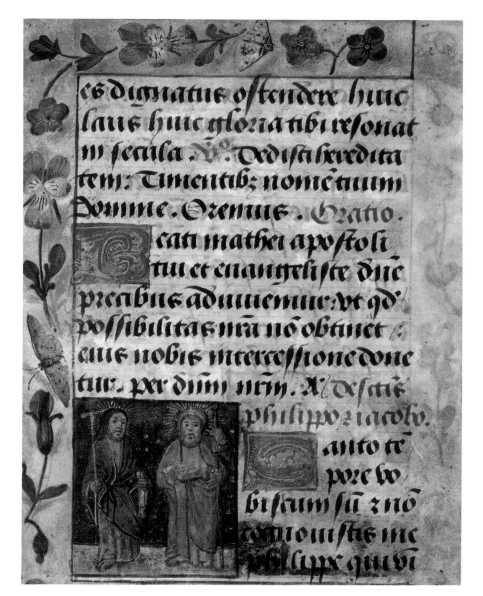

PLATE 25. ST. PHILIP AND ST. JAMES, 3 MAY. BODLEIAN LIBRARY, MS LAUD MISC. 7, F. 166.

5 MAY

St. Hilary
ARCHBISHOP OF ARLES
A.D. 449

This saint was nobly born about the year 401. His kinsman, St. Honoratus, who had forsaken his country to seek Christ in the solitude of the isle of Lérins, where he had founded a great monastery, was the instrument made use of by the Almighty to open his eyes. This holy man had always loved Hilary. He therefore left his retirement for a few days to seek him out and endeavoured to move him to break the chains of this world. Honoratus finding his endeavours ineffectual, they took leave of each other. Hilary was not long before he began to feel a violent conflict within himself. 'On one side,' says he, 'methought I saw the Lord calling me; on the other the world offering me its seducing charms.' He then went to seek Honoratus, and appeared before him as humble and tractable as the saint had left his haughty and indocile.

St. Honoratus having been chosen Archbishop of Arles in 426 Hilary followed him to that city, but it was not long before his love of solitude occasioned his return to Lérins. St. Honoratus begged his assistance; and as he did not yield to entreaties, went himself to fetch him from Lérins. Soon after God called Honoratus to himself in 428 or 429. Hilary, though sensibly afflicted, set out directly for Lérins. But he was overtaken, brought back, and consecrated archbishop, though only twenty-nine years of age.

In this high station he reduced himself in everything to the strictest bounds of necessity. He bore the weak with tenderness, but never indulged the passions or sloth of any. He visited the bishops of his province and endeavoured to make them walk in the perfect spirit of Christ. He established many monasteries and took particular care to enforce a strict obedience of monastic discipline. He had a close friendship with St. Germanus, whom he called his father.

His zeal exasperated several tepid persons, and some of these gave the pope St. Leo a disadvantageous character of him. Chelidonius, Bishop of Besançon, had been deposed by Hilary upon an allegation that before he was consecrated he had married a widow. Chelidonius set out from Rome to justify himself to the pope who received his appeal and acquitted him. St. Hilary pretended that the cause ought to be judged by commissaries deputed by the pope. This plea was overruled. Another affair brought Hilary into a greater difficulty. Projectus, a bishop of his province being sick, Hilary hastened to his see and ordained a new bishop; after which Projectus recovering, there were two bishops contending for the same see. St. Leo judged such an ordination irregular and productive of schisms. Wherefore he forbade St Hilary to ordain any more bishops for the future.

Exhausted by austerities and labours, St. Hilary passed to a better life on the 5th of May, 559, being only forty-eight years old.

7 MAY

St. John
OF BEVERLEY
A.D. 721

This illustrious saint was born at Harpham, a village in Yorkshire. An earnest desire of qualifying himself for the service of God drew him young into Kent, where he made great progress in the famous school of St. Theodorus, the archbishop, under the direction of the holy abbot Adrian. Returning to his own country, he pursued the exercises of piety in the monastery of men under St. Hilda at Whitby, till, in the beginning of the reign of King Alfred, upon the death of Eata he was made Bishop of Hexam. What time he had to spare from his functions he consecrated to heavenly contemplation, retiring into the churchyard of St. Michael's beyond the river Tyne, especially during Lent. He was accustomed to take with him some poor person whom he served during that time. Once he took with him a dumb youth whose head was covered with hideous scabs and scales, without any hair. The saint caused a mansion to be built for this youth within his enclosure and often admitted him to his own cell. On the second Sunday he made the sign of the cross upon his Tongue and loosed it. Then he taught him the letters of the alphabet and afterwards syllables and words. The youth miraculously obtained his speech. Moreover, by the saint's blessing the remedies prescribed by a physician whom he employed, his head was entirely healed and became covered with hair.

Upon the death of Bosa, as Bede testifies, he was placed in the chair of York. Venerable Bede who received the holy orders of deacon and priest from his hands, gives ample testimony to his sanctity and relates several miracles performed by him, from the testimony of Berethun, Abbot of Beverley, and Herebald, Abbot of Tynemouth, who had been eye-witnesses to several of them. St. John made frequent retirement his delight, to renew thereby his spirit of devotion. He chose for his retreat a monastery which he had built at Beverley, then a forest twenty-seven miles from York. This monastery, according to the customs of those times, he erected for the use of both sexes and put it under the government of his disciple Berethun.

In 717, being much broken with age and fatigues he resigned his bishopric to his chaplain, St. Wilfrid the Younger, and having ordained him Bishop of York, he retired to Beverley, where he spent the remaining four years of his life in the punctual performance of all monastic duties. He died there the death of the just on the 7th of May, 721. The monastery of Beverley having been destroyed by the Danes, King Athelstan, who had obtained a great victory over the Scots by the intercession of St. John, founded in his honour, in the same place, a rich collegiate church of canons.

8 MAY

St. Peter
ARCHBISHOP OF TARENTAISE
A.D. 1174

Peter was a native of Dauphiné. At twenty he took the Cistercian habit at Bonnevaux, a monastery that had been lately filled by a colony from Clairvaux. They employed a great part of the day in hewing wood and tilling the ground, in perpetual silence and interior prayer. The year after Peter had taken the monastic habit, his example was followed by Amedeus, nearly related to the Emperor Conrad III. Amedeus built four monasteries of his order; among which was that of Tamies in the desert mountains of Tarentaise, of which he procured his friend St. Peter, not then quite thirty, to be appointed the first abbot in 1140.

The monastery of Tamies seemed a house of terrestrial angels. St. Peter, by the help of Amedeus, founded in it a hospital to receive all the poor sick persons of the country and all strangers; and would himself attend them. In 1142 the Count of Savoy procured his election to the archbishop of Tarentaise, and he was compelled by St. Bernard and the general chapter of his Order, though much against his own inclinations, to accept. Indeed that diocese stood extremely in need of such an apostolic pastor, having been usurped by an ambitious wolf named Idrael, whose deposition left it in the most desolate condition. The parish churches tithes were held by laymen, the chapter of the cathedral full of irregularities. Peter recovered the tithes; made many foundations for the education of youth and relief of the poor and restored everywhere the decent service of God. In 1155, after he had borne the weight of the episcopal character thirteen years, he disappeared of a sudden and made his way to a monastery in Germany, where he was not known. Inquiry was made in all the neighbouring provinces, but in vain, till a young man who had been brought up in his care came to the monastery in which he lay concealed and made him known. The saint was forced to go back to his diocese where he applied himself to his functions with greater vigour than ever. He founded hospitals on the Alps, for poor travellers, often reconciled sovereign princes where they were at variance, and prevented several bloody wars. The Emperor Frederic I set up a schismatical pope under the name of Victor against Alexander III. St. Peter was almost the only subject of the empire who had the courage openly to oppose the tyrant.

He was ordered by the pope to go into Normandy to endeavour a reconciliation between the kings of England and France who had quarrelled. Though then very old he went to Chaumont and prevailed on the two kings to put an end to their differences, but was some time after sent again by the pope to the King of England to compose the difference between him and his son. His journey had not the desired effect, he fell sick on his return and died in Besançon in 1174.

9 MAY (14 MAY)

St. Pachomius
ABBOT
A.D. 348

St. Pachomius was born in Upper Thebais about the year 292 of idolatrous parents. Being about twenty, he was pressed into the emperor's troops and, with several other recruits, put on board a vessel falling down the river to Thebes, in which dwelt many Christians. Those true disciples of Christ were moved with compassion towards the recruits, who were kept close confined and very ill treated. They took all possible care of them and supplied them with money and necessaries. Such virtue made a great impression on Pachomius. When the forces were disbanded, he was no sooner returned home but he repaired to a town in which there was a Christian church and there entered his name among such as were preparing for baptism.

When Pachomius was baptized he began to consider how he should fulfil the obligations which he had contracted. Hearing that a venerable old man named Palemon served God in the desert, he sought him out and begged to live under his direction. The hermit having set before him the difficulties of his way of life, advised him to make a trial of his fervour in some monastery; and he added, 'Consider, my son, that my diet is only bread and salt: I drink no wine, use no oil, and sometimes pass the whole night without sleeping.' Pachomius was not discouraged and promised to observe whatever Palemon should think fit to enjoin them, who thereupon admitted him into his cell.

Pachomius used sometimes to go into a vast uninhabited desert on the banks of the Nile called Tabenna. Whilst he was there one day in prayer he heard a voice which commanded him to build a monastery in that place. He received about the same time from an angel certain instructions relating to a monastic life. Pachomius imparted to Palemon this vision; and both of them coming to Tabenna, built there a little cell. After a short time Palemon returned to his former dwelling.

Pachomius received first his own brother, John, and after his death many others, so that he enlarged his house. He built six other monasteries in Thebais, and from the year 336 chose often to reside in that of Pabau near Thebes. He built a church in a village for the benefit of the poor shepherds in which he performed the office of Lector. He zealously opposed the Arians and in 333 was favoured with a visit from St. Athanasius. His sister came to his monastery desiring to see him; but he sent her word at the gate that no woman could be allowed to enter. However, he built her a nunnery on the other side of the Nile. In 348 God afflicted his monasteries with a pestilence which swept off a hundred monks. The saint himself fell sick and resigned his soul to his Creator in the fifty-seventh year of his age. He lived to see in his different monasteries seven thousand monks.

10 MAY

St. Antoninus

ARCHBISHOP OF FLORENCE

A.D. 1459

St. Antonius, or Little Antony, was born at Florence in 1389. His parents were noble citizens of that place. F. Dominic, a preacher of the Order of St Dominic, afterwards made Cardinal Archbishop of Ragusa, was then employed in building a convent at Fiesoli, two miles from Florence. Antoninus was wonderfully delighted with his sermons and applied for the Dominican habit. The father, judging him too young, advised him to wait and bid him first study canon law, adding that when he should have learned Gratian's decree by heart his request should be granted. In less than a year Antoninus presented himself again to the prior and by answering his examination upon the whole decree of Gratian, gave him surprising proof of his capacity. The prior hesitated no longer, but gave him the habit, he being then sixteen.

Being advanced to the priesthood, Antoninus was chosen very young to govern the great convent of the Minerva in Rome; and after that was successively prior at Naples, Cortona, Siena and Florence. The work which he published increased his reputation. He was consulted from Rome and Pope Eugenius IV called him to the general council of Florence. While employed in introducing the primitive discipline of his Order in Naples, the sea of Florence became vacant. The intrigues of several candidates protracted the election of a successor. But Pope Eugenius no sooner named F. Antoninus to the Florentines than they all acquiesced in his choice. Antoninus was surprised that he should have been thought of for so eminent a dignity and so averse that all entreaties to take it upon him were to no purpose till the pope sent him an order to obey. Antoninus at last complied and was consecrated in March 1446.

He practised all the observance of his rule as far as compatible with his functions. He declared himself the protector of the poor and founded the College of St. Martin to assist persons of reduced circumstances, suppressed games of hazard and visited his whole diocese every year, always on foot. In 1447 a pestilence began to show itself, which raged the whole year following. The holy archbishop exposed himself and his clergy in assisting the infected so that almost all the friars were swept away by the contagion. The famine followed this first scourge and the archbishop obtained from Rome great succours for the relief of the distressed. Florence was shook by frequent earthquakes during three years from 1453. The saint set up again and most distressed and rebuilt their houses. But he laboured most assiduously to render these public calamities instrumental to the reformation of his people's manners.

God called him to the reward of his labours on the 2nd of May, 1459.

13 MAY

St. John

THE SILENT

A.D. 559

John was born at Nicopolis in Armenia in the year 454. His descent by both parents was from the most illustrious generals and governors of that part of the empire. After their death, he built a monastery in which, with ten fervent companions, he shut himself up when only eighteen. His mildness, prudence and piety won him the esteem and affection of all his brethren; but when he was only twenty-eight years old the Archbishop of Sebaste obliged him to quit his retreat and ordained him Bishop of Colonian, in 482. St. John fulfilled all the duties of a holy bishop nine years. He instructed his flock by preaching. He was the comforter of all that were in affliction. Certain evils which he found it impossible to remedy gave him an ernest desire to resign his charge. He went first to Jerusalem and retired to the neighbouring Laura of St. Sabas, which at that time contained one hundred and fifty monks. St John was then thirty-eight years old.

St. Sabas first placed him under the steward of the Laura, to serve the workmen in building a new hospital. After this trial the superior appointed him to receive and entertain strangers. St. Sabas observed every step, and by this time clearly perceived that his novice was already eminently endowed with the spirit of his vocation. Therefore, to afford him opportunities of uninterrupted contemplation, he allowed him a separate hermitage. During five days in the week, John never left his cell; but on Saturdays and Sundays he attended the public worship in church. After passing three years in this eremitical life, he was made steward of the Laura.

Our saint had discharged this office four years when St. Sabas, judging him worthy to be promoted to the priesthood, presented him to the patriarch Elias. When they came to the church where the ordination was to take place John said to the patriarch 'Father, I have been ordained a bishop; but on account on the multitude of my sins have fled, and am come into this desert to wait the visit of the Lord.' The patriarch was startled and, calling in St. Sabas, said to Him 'I desire to be excused from ordaining this man.' St. Sabas went back much afflicted, fearing lest John had been guilty of some grievous crime. Under this uncertainty God revealed to him the state of the affair. Finding himself discovered, John lived four years in his cell without speaking to any one. In 503 the factious spirit of certain disciples obliged St. Sabas to quit his Laura. St. John withdrew into a neighbouring wilderness where he spent six years. When St. Sabas was called home again he brought John back in 510. The saint confined himself forty years to his cell and died soon after 558, having lived seventy-six years in the desert, interrupted only by the nine years of his episcopal dignity.

14 MAY (24 FEBRUARY)

St. Matthias

APOSTLE

First century

We learn from the Acts of the Apostles that Matthias was a constant attendant on our Lord from the time of his baptism by St. John to his ascension. St. Peter having, in a general assembly of the faithful held soon after, declared from holy scripture the necessity of choosing a twelfth apostle in the room of Judas, two were unanimously picked upon by the assembly as most worthy of the dignity – Joseph called Barsabas, and on account of his piety, surnamed the Just, and Matthias. After devout prayer to God that he would direct them in their choice, they proceeded in it by way of lot, which falling on Matthias he was accordingly associated with the eleven and ranked among the apostles. When in deliberations each side appears equally good lots may sometimes be lawfully used. However, the miraculous dreams or lots which we read of in the prophets must no ways authorize any rash superstitious use of such means in others who have not the like authority.

St. Matthias received the Holy Ghost with the rest soon after his election; and after the dispersion of the disciples applied himself with zeal to the functions of his apostleship in converting nations to the faith. He is recorded by St. Clement of Alexandria to have been remarkable for inculcating the necessity of the mortification of the flesh with regard to all its sensual and irregular desires, an important lesson he had received from Christ, and which he practised assiduously on his own flesh.

The tradition of the Greeks in their menologies tells us that St. Matthias planted the faith about Cappadocia and on the coasts of the Caspian Sea, residing chiefly near the port Issus. He must have undergone great hardships and labours amidst so savage a people. The same authors add that he received the crown of martyrdom in Colchis, which they called Ethiopia.

15 MAY

St. Isidore

PATRON OF MADRID

A.D. 1170

Isidore was born at Madrid, of poor parents, and was christened from the name of their patron, St. Isidore of Seville. They had not the means to procure him learning or a polite education, but they infused into his tender soul the utmost horror of all sin and the most vehement ardour for every virtue. Good books are a great help to holy meditation; but not indispensably requisite. In his youth Isidore was retained servant by a gentleman named John de Vargas of Madrid, to till his land and do his husbandry work. The saint afterwards took a most virtuous woman to wife, named Mary Toribia. After the birth of one child, which died young, the parents by mutual consent served God in perfect continency.

St. Isidore continued always in the service of the same master. Don John de Vargas, after long experience of the treasure he possessed in his faithful ploughman, treated him as a brother. He allowed him the liberty of assisting daily at the public office of the church. On the other side, Isidore was careful by rising very early, to make his devotions no impediment to his business, nor any encroachment upon what he owed to his master. He also inspired his wife with the same confidence in God, the same love of the poor, and the same disengagement from the things of this world. She died in 1175 and is honoured in Spain among the saints.

St. Isidore being seized with the sickness of which he died, foretold his last hour and prepared himself for it with redoubled fervour, and with the most tender devotion, patience and cheerfulness. The piety with which he received the last sacraments drew tears from all that were present. Repeating inflamed acts of divine love he expired on the 15th of May, 1170, being near sixty years of age. His death was glorified by miracles. After forty years his body was removed out of the churchyard into the church of St. Andrew. It has since been placed in the bishop's chapel, being honoured with a succession of frequent miracles down to this time.

16 MAY

St. John

NEPOMUCEN

A.D. 1383

This servant of God was born at Nepomuc, a little town in Bohemia some leagues from Prague, about the year 1330. When he had learned the first elements at home he was sent to Staaze to study Latin. He excelled his schoolfellows in grammar, but surpassed himself in rhetoric. Charles IV, Emperor of Germany, had lately founded the University of Prague. John being sent thither, distinguished himself in philosophy, divinity, and canon law, in which two last faculties he proceeded doctor. He had from his tender years regarded the priesthood as the great object of his ambition. He increased the fervour of his preparation for this holy order, which he received at the hands of his bishop. This prelate, being acquainted with his extraordinary talents, commanded him immediately to employ them in preaching. The whole city flocked to hear him, the students thronged to his discourses and many hardened libertines returned from hearing him full of compunction.

The Emperor Charles died in 1378 and his son Wenceslas succeeded him, being only sixteen. He resided at Prague and, hearing high commendations of St. John, pitched upon him to preach the Lent to his court. The Empress Jane was a most virtuous princess, and chose him for the director of her conscience. He also took upon him the direction of the nuns of the Catle of Prague. The empress became much more devout after she began to follow his advice and was not afraid to appear such. Her prayers were only interrupted by charity to the poor.

Wenceslas grew the more impatient by the piety of his consort and made her conduct an argument for his suspicions. He formed a design of extorting from St. John what she had disclosed to him in confession. The saint represented to him how notoriously injurious such a sacrilege was, and Wenceslas commanded him to be thrown into a dungeon. He was stretched on a rack, burnt at a slow fire and tormented in other ways. In the mean time the empress was informed, and by her prayers obtained of Wenceslas the enlargement of the servant of God. He therefore appeared at court again, but like a persecuted saint prepared himself for death. He visited a place of great devotion among the Bohemians and was returning home when the emperor saw him pass. The sight of the holy man renewed his indignation and the emperor cried out, 'Take away this man and throw him into the river as soon as it shall be dark, that his execution may not be known by the people.' The barbarous order was executed and the martyr was thrown off the bridge which joins the Great and Little Prague into the river Muldaw, with his hands and feet tied on the 16th of May, 1383. The martyr was no sooner stifled in the water but a heavenly light appeared over his body.

17 MAY

St. Paschal

BAYLON
A.D. 1592

St. Paschal Baylon was born in 1540, at Torre-Hermosa, a small country town in the kingdom of Arragon. His parents were day-labourers and their circumstances were too narrow to afford his being sent to school; but the pious child carried a book with him into the fields where he watched the sheep, and desired those that he met to teach him the letters; and thus, in a short time, being yet very young, he learned to read.

When he was of a proper age, he engaged with a master to keep his flocks as under shepherd. That solitary life had charms for him. He read continually in the great book of nature and, besides external objects, had almost continually a spiritual book in his hands. His master was charmed with his conduct, and made him an offer to adopt him for his son, and to make him his heir. But Paschal, who desired only the good of another life, modestly declined the favour. How great soever his love was for his profession, he found, however, several difficulties in it which made him think of leaving it. Some of his companions were too much addicted to cursing, quarrelling and fighting; nor were they to be reclaimed by his gentle rebukes. He was therefore determined to leave them and to become a religious man.

Being at that time twenty years of age, he left his master, his friends and his country and went into the kingdom of Valencia where was an austere convent of barefoot reformed Franciscans which stood in a desert solitude, at no great distance from the town of Montfort. To sequester himself from the world he made the more haste to petition for the habit of a lay-brother in the house, and was admitted in 1564. The fathers desired to persuade him to enter himself among the clerks; but they were obliged to yield to his humility and admit him among the lay-brothers. He was not only a fervent novice, but also a most fervent religious. Whenever he changed convents, according to the custom of his Order, the better to prevent any secret attachments of the heart, he never complained of anything.

The general of the Order happening to be at Paris, Paschal was sent thither to him about some business. Many of the cities through which he was to pass in France were in the hands of the Huguenots, who were then in arms. Yet he travelled in his habit, without so much as sandals on his feet, was often pursued by the Huguenots and received a wound on one shoulder. On the very day he arrived at his convent from this tedious journey he went out to his work and other duties as usual, and never spoke of anything that had happened in his journey unless asked.

He died at Villa Reale, near Valencia, on the 17th of May, in 1592, being fifty-two years old.

18 MAY

St. Eric

KING OF SWEDEN
A.D. 1151

Eric was descended of a most illustrious Swedish family; in his youth he had a solid foundation of virtue and learning, and took to wife Christina, daughter of Ingo IV, King of Sweden. Upon the death of King Smercher in 1141 he was placed upon the throne by the election of the states, according to the ancient laws of that kingdom. His first care in that exalted and dangerous station was to watch over his own soul. He treated his body with great severity, fasting and watching much, in order to keep his domestic enemy in due subjection to the spirit and to fit himself for the holy exercises of heavenly contemplation and prayer. He was truly the father and servant of all his people. With indefatigable application he himself administered to them justice, especially to the poor, to whose complaints his ears were always open, and whose grievances and oppressions he took care himself to redress. He often visited the poor that were sick, and relieved them with bountiful alms. Content with his own patrimony, he levied no taxes. He built churches, and by wholesome laws restrained the brutish and savage vices of his subjects. The frequent inroads of the idolatrous Finlanders upon his territories obliged him to take the field against them. He vanquished them in a great battle; but after his victory he wept bitterly at the sight of the dead bodies of his enemies which covered the field, because they had been slain unbaptized.

When he had subdued Finland, he sent St. Henry, Bishop of Upsal, to preach the faith of God to that savage infidel nation, of which he may be styled the apostle. Among the subjects of this good king were certain sons of Belial, who made his piety the subject of their ridicule, being mostly obstinate idolaters. Magnus, son of the King of Denmark, blinded by ambitious views to the crown of Sweden, put himself at the head of these malcontents, and engaged them in a conspiracy to take away the life of their sovereign. The holy king was hearing mass on the day after the feast of the Ascension, when the news was brought him that the rebels were in arms, and on the march against him. He calmly answered, 'Let us at least finish the sacrifice; the remainder of the festival I shall keep elsewhere.' After mass he recommended his soul to God, made the sign of the cross, and to spare the blood of the citizens who were ready to defend his life at the expense of their own, marched out alone before his guards. The conspirators rushed upon him, beat him down from his horse, and struck off his head. His death happened on the 18th of May, 1151. St. Eric was honoured as chief patron of the kingdom of Sweden till the change of religion in the sixteenth century.

19 MAY

St. Dunstan
ARCHBISHOP OF CANTERBURY
A.D. 988

St. Dunstan was a native of the town of Glastonbury and received his education under certain Irish monks who at that time resided at Glastonbury, which the wars had left in a ruinous condition. Through the recommendation of Athelmus, Archbishop of Canterbury, his uncle, with whom he had lived some time, he was called to the court of the great King Athelstan. Dunstan had in his youth received the clerical tonsure and the lesser orders. After he left the court he took the monastic habit, being advised thereto by Elphegus the Bald, Bishop of Winchester, also his uncle, who not long after ordained him priest. When he was well grounded in his profession, the bishop sent him to Glastonbury with the view of serving that church. Here he built for himself a small cell and in this hermitage he spent his time in prayer and fasting. His labour consisted in making crosses, vials, censers and sacred vestments; he likewise painted and copied books.

King Athelstan dying, his brother Edmund succeeded to the crown in 900, and having been long acquainted with the sanctity of Dunstan he installed him Abbot of Glastonbury. King Edmund had reigned only six years when he was murdered. His sons Edwi and Edgar being too young to govern, his brother Edred was called to the crown, who did nothing but by the advice of Dunstan. He died in 955 and was succeeded by Edwi, a most debauched youth, who on the very day he was anointed king, left his nobles at the banquet to go to see his harlot. St. Dunstan followed him and endeavoured to put him in mind of the duty he owed to God and men. In requital the tyrant banished him, persecuted all the monks in his kingdom and ruined all the abbeys which had escaped the devastation of the Danes, except Glastonbury and Abingdon.

St. Dunstan spent one year in exile; but the Mercians shaking off the yoke of the tyrant, placed the crown on Edgar who immediately recalled Dunstan, and in 957 preferred him to the bishopric of Worcester. King Edwi ended a wicked life in 959, when Edgar became sole monarch of the English. In 961 Dunstan was raised to the see of Canterbury. He was moreover appointed by the pope legate of the holy see. He set about re-establishing every where ecclesiastical discipline which had been much impaired by the Danish invasions and restoring the monasteries. The reformation of the clergy was no less the object of his zeal. He frequently visited the churches over the whole kingdom, everywhere preaching and instructing the faithful. Glastonbury was his dearest solitude and thither he would often retire from the world. At Canterbury, finding himself taken ill on the feast of Ascension he preached thrice, then took to his bed, and on the Saturday following calmly expired. His death happened on the 19th of May, 988.

20 MAY

St. Bernardin
OF SIENA
A.D. 1444

St. Bernardin was born at Massa in 1380. He lost his mother when he was but three, and his father, who was chief magistrate of Massa, before he was seven. The care of his education devolved on a virtuous aunt who loved him as if he had been her own son. At seventeen, he enrolled in the confraternity of our Lady in the hospital of Scala to serve the sick. He had served this hospital four years, when, in 1400, a dreadful pestilence which had already made great havoc in others parts of Italy, reached Siena; insomuch that twelve, eighteen or twenty persons died every day in this hospital, and among others were carried off almost all the priests, apothecaries and servants. Bernardin therefore persuaded twelve young men to bear him company and was intrusted with the whole care of the hospital, which, in the space of four months, he put into excellent order. He then returned home, but sick of a fever which he had contracted by his fatigues, which obliged him to keep his bed four months.

He was scarce well recovered when he returned to the like works of charity and attended a dying aunt for fourteen months. When God had called her, Bernardin retired to a house at some distance from the city, and here in solitude, fasting and prayer, he endeavoured to learn the will of God. After some time he took the habit of the Order of St. Francis and made his profession on the 8th of September 1404. Having been born on the feast of the Nativity of the blessed Virgin, he chose the same day for the principal actions of his life; on it he took the religious habit, made his vows, said his first mass and preached his first sermon.

Having in retirement prepared himself for the office of preaching, his superiors ordered him to employ his talent that way. For fourteen years his labours were confined to his own country, but when the reputation of his virtue was spread abroad, he shone as a bright light to the whole church. Often at the end of his sermons he showed to the people the sacred name of Jesus curiously cut on a board with gold letters, inviting them to adore Christ with him. This was misconstrued by some, and upon their complaints Pope Martin V summoned him to appear. But his holiness after a full examination of his doctrine dismissed him with leave to preach everywhere. The same pope pressed him to accept the bishopric of Siena in 1427, but he declined. In 1431 he no less resolutely refused that of Ferrara and again that of Urbino in 1435.

St Bernardin preached several times through the great part of Italy. He was appointed vicar-general of his Order in 1438, but after five years obtained a discharge and in his old age continued preaching. He died on the 20th of May, 1444.

PLATE 26. ST. BERNARDINO, 20 MAY. BODLEIAN LIBRARY, MS LAT. LITURG. G5, P. 314.

23 MAY

St. Julia

VIRGIN AND MARTYR
FIFTH AGE

Julia was a noble virgin at Carthage, who, when that city was taken by Genseric in 439, was sold for a slave to a pagan merchant of Syria. Under the most mortifying employments of her station, by cheerfulness and patience she found a present happiness and comfort. All the time she was not employed in her master's business was devoted to prayer and reading books of piety. She fasted every day but Sunday, nor could all the entreaties of her master, nor the hardships of her situation, prevail with her to be more tender of herself.

The merchant thought proper to carry her with him in one of his voyages to Gaul. Having reached the northern part of Corsica he cast anchor and went to shore to join the pagans of the place in a festival. Julia was left at some distance because she would not be defiled by the superstitious ceremonies. Felix, the governor of the island, asked the merchant who this woman was who dared to insult the gods. He informed him that she was a Christian and that all his authority over her was too weak to prevail with her to renounce her religion; but that he found her so diligent and faithful he could not part with her. The governor offered him four of his best female slaves in exchange for her. But the merchant, whose name was Eusebius, replied, 'No; all you are worth will not purchase her; for I would freely lose the most valuable thing I have in the world rather than be deprived of her.'

However, the governor, whilst Eusebius was drunk and asleep, took upon him to compel her to sacrifice to his gods. He proffered to procure her liberty if she could comply. The saint made answer that she was as free as she desired to be, as long as she was allowed to serve Jesus Christ; and whatever should happen she would never purchase her liberty by so abominable a crime. Felix thinking himself derided by her undaunted and resolute air, in a transport of rage caused her to be struck on the face, and the hair of her head to be torn off; and lastly, ordered her to be hanged on a cross till she expired. Certain monks of the isle of La Gorgona (which lies between Corsica and Leghorn) carried off her body.

PLATE 27. ST. JULIA, 23 MAY. BUTLER, *LIVES OF THE SAINTS,* **TWO-VOLUME ILLUSTRATED 19TH-CENTURY EDITION.**

24 MAY

St. Vincent
OF LÉRINS

A.D. 450

St. Vincent was of Gaulish extraction, had a polite education, was for some time an officer in the army and lived with dignity in the world. Having been some time tossed about in the storms of a military life he desired to take shelter in the harbour of religion. In these dispositions he retired to a small remote island. This Gennadius assures us to have been the famous monastery of Lérins, in the lesser of two islands not far from the coast of Provence towards Antibes. In this place he shut himself up and writ a book, which he enitled *A Commonitory against Heretics*, which he composed in 434, three years after the general council of Ephesus had condemned the Nestorians. He had chiefly in view the heretics of his own times, but he confuted them by general clear principles which overturn all heresies to the end of the world. Together with the ornaments of eloquence and erudition, the inward beauty of his mind and the brightness of his devotion sparkle in every page.

Out of humility he disguises himself under the name of Peregrinus, to express the quality of being a pilgrim, and layeth down this fundamental principle that such doctrine is truly Catholic as hath been believed in all places, at all times, and by all the faithfull. He saith, 'They who have made bold with one article of faith will proceed on to others; and what will be the consequence of this reforming of religion, but only that these refiners will never have done till they have reformed it quite away.' He takes notice that heretics quote the sacred writings at every word, but in this are like those poisoners or quacks who put off their destructive potions under inscriptions of good drugs, and under the title of infallible cures.

If a doubt arise in interpreting the meaning of the scriptures, we must summon in the holy fathers who have lived and died in the faith and communion of the Catholic church. After a point has been decided in a general council the definition is irrefragable. These general principles by which all heresies are easily confounded, St. Vincent explains with perspicuity; and no controversial book ever expressed so much and such deep sense in so few words. The same rules are laid down by Tertullian in his book of Prescriptions, by St. Irenaeus and other fathers. St. Vincent died in the reigns of Theodosius II and Valentian III, consequently before the close of 450. His relics are preserved with respect at Lérins and his name occurs in the Roman Martyrology.

25 MAY (27 MAY)

St. Bede
FATHER OF THE CHURCH

A.D. 735

Venerable Bede (who is not to be confounded with a monk of Lindisfarne of the same name, but older) was born in 673 in a village which became part of the estate of the monastery of Jarrow, but was gained upon by the sea before the time of Simeon of Durham. St. Bennet Biscop founded the abbey of St. Peter's at Weremouth in 674 and that of St. Paul's at Jarrow in 680 on the banks of the Tyne, below the *Caprae caput*, still called Goat's head or Gateshead. To his care Bede was committed at seven years of age, but was afterwards removed to Jarrow, where he prosecuted his studies under the direction of the Abbot Ceolfrid.

His endowments supplying the defect of age, he was ordained deacon in 691 at nineteen, and from this time continued his studies, till in 702 he was ordained priest. From this time he began to compose books; and he had a great school in which he brought up many eminent and holy scholars and instructed his fellow monks, who amounted to the number of six hundred. He says that from the time of being made priest to the fifty-ninth year of his age, he had compiled forty-five different works, of which thirty consist of comments on the Old and New Testaments. All the sciences and every branch of literature were handled by him: natural philosophy, astronomy, arithmetic, grammar, ecclesiastical history and the lives of the saints.

His life was a model of devotion, obedience, humility and penance. He declined the abbatial dignity which was pressed upon him. Malmesbury gives us a letter of Pope Sergius, by which he was invited to Rome. What hindered his journey we know not; but we have his word for it that he lived from his childhood in his monastery without travelling abroad. His reputation drew to him many visits from all the greatest men in Britain. Egbert, who was consecrated Archbishop of York in 734, had been a scholar of Bede, and at his pressing invitation our saint went to York, and taught there some months, but excused himself from leaving his monastery the following year. This school set up at York became very flourishing, and Alcuin, one of its greatest ornaments, is said to have been himself a scholar of Bede.

St. Bede died in the year 735, of his age sixty-two, on Wednesday evening, the 26th of May, after the first vespers of Our Lord's Ascension; whence many authors say he died on the feast of Ascension for our Saxon ancestors reckoned festivals from first vespers. Bede was buried in St. Paul's church in Jarrow. In 1020 his remains were conveyed to Durham and laid in a wooden trunk in the shrine of St. Cuthbert.

26 MAY

St. Philip
NERI
A.D. 1595

Philip Neri was born at Florence in 1515, the son of Francis Neri, a lawyer. Having finished his grammar studies when he was eighteen, he was sent by his father to an uncle who was very rich, to be his heir. Philip soon left his uncle and went to Rome in 1533. There, being taken into the house of Galleotto Caccia, a Florentine nobleman, as preceptor to his children, he led so edifying a life that the reputation of his sanctity spread very wide. He spent much time retired in a little chamber, passing sometimes whole nights in prayer. He made the study of the canon law a part of his care and became one of the best scholars of the age; but being desirous to approach nearer to Jesus Christ, at twenty-three years of age he sold even his books for the relief of the poor.

He often visited the hospitals to serve the sick, and lamented to see the custom of waiting on poor sick persons disused in the world. He therefore desired to revive it, and with that view commenced the confraternity of the Blessed Trinity in Rome, with the assistance of his confessarius, Persiano Rosa. He laid the first foundation of this establishment with fourteen companions in 1548 in the church of Our Saviour del Campo. In the year 1550 he translated this confraternity to the church of the Holy Trinity and erected a new hospital under the name of the Blessed Trinity which to this day subsists and is one of the best regulated hospitals in the world. Humility made the saint think of devoting himself to the service of God in a laical state, but he was most urgently pressed by Rosa to enter into holy orders, and after a long preparation was ordained priest in June 1551. From which time he chose his dwelling in a small community where Rosa and certain other priests lived.

Desiring by all means in his power to help his neighbour, he laid the foundation of the Congregation of Oratorians in 1551. Several priests and young ecclesiastics began to assist him in his conferences and in reading prayers to the people in the church of the Holy Trinity. They were called Oratorians because at certain hours every morning and afternoon, by ringing a bell, they called the people to church. In 1564 the saint formed his Congregation into a regular community, using one common purse and table, and he gave them rules and statutes. St. Philip obtained of Pope Gregory XIII the approbation of his Congregation in 1575 and lived to see many houses of his Oratory erected at Florence, Naples, Lucca, etc.

St Philip was of sickly constitution and was usually visited every year by one or two fevers. In 1595 he laid all April sick and in May was taken with a vomiting of blood. He expired just after midnight between the 25th and 26 of May, 1595.

27 MAY

St. Augustine
APOSTLE OF THE ENGLISH
A.D. 604

The Saxons, English and Jutes had reigned in this island about one hundred and fifty years when God was pleased to open their eyes to the light of the gospel. St. Gregory the Great, when he was placed in the apostolic chair, turned his thoughts towards this abandoned part of the vineyard, and resolved to send thither a number of zealous labourers. For this great work none seemed better qualified than Augustine, then prior of St. Gregory's monastery of St Andrew in Rome. Him the pope appointed superior of the mission, allotting him several assistants who were Roman monks.

When the missionaries were advanced several days journey, certain persons exaggerated to them the ferocity of the English people in such a manner that they deliberated whether it was prudent to proceed and Augustine was deputed back to St. Gregory to beg leave to return to Rome. St. Gregory sent Augustine back with a letter of encouragement, representing to them the cowardice of abandoning a good work when it is begun. The labourers pursued their journey and taking some Frenchmen for interpreters with them, landed in the Isle of Thanet in 596. From this place St. Augustine sent to Ethelbert, King of Kent. After some days the king went in person to the isle, listened attentively to the word of life, but answered that their premises were fair, but to him uncertain. However they should not be molested, nor hindered from preaching. He also appointed them necessary subsistence and a dwelling place in Canterbury. Several among the people were converted and in a short time the king himself.

St. Augustine sent Laurence and Peter to Rome to solicit a supply of labourers and they brought over several disciples of Pope Gregory. The good King Ethelbert laboured himself in promoting the conversion of his subjects, built Christchurch, the cathedral in Canterbury and the Abbey of SS. Peter and Paul, since called St. Augustine's. St. Gregory in the year 600 sent a letter of congratulation to King Ethelbert and to St. Augustine authority to ordain twelve bishops. By virtue of his metropolitan authority St. Augustine took upon him to make a general visitation of his province. He desired very much to see the ancient Britons reclaimed from certain abuses which had crept in among them, and to engage them to assist in converting the English. Being on the edge of Worcestershire, he invited the British bishops and doctors to a conference but they said that without the consent of their nation, they could not quit their ancient rites. Accordingly a second more numerous council was assembled, but when the British bishops entered the synod Augustine did not rise from his seat and, concluding from this that he lacked humility, they remained obstinate.

St. Augustine, whilst yet living, ordained Laurence his successor in the see of Canterbury, not to leave an infant church destitute of a pastor. He died on the 26th of May, 604.

28 MAY

St. Germanus
BISHOP OF PARIS
A.D. 576

St. Germanus was born in the territory of Autun about the year 469. Being ordained priest by St. Agrippinus, Bishop of Autun, he was made abbot of St. Symphorian's, in the suburbs of that city. In 554, happening to be in Paris when that see became vacant on the demise of the bishop, he was exalted to the episcopal chair. His promotion made no alteration in his austerities; and the same simplicity and frugality appeared in his dress, table and furniture. His house was perpetually crowded with the poor and the afflicted, and he had always many beggars at his own table. God gave his sermons a wonderful influence over the minds of all ranks of people. King Childebert, who till then had been an ambitious worldly prince, was entirely converted to piety, reformed his whole court, and, not content with making many religious foundations and with sending money to the bishop to be distributed among the indigent, melted down his silver plate and gave away the chains about his neck.

The king built a church in honour of St. Vincent and of the Holy Cross, which is now called St. Germain's-in-the-Meadow, and stands in the suburbs of Paris. The saint performed the ceremony of dedication on the 23rd of September, 558. The king likewise built a large monastery joining to his new church which he endowed most liberally with the fief of Issy and other lands, on part of which a considerable suburb of Paris has been since built, and committed the monastery and church to the care of our saint, who placed there monks under the holy Abbot Droctoveus whom he had invited from Autun.

Clotaire, who succeeded his brother Childebert, at first seemed to treat the holy bishop coldly; but falling ill of a violent fever was put in mind to send for St. Germanus. He did so, took hold of his clothes and applied them to the parts of his body where he felt pain and recovered immediately. That prince dying in 561, Paris was given to Charibert who sunk into a vicious indolence, yet was obstinate and headstrong in his passions. Our saint, finding all his remonstrances lost on him, proceeded to excommunicate him. Upon the death of Charibert his three brothers divided his dominions. St. Germanus found his flock involved by this agreement in great difficulties, and the city divided into three different parties, always plotting against one another. He did all he could to preserve the peace and wrote to Queen Brunehaut conjuring her to employ her interest with her husband, but her passion rendered her deaf to all remonstrances.

In his old age St. Germanus lost nothing of that activity with which he had filled his station in the vigour of his life. By his zeal, the remains of idolatry were extirpated in France and he was called to receive his reward on the 28th of March, 576, being eight years old.

30 MAY

St. Ferdinand
III, KING OF CASTILE AND LEON
A.D. 1252

Ferdinand was eldest son to Alphonsus, King of Leon, and Berengera of Castile, and was born about the end of 1198, or some time in 1199. Berengera had been obliged to a separation from Alphonsus after having borne him two sons and two daughters, because, though in the third degree of consanguinity, they had been married without a dispensation. But because the marriage had been contracted *bona fide* their children were declared lawful heirs. Berengera returned to her father Alphonsus of Castile. He dying in 1214, his son Henry succeeded and Berengera was charged with the regency. The young King Henry died in 1217, and Berengera put in her claim to the crown, transferring her right upon Ferdinand who was in the eighteenth year of his age proclaimed king.

By Berengera's advice Ferdinand took to wife, in 1219, Beatrix, daughter of Philip, Emperor of Germany, and their marriage was blessed with seven sons and three daughters. Nothing ever so much troubled our saint as when his own father, King of Leon, laid claim to and invaded his dominions. St. Ferdinand endeavoured, by the most dutiful letters, to gave him satisfaction, and lent him his own forces to fight against the Moors. He founded several bishoprics and contributed munificently to the building or repairing of many cathedrals, churches, monasteries and hospitals.

St. Ferdinand was marching to lay siege to Jaen in 1230 when he received news of the death of his father and was called to take possession of Leon. It cost him three years to settle the affairs of his new kingdom, but in 1234 he recommended his wars against the Moors and completed the conquest of the two Moorish kingdoms of Baeza and Cordova. This last city had been in the hands of those infidels five hundred and twenty-four years and had long been the capital of their empire in Spain.

In the campaigns that followed he made himself master of twenty-four other towns. The rich city of Seville had formed itself into a republic when Ferdinand resolved to turn his forces against that place, far the most important which the Moors at that time possessed in Spain. The death of his mother interrupted his preparations for a short time; but motives of religion moderating his grief, he had no sooner settled the administration but he resumed his expedition with greater vigour than ever. The siege held sixteen months, Seville being the largest and strongest city in Spain. The city surrendered in 1249. St. Ferdinand after the most solemn thanksgivings to God, refounded the cathedral with such magnificence that it yielded to no church in Christendom but that of Toledo.

The three years which he survived he resided at Seville, and was preparing an expedition against the Moors in Africa when he was taken with his last sickness and died on the 30th of May, 1252.

FERDINANDVS REX LEGIENSIS ETCASTILLIÆ

PLATE 28. ST. FERDINAND, 30 MAY. BUTLER, *LIVES OF THE SAINTS*, TWO-VOLUME ILLUSTRATED 19TH-CENTURY EDITION.

1 JUNE

St. Justin

THE PHILOSOPHER, MARTYR
A.D. 167

St. Justin was born at Neapolis, the capital of Samaria. Vespasian, having endowed its inhabitants with the privileges belonging to Roman citizens, gave it the name Flavia. His son Titus sent thither a colony of Greeks, among whom were the father and grandfather of our saint. St. Justin spent his youth reading the poets, orators and historians. Having gone through the usual course of these studies, he gave himself up to that of philosophy in quest of truth. He made great progress in the Platonic philosophy and flattered himself with the hope of arriving at the sight of God. Upon inquiry into the credibility of the Christian religion he embraced it soon after. His discourse or *Oration to the Greeks* he wrote soon after his conversion, in order to convince the heathens of the reasonableness of his having deserted paganism. His second work is called his *Exhortation to the Greeks*, which he drew up at Rome.

Justin made a long stay in Rome. The Christians met in his house to perform their devotions and he applied himself with great zeal to the instruction of all those who resorted to him. The martyr, after his first *Apology*, left Rome and probably performed the functions of an evangelist in many countries for several years. But the *Apologies* of this martyr have chiefly rendered his name illustrious. The first he addressed to the Emperor Antoninus Pius, his two adopted sons, and the senate about the year 150. That mild emperor had published no edicts against the Christians; but by virtue of former edicts they were often persecuted by the governors. Justin in his *Apology* boldly declares himself a Christian and an advocate for his religion. He exhorts the emperor to hold the balance even in the execution of justice and sets forth the sanctity of the doctrine and manners of Christians. It appears that this had its desired effect, the quiet of the church.

He composed his second *Apology* near twenty years after, in 167, on account of the martyrdom of one Ptolemy and two other Christians. The apologist added that he expected death would be the recompense of his *Apology*. Justin and others that were with him were apprehended and brought before the prefect of Rome who said, 'Obey the gods.'

Justin replied, 'No one can be justly blamed or condemned for obeying the commands of Jesus Christ. I have tried every kind of discipline and learning, but I have finally embraced the Christian discipline.' The prefect seeing it was to no purpose to argue, bade them go together and unanimously sacrifice to the gods, and told them that in the case of refusal they should be tormented without mercy. Upon their refusal the martyrs were led to the place where criminals were executed, and there scourged and beheaded.

3 JUNE

St. Clotildis

QUEEN OF FRANCE
A.D. 545

Clotildis was daughter of Chilperic, younger brother to the tyrannical King of Burgundy, who put him, his wife, and the rest of his brothers except one, to death in order to usurp their dominions. In this massacre he spared Chilperic's two daughters, then in their infancy. One of them became a nun; the other, Clotildis, was brought up in her uncle's court and instructed in the Catholic religion, though she was educated in the midst of Arians. She was adorned with all virtues and the reputation of her wit, beauty, modesty and piety made her the adoration of all the neighbouring kingdoms, when Clovis I, the victorious king of the Franks, demanded and obtained her of her uncle in marriage, granting her all the conditions she could desire for the free and secure exercise of her religion.

The marriage was solemnized at Soissons in 493. Clotildis made herself a little oratory in the royal palace in which she spent much time in fervent prayer. She honoured her royal husband; and when she saw herself mistress of his heart she did not defer the great work of endeavouring to win him to God, and often spoke to him on the vanity of his idols, and on the excellency of the true religion, but the moment of his conversion was not yet come.

After the baptism of their second son, Clodomir, and the infant's recovery from a dangerous indisposition, she pressed the king more boldly to renounce his idols. But the fear of giving offence to his people made him delay. His miraculous victory over the Alemanni, and his entire conversion in 496, were at length the fruit of our saint's prayers.

Clotildis having gained to God this great monarch never ceased to excite him to glorious actions for the divine honour. He built in Paris, at her request, the great church of SS. Peter and Paul. He died in 511. His eldest son, Theodoric, whom he had by a concubine before his marriage, reigned over the eastern parts of France. As to the three sons of Clotildis, Clodomir reigned at Orleans, Childebert at Paris, and Clotaire at Soissons. This division produced wars and jealousies, till in 560 the whole monarchy was reunited under Clotaire. The most sensible affliction of this pious queen was the murder of the two eldest sons of Clodomir in 526 by their uncles. This tragical disaster contributed to wean her heart from the world. She spent the remaining part of her life at Tours, near the tomb of St. Martin, in exercises of prayers, watching, fasting and penance, seeming totally to forget that she had been a queen. In her last illness she sent for her sons and exhorted them to honour god and keep his commandments. She ordered all she had left to be distributed among the poor. On the thirtieth day of her illness, she departed to the Lord on the 3rd of June in 545.

CLOTILDIS

BAPTISMVS CLODOVEI

PLATE 29. ST. CLOTILDIS, 3 JUNE. BUTLER, *LIVES OF THE SAINTS*, TWO-VOLUME ILLUSTRATED 19TH-CENTURY EDITION.

4 JUNE

St. Optatus

BISHOP OF MILEVUM
FOURTH AGE

This father was an African, and an illustrious champion of the Church of Christ in the fourth age. He was Bishop of Milevum in Numidia and the first catholic prelate who undertook by writing to stem the tide of the Donatist schism in Africa. Parmenian, the third bishop of that sect at Carthage, wrote five books in defence of his party. He was a man of learning and abilities, well versed in the art of sophistry, and capable of covering the worst cause with spacious glosses. Against this Goliath, St. Optatus stepped forth and turned all his artillery against himself. This he performed by six books against Parmenian, to which he several years after, about the year 285, added a seventh. To set this controversy in a clear light, it is necessary to take a short view of the Donatist schism, which took its rise from a circumstance that happened in the persecution of Diocletian.

The Traditors, or Christians who, for fear of torments, delivered the holy scriptures into the hands of the persecutors that they might be burnt, were guilty of a crime which bordered upon apostasy. Upon their repentance they were, if in holy orders, to be deposed. But in this the bishops had power to grant an indulgence. Mensurius, primate of Carthage admitted penitent priests to their functions alleging the danger of a schism. Certain Numidian zealots took offence at this mildness and drew many into schism. Donatus, Bishop of Casae-Nigrae began this breach and refused to communicate with Mensurius and accused him of having given up the scriptures into the hands of the heathen. The Donatists called the Catholics pagans, and rebaptized all who came over to them. To condemn this their capital error, the great council of Arles was assembled in 314.

In his books against Parmenian, who had succeeded Donatus, our saint gives the history of the origin and follies of the Donatist sect, and enlarges upon the universality of the church. 'Wherefore', says he, 'would you unchurch an infinite number of Christians that are in the East and the West? You are but a small number of rebels who have opposed all the churches of the world.' He confutes the errors of the Donatists, who pretend that the sacraments are null if given out of the true church.

St. Optatus survived the year 384, but the time of his death is not known.

5 JUNE

St. Boniface

ARCHBISHOP OF MENTZ, APOSTLE OF
GERMANY, AND MARTYR
A.D. 755

St. Boniface was born at Crediton in Devonshire about the year 690 and at his baptism named Winfrid. He was educated from thirteen years of age in the monastery of Exeter. The reputation of the schools of the monastery of Nutcell in Winchester, drew him to that house. At thirty he was promoted to the priesthood, and from that time was chiefly employed in preaching.

With the leave of his abbot he passed over into Friseland to preach the gospel to the infidels in 716. But a war breaking out between Charles Martel and the King of Friseland threw insuperable difficulties in his way and he was obliged to return to his monastery, where he was chosen abbot. Having stayed two years in England, he set out for Rome in 719 and presented himself to Pope Gregory II, begging his authority that he might preach the faith to infidels. Gregory bestowed on him many holy relics and dismissed him with letters of recommendation to all Christian princes in his way.

The holy missionary lost no time but crossed the Lower Alps and travelling through Bavaria and Thuringia, there began his apostolical functions. He baptized great numbers, but also brought the Christians he found to reform many irregularities. During three years he joined his labours with St. Willebrord in Friseland, then went to Hesse and part of Saxony. The pope commanded him to repair to Rome and ordained him bishop. The saint returning to Hesse, cut down a tall oak consecrated to Jupiter, the timber of which he employed in building a chapel. He founded many churches, and a monastery at Orfordt. The pope now constituted him Primate of all Germany with the power to erect new bishoprics.

Gregory dying St. Boniface went to Rome where he received from the hands of Pope Zachary the monastic habit, and withdrew to Mount Cassino for several years. Pepin the Short in 752 was chosen King of France and desiring to be crowned by the most holy prelate in his dominions, insisted upon the ceremony being performed by St. Boniface. This was done at Soissons, where our saint presided in a synod. From the councils of Lessines and Soissons he appears to have been a legate of the apostolic see in France no less than in Germany. To assist him in planting the spirit of Christian piety St. Boniface invited over from England many holy men and religious women. In 746 he laid the foundation of the great abbey of Fuld, which continued long the most renowned seminary in that part of the world.

Having set out with certain zealous companions to preach to the savage inhabitants of East Friseland, a band of enraged infidels appeared and rushed into his tent. The servants were for defending his life by fighting, but he would not suffer it. The pagans attacked them and put them all to death. St. Boniface suffered on the 5th of June 755.

6 JUNE

St. Norbert

ARCHBISHOP OF MAGDEBURG, FOUNDER OF
THE PREMONSTRATENSIAN ORDER
A.D. 1134

St. Norbert was born at Xanten in Cleves in 1080. His father was related to the emperor. Being at first blinded by the flattery of the world, he suffered himself to be carried away by its pleasures and pastimes. He even received the tonsure with a worldly spirit; and though he was instituted to a canonry and ordained subdeacon, he neither changed his spirit nor his conduct.

God awakened him from his spiritual lethargy by an alarming accident. Norbert was riding to a village in Westphalia when he was overtaken by a violent storm. A ball of lightning fell just before his horse's feet and the poor beast threw his rider, who lay like one dead for near an hour. At last, coming to himself, like another Saul, he cried out to God, 'Lord, what wouldst thou have me to do?' To which the divine grace interiorly suggested this reply, 'Turn away from evil and do good.' He became on the spot a sincere penitent and withdrew to his canonry at Xanten. His conversion was completed by a retreat which he made in St. Sigebert's monastery near Cologne. Norbert was this time in the thirtieth year of his age.

After his conversion he employed two years in preparing himself for the priesthood. After his ordination he made a sermon on the vanity of the world. Some accused him to the pope's legate as a hypocrite. He purged himself in a council held at Fritzlar in 118, sold his own estate and travelled to Languedoc where Pope Gelasius II was at that time. He obtained of the pope faculties to preach the gospel where he judged proper. It was then the death of winter. Yet he walked barefoot through the snow, and seemed insensible to the rigours of the season. He preached penance with incredible fruit over Languedoc, Guienne, Poitou and Orleanois.

Pope Calixtus II having succeeded Gelasius in 1119 Norbert went to Rheims where his holiness held a council. The Bishop of Laon gave Norbert the choice of several places to build a house and he pitched upon a lonesome valley called Prémontré in the forest of Coucy. The bishop there built a monastery for the saint who assembled thirteen brethren. Their number soon increased and the Order was soon spread over several parts of Europe. Norbert, having completed the establishment of his Order, was obliged to quit his monastery to be in a more exalted station for the benefit of many as archbishop of Magdeburg. But his zeal made enemies and some even made attempts upon his life. He continued still to superintend the observance of discipline in his Order, though upon his episcopal consecration he had left the government thereof to his first disciple, Hugh. The fourth general chapter consisted of eighteen abbots. The saint died in Magdeburg on the 6th of June, 1134.

8 JUNE

St. William

ARCHBISHOP OF YORK
A.D. 1154

William was the son of Earl Herbert and Emma, sister to King Stephen. He renounced the world in his youth, employing his riches to purchase treasures in heaven by works of mercy to the poor, and giving himself wholly to the study and practice of religion. Being promoted to holy orders, he was elected treasurer in the church of York, under the learned and good Archbishop Thurstan. When that prelate, after having held his dignity twenty years, retired among the Cluniac monks at Pontefract, to prepare himself for his death which happened the year following, St. William was chosen archbishop by the majority of the chapter, and consecrated at Winchester in September 1144.

But Osbert, the archdeacon, a turbulent man, procured Henry Murdach, a Cistercian monk of the abbey of Fountains, who was also a man of great learning and a zealous preacher, to be preferred at Rome, whither William went to demand his pall and to plead the cause of his constituents rather than his own. Being deprived by Pope Eugenius III in 1147, he, who had always looked upon this dignity with trembling, appeared much greater in the manner in which he bore this repulse than he

could have done in the highest honours. Being returned into England, he went privately to Winchester, to his uncle Henry, bishop of that see, where he led a penitential life in silence, solitude and prayer in a retired house belonging to the bishop, bewailing the frailties of his past life, for seven years.

The Archbishop Henry then dying, in 1153, and Anastasius IV having succeeded Eugenius in the see of Rome, St. William, to satisfy the importunity of others, by whom he was again elected, undertook a second journey to Rome and received the pallium from his holiness.

The saint on his return was met on the road by Robert, dean, and Osbert, archdeacon of the church of York, who insolently forbade him to enter that city or diocese. He received the affront with meekness but pursued his journey. He was received with incredible joy by his people. The great numbers who assembled to welcome him broke down the wooden bridge over the river Ouse in the middle of the city and a great many persons fell into the river. The saint made the sign of the cross over the river and addressed himself to God, and all the world ascribed to his prayers the miraculous preservation of the whole multitude, who all escaped out of the waters without hurt.

St. William sought no revenge against his enemies who had obstructed his good designs. He formed a great many projects for the good of his diocese, but within a few weeks after his installation was seized with a fever, of which he died on the 8th of June, 1154.

9 JUNE

St. Columba

OR COLUMKILLE, ABBOT
A.D. 597

St. Columba was of noble extraction and was born at Garton in the county of Tyrconnel in 521. He learned the divine scriptures and the lessons of an ascetic life under the holy bishop St. Finian in his great school of Cluain-iraid. Being advanced to the order of priesthood in 546 he began to give admirable lessons of sacred learning, and in a short time formed many disciples. He founded, about 550, the great monastery of Durrogh, and besides many smaller. St. Columba composed a rule which he settled in the hundred monasteries which he founded in Ireland and Scotland. It was chiefly borrowed from the ancient oriental monastic institutions.

King Dermot, being offended at the zeal of St. Columba in reproving public vices, the holy abbot left his native country and passed into Scotland. He took along with him twelve disciples and arrived there, according to Bede, in the year 565. The Picts, having embraced the faith, gave St. Columba the little island of Iona, twelve miles from the land, in which he built the great monastery which was for several ages the chief seminary of North Britain, and continued for long the burying place of the kings of Scotland. This monastery, several ages afterwards, embraced the rule of St. Bennet.

St. Columba's manner of living was always most austere. He lay on the bare floor with a stone for his pillow. Yet his devotion was neither morose nor severe. His countenance always appeared wonderfully cheerful and his incomparable mildness and charity towards all men and on all occasions won the hearts of all who conversed with him. He was of such authority that neither king nor people did any thing without his consent.

When King Aedhan succeeded to his cousin Conall in the throne of Scotland in 574, he received the royal insignia from St. Columba.

Four years before his death St. Columba was favoured with a vision of angels which left him in tears, because he learned from those heavenly messengers that God, moved by the prayers of the British and Scottish churches, would prolong his exile on earth yet four years. Having continued his labours in Scotland thirty-four years, he, on Saturday the 9th of June said to his disciple Diermit, 'This day is called the Sabbath, that is, the day of rest, and such will it truly be to me; for it will put an end to my labours.' He was the first in the church at matins at midnight; but knelt before the altar, received the viaticum, and having given his blessing to his spiritual children, sweetly slept in the Lord in the year 597, the seventy-seventh of his age. His body was buried in this island, but some ages after removed to Down in Ulster and laid in one vault with the remains of St. Patrick and St. Brigit.

11 JUNE

St. Barnabas

APOSTLE
FIRST CENTURY

St. Barnabas, though not of the twelve chosen by Christ, is nevertheless styled an apostle by the primitive fathers and by St. Luke. His singular vocation by the Holy Ghost, and the great share he had in the apostolic labours have obtained him this title. He was of the tribe of Levi, but born in Cyprus where his family was settled. He was first called Joses. After the Ascension the apostles changed his name into Barnabas. The first mention of him is in the Acts of the Apostles where it is related that the converts at Jerusalem lived in common, and that as many as were owners of lands or horses sold them and brought the price and laid it at the feet of the apostles. No one is mentioned in particular but St. Barnabas; doubtless because he was possessed of a large estate.

St. Paul coming to Jerusalem after his conversion and not easily getting admittance into the church because he had been a violent persecutor, addressed himself to Barnabas who introduced him to the apostles Peter and James. About four or five days after this, certain disciples having preached the faith with great success at Antioch, someone was wanted to form the church and to confirm the neophytes. Whereupon St. Barnabas was sent from Jerusalem. St. Paul being then at Tarsus, Barnabas invited him to share in his labours at Antioch. The Church was so much increased at Antioch that the name Christians was first given to the faithful in that city.

As they were ministering to the Lord, the Holy Ghost said to them, 'Separate me Paul and Barnabas for the work whereunto I have taken them.' Paul and Barnabas having thus received their mission, left Antioch and went to Seleucia, a city adjoining to the sea, whence they set sail for Cyprus. Having there preached Christ, they sailed to Pamphylia and Pisidia. The apostles went next to Iconium and to Lystra, in which city the idolaters, surprised to see a cripple miraculously healed by St. Paul, declared the gods were come among them. They gave to Paul the name of Mercury, because he was the chief speaker, and to Barnabas that of Jupiter. They at length arrived at Antioch in Syria. During their abode in this city arose the dispute relating to the necessity of observing the Mosaic rites. This weighty question gave occasion to the council of the apostles at Jerusalem in 51, where in SS. Paul and Barnabas gave a full account of the success of their labours among the Gentiles. At last a difference in opinion produced a separation, without the least breach of charity in their hearts. St. Paul travelled into Syria and Cilicia, and Barnabas betook himself to his native island, Cyprus. Here the sacred writings dismiss his history. Alexander, a monk of Cyprus, hath written an account of his death in which the saint was taken by the mob and stoned to death.

13 JUNE

St. Antony

OF PADUA
A.D. 1231

St. Antony, though a native of Lisbon, received his surname from his long residence at Padua. He was born in 1195 and christened by the name of Ferdinand, which he changed for that of Antony when he entered the order of St. Francis. His father was Martin de Bullones, an officer in the army of Alphonsus I.

At fifteen years of age he entered among the regular canons of St. Austin, near Lisbon, but he desired, two years after, to be sent to the convent of the Holy Cross, at Coimbra, a hundred miles from the former city. He had lived at Coimbra near eight years when Don Pedro brought over from Morocco the relics of the five Franciscans who had been lately there crowned with martyrdom. Ferdinand was strongly affected at the sight and conceived an ardent desire to lay down his life for Christ. After some time spent in solitude, he obtained leave to go into Africa. He was scarce arrived there when God visited him with a severe illness which obliged him to return to Spain. But the vessel on which he was embarked was driven to Sicily, where he was informed that St. Francis was then holding a general chapter at Assisium. When he had seen St. Francis he offered himself to the provincials of Italy. He took care to conceal his learning and presented himself only to serve in the kitchen.

An assembly of the neighbouring friars was held at Forli. St. Antony's guardian ordered him to speak. The saint begged to be excused; but the superior insisting, he spoke with such eloquence as astonished the whole company. St. Francis was informed and sent him to Vercelli to study theology. St. Antony taught divinity some years with great applause at Bologna, Toulouse, Montpellier and Padua, and was appointed guardian at Limoges. He at length forsook the schools to apply himself wholly to the functions of a missionary preacher. The saint was no less admirable in the confessional than in the pulpit.

St. Francis dying in 1226, brother Elias, a man of worldly spirit, was chosen general; who abusing his authority, began to introduce several relaxations of the rule. Only St. Antony and an Englishman named Adam boldly opposed and condemned these abuses; but were loaded with injuries and ill-treatment. They addressed themselves to Pope Gregory IX by whom they were graciously received. Antony returned to his convent at Padua, but finding his health and strength declining very fast retired out of town. His distemper increasing very much upon him he desired to be carried back to his convent in Padua; but the crowds of people pressing to kiss the hem of his habit were so great that he stopped in the suburbs and was laid in the chamber of the director of the nuns of Arcela where he gave up his happy soul on the 13th of June 1231, being only thirty-six years old.

PLATE 30. ST. ANTHONY OF PADUA, 13 JUNE. BUTLER, *LIVES OF THE SAINTS*, TWO-VOLUME ILLUSTRATED 19TH-CENTURY EDITION.

15 JUNE

SS. Vitus

OR GUY, CRESCENTIA AND MODESTUS, MARTYRS

IN THE BEGINNING OF THE FOURTH CENTURY

These saints are mentioned with distinction of the ancient martyrologies. According to their acts they were natives of Sicily. Vitus was a child nobly born, who had the happiness to be instructed in the faith, and inspired with the most perfect sentiments of his religion by his Christian nurse, named Crescentia, and her faithful husband Modestus. His father, Hylas, was extremely incensed when he discovered the child's invincible aversion to idolatry; and finding him not to be overcome by stripes and such like chastisements, he delivered him up to Valerian, the governor, who in vain tried all his arts to work him into compliance with his father's will and the emperor's edicts. He escaped out of their hands, and together with Crescentia and Modestus, fled into Italy. They there met with the crown of martyrdom in Lucania, in the persecution of Diocletian.

[Editorial note: St. Vitus is the patron of sufferers from epilepsy and from nervous diseases, including 'St. Vitus's Dance', a form of chorea, and is said to protect against the bites of snakes and rabid dogs. Although the cult of these martyrs dates back to very early times, their exact identity and place of death remains confused, suggesting that there may have been two people named Vitus, one who died in Lucania and the other in Sicily. Most of the English abbeys of the Middle Ages venerated Vitus and Modestus alone.]

16 JUNE

St. Quiricus

OR CYR, AND JULITTA, MARTYRS

A.D. 304

Domitian, the governor of Lycaonia, executing with great cruelty the edicts of Diocletian against the Christians, Julitta, a lady of that country, withdrew to Seleucia with her little son, Cyr, or Quiricus, only three years old, and two maids. Alexander, the governor of Seleucia, was not less a persecutor than Domitian. Wherefore Julitta went on to Tarsus in Cilicia. Alexander happened to enter that city about the same with her, and she was immediately apprehended holding her infant in her arms and conducted to the tribunal of this governor.

She was of royal blood, the granddaughter of kings, and she possessed great riches; out of all of which she carried nothing with her but present necessaries. Her two maids fled and hid themselves. Alexander demanded her name, quality and country; to all of which questions she answered only, 'I am a Christian'. The judge, enraged, ordered her child to be taken from her, and that she should be extended and cruelly whipped with thongs; which was accordingly executed.

Nothing could be more amiable than the little Cyr, a certain air of dignity spoke his illustrious birth; and this, joined to the sweetness and innocence of his tender age and looks, moved all present exceedingly. It was a difficult thing to tear him from the arms of his mother; and he continued still to stretch his little hands towards her. The governor held the infant on his knees, and endeavoured to kiss and to pacify him; but the innocent babe, having his eyes still fixed upon his mother, and striving to get back to her, scratched the face of the inhuman judge; and when the other, under her torments, cried out that she was a Christian, he repeated as loud as he was able, 'I am a Christian.'

The governor, being enraged, took him by the foot and throwing him to the ground from off his tribunal, dashed out his brains against the edge of the steps, and all the place round about was sprinkled with blood. Julitta, seeing him thus expire, rejoiced at his happy martyrdom and gave thanks to God. Her joy increased the rage of the governor, who commanded her sides to be torn with hooks, and scalding pitch to be poured on her feet, while proclamation was made by a crier, 'Julitta, take pity on thyself and sacrifice to the gods.' She always answered, 'I do not sacrifice to devils or to dumb and deaf statues; but I worship christ.'

Whereupon the governor commanded her head to be struck off, and the body of the child to be carried out of the city and thrown where the carcases of malefactors were usually cast. Julitta, being led to the place of execution, prayed aloud. She concluded by saying 'Amen'; at which her head was severed. She suffered in the year 304 or 305. The two maids came privately and buried both martyrs in a field near the city.

19 JUNE

St. Juliana

FALCONIERI

A.D. 1340

Juliana's father, Charissimus Falconieri, and his pious lady Reguardata, were both advanced in years, and seemed to have lost all hopes of issue, when in 1270, they were blessed with the birth of our saint. Afterwards they built and founded at their own expense the stately church of the Annunciation of our Lady in Florence, which may at this day be ranked among the wonders of the world. Alexius, the only brother of Charissimus, and uncle of our saint, was, with St. Philip Beniti, one of the seven first propagators of the Order of Servites, or persons devoted to the service of God under the special patronage of the Virgin Mary.

In the sixteenth year of her age Juliana, despising, whatever seemed not conductive to virtue, bid adieu to all worldly thoughts and pleasures, renounced her great estate and fortune, and the better to seek the inestimable jewel of the gospel, she consecrated her virginity to God, and received from the hands of St. Philip Beniti, the religious veil of the Mantellatae. The religious men among the Servites are called the first Order. St. Philip Beniti constituted his second Order, which is that of nuns, in favour of certain devout ladies. The Mantellatae are a third Order of Servites, and take their name from a particular kind of short sleeves which they wear as fittest for their work. They were instituted to serve the sick, and for other offices of charity, and in the beginning were not obliged to strict enclosure.

Of this third Order St Juliana was the first plant. And as she grew up, the great reputation of her prudence and sanctity drawing to her many devout ladies who desired to follow the same institute, she was obliged to accept the charge of prioress.

Though she was the spiritual mother of the rest, she made it her delight and study to serve all her sisters. St. Juliana practised incredible austerities. In her old age she was afflicted with various painful distempers which she bore with cheerfulness. One thing afflicted her in her last sickness, that she was deprived of the comfort of uniting her soul with her divine Spouse in the sacrament of the altar which she was not able to receive by reason that her stomach could not retain any food.

The sacred host, however, was brought to her cell, and there suddenly disappeared out of the hands of the priest. After her death, the figure of the host was found imprinted on the left side of her breast; by which prodigy it was judged that Christ had miraculously satisfied her holy desire. She died in her convent, at Florence, in the year 1340.

21 JUNE

St. Aloysius

GONZAGA

A.D. 1591

Aloysius Gonzaga was son of Ferdinand Gonzaga, Marquis of Castiglione. His mother was lady of honour to Isabel, wife of Philip II of Spain. Our saint was born in the castle of Castiglione in the diocese of Brescia on the 9th of March, 1568. His father, designing to train him up to the army, furnished him with little guns. Being eight years old, his father placed him and his younger brother in the court of the Grand Duke of Tuscany that they might learn Latin and other exercises suitable to their rank. At Florence the saint made such progress in the science of the saints that he afterwards used to call that city the mother of his piety.

The two young princes had stayed there two years when their father removed them to Mantua and placed them in the court of the Duke William Gonzaga. Aloysius left Florence in November 1579 when he was eleven years. He at that time took a resolution to resign to his brother his title to the marquisate. In the mean time he fell sick of an obstinate retention of urine and took the opportunity of this indisposition to spend most of his time reading books of devotion. Falling at last on a little book which treated on certain letters of the Jesuit missionaries, he felt a strong inclination to enter the Society of Jesus.

In 1581 his father attended the Empress Mary of Austria in her journey to Spain and took with him his children. Aloysius continued her studies but never neglected long his devotions. He at length determined to enter the Society of Jesus. His mother rejoiced but his father was enraged. However the consent of the marquis was at length extorted through the mediation of friends and Aloysius entered his novitiate at St. Andrew's in Rome in 1585. Being conducted to his cell, he repeated, 'This is my rest for ever: here will I dwell, for I have chosen it.' His health decaying, he was forbid to meditate or pray, except at regular times and was sent to Naples where he stayed half a year, then returned to Rome where he made his vows in November, 1587 and soon after received minor orders.

On the direction of his superior he went to Milan. One day he was favoured with a revelation that he had only a short time to live and by this found his mind more than ever weaned from all transitory things. The general recalled him to Rome to perform the fourth year of his theological course. In 1591 an epidemical distemper swept off great multitudes in Rome. In this public distress the fathers of the Society erected a new hospital in which the general and other assistants served the sick. The distemper being contagious, Aloysius fell sick. He recovered, but an hectic fever reduced him to excessive weakness. He expired a little after midnight between the 20th and 21st of June, 1591.

23 JUNE

St. Etheldreda

OR AUDRY

A.D. 679

St. Etheldreda, commonly called Audry, was third daughter of Annas, the holy king of the East Angles, and St. Hereswyda, younger sister to St. Sexburga and St. Ethelburga, and elder sister to St. Withburga. She was born at Ermynge, a famous village in Suffolk. In compliance with the desire of her friends she married Tonbercht, prince of the Southern Girvij. Three years after her marriage, and one year after the death of her father, Audry lost her husband, who for her dowry settled upon her the Isle of Ely. The holy widow retired into that solitude and there lived five years.

Egfrid, the powerful King of Northumberland, hearing the fame of her virtues, by the most earnest suit extorted her consent to marry him. St. Audry, during twelve years that she reigned with her husband, lived with him as if she had been his sister, not as his wife, and devoted her time to the exercises of devotion and charity. At length, having taken the advice of St. Wilfrid, and received from his hands the religious veil, she withdrew to the monastery of Coldingham beyond Berwick, and there lived in holy obedience.

Afterwards, in the year 672, she returned to the Isle of Ely, and there founded a double monastery upon her own estate. The nunnery she governed herself and was by her example a living rule of perfection to her sisters. She ate only once a day, except on great festivals or in time of sickness; never wore any linen, but only woollen clothes; never returned to bed after matins, which were sung at midnight, but continued her prayers in the church till morning. She rejoiced in pains and humiliations, and in her last sickness thanked God for being afflicted with a painful red swelling in her neck, which she regarded as a just chastisement for her vanity — when in her youth at court she wore rich necklaces studded with brilliants.

After a lingering illness she breathed out her pure soul on the 23rd of June, 679. She was buried according to her direction, in a wooden coffin. Her sister, Sexburga, succeeded her in the government of her monastery, and caused her body to be put into a stone coffin and translated into the church, on which occasion it was found uncorrupt; and the same physician who had made a ghastly incision in her neck a little before her death, was surprised to see the wound then perfectly healed.

PLATE 31. ST. ETHELDREDA, 23 JUNE. BRITISH LIBRARY.
KINGS MS 9, F. 64V.

24 JUNE

NATIVITY OF ST. JOHN THE BAPTIST

John's father, Zachary, was holy priest of the family of Abia, one of the twenty-four sacerdotal families into which the children of Aaron were divided. Elizabeth, the wife of this virtuous priest, was also descended of the house of Aaron, though probably her mother was of the tribe of Juda, she being cousin to the Blessed virgin.

Zachary lived probably at Hebron about twenty miles from Jerusalem. It was usual for the priests of each family to choose by lot among themselves the men who were to perform the several parts of the service that week. It happened that while Zachary was offering the incense one day he was favoured with a vision, the angel Gabriel appearing to him. Zachary being struck with exceeding terror and amazement, the angel encouraged him, assuring him that his prayer was heard, and that in consequence thereof his wife, though she was called barren,

should conceive and bear him a son, adding, 'Thou shalt call his name John, and he shall be great before God.'

Zachary was amazed at the apparition, and begged a sign might be given him. The angel answered that from that moment he should continue dumb until such time as the child was born. Elizabeth conceived, and in the sixth month of her pregnancy was honoured with a visit from the mother of God in which the Baptist was sanctified while yet in his mother's womb. Elizabeth, after nine months, brought forth her son, who was circumcised on the eighth day. On that occasion the rest of the family were for having him called Zachary; but his mother said his name should be John. The father confirmed the same by writing, and immediately recovering the use of his speech, broke out into the divine praises and joyfully proclaimed the infinite mercy with which God was pleased to visit his people Israel.

The Baptist was inspired by the Holy Ghost to retire in his tender years into the wilderness. There he devoted himself to the exercises of holy prayer, leading a most austere penitential life. His garment was of rough camel's hair, girt about him with a leather girdle and he allowed himself no other food than what he found in the desert, wild honey and locusts.

27 JUNE (28 JANUARY)

St. Cyril

PATRIARCH OF ALEXANDRIA
A.D. 444

St. Cyril studied under his uncle Theophilus and testifies that he made it his rule never to advance any doctrine which he had not learned from the ancient Fathers. He often says himself that he neglected human eloquence; and it is to be wished that he had wrote in a clearer style and with greater purity of the Greek tongue. Upon the death of Theophilus in 412 he was raised to the patriarchal dignity.

He began to exert his authority by causing the churches of the Novatians in the city to be shut up. He next drove the Jews out, who were very numerous. Seditions and several acts of violence committed by them excited him to this, which was approved by the Emperor Theodosius; and the Jews never returned. This produced pernicious effects. Hypatia, a pagan lady, kept a public school of philosophy in the city. Her reputation for learning for so great that disciples flocked to her from all parts. The mob, upon a suspicion that she incensed the governor against their bishop, seditiously rose, pulled her out of her chariot, and tore her body to pieces in 415, to the grief of all good men, especially the pious bishop.

Nestorius, a priest of Antioch, was made Bishop of Constantinople in 428. Nestorius and his mercenary priests broached new errors from the pulpit, teaching two distinct persons in Christ, that of God and that of man, only joined by a moral union. His homilies gave great offence and excited clamours against the blasphemies they contained. St. Cyril, having read them, sent him a mild expostulation on the subject, but was answered with contempt. Pope Celestine, being applied to by both parties, examined his doctrine in a council at Rome, condemned it and pronounced a sentence of excommunication against the author, unless within ten days after notification of the sentence, he publicly retracted, appointing St. Cyril to see that the sentence was put in execution. But the heresiarch

IOHANNES: BAPTISTA

PLATE 32. ST. JOHN BAPTIST, 24 JUNE. BUTLER, *LIVES OF THE SAINTS*, TWO-VOLUME ILLUSTRATED 19TH-CENTURY EDITION.

appeared more obstinate than ever. This occasioned the calling of the third general council at Ephesus in 431, with two hundred bishops, with St. Cyril at their head. Nestorius, though in the town, thrice refused to appear and the sentence of excommunication was pronounced against him. Six days after, John, Patriarch of Antioch, arrived with forty-one oriental bishops, who assembled by themselves and presumed to excommunicate St. Cyril. Both sides had recourse to the emperor, by whose order St. Cyril and Nestorius were both arrested. Our saint was on the point of being banished when three legates from Pope Celestine arrived, confirmed the condemnation of Nestorius and approved St. Cyril's conduct. The Orientals continued their schism till 433 when they made peace with St. Cyril.

He arrived at Alexandria in October 431 and spent the remainder of his days maintaining the faith of the church till his death in 444, on the 28th of June.

28 JUNE

St. Irenaeus
BISHOP OF LYONS
A.D. 202

This saint was a Grecian, probably a native of Lesser Asia. His parents, who were Christians, placed him under the care of St. Polycarp, Bishop of Smyrna. St. Polycarp cultivated his genius and formed his mind to piety by precepts and example.

The great commerce between Marseilles and the ports of Lesser Asia made the intercourse between those places very open. The faith of Christ was propagated in that part of Gaul in the times of the apostles; and from thence soon reached Lyons. St. Polycarp himself sent St. Irenaeus into Gaul, perhaps in company with some priest. He was himself ordained priest of the church of Lyons by St. Pothinus, and in 177 he was sent in the name of that church to Pope Eleutherius, to entreat him not to cut off from the communication of the church the Orientals, on account of their difference about the celebration of Easter.

The multitude and zeal of the faithful at Lyons stirred up the rage of the heathens, and gave occasion to a most bloody persecution. St. Irenaeus gave proofs of his zeal in those times of trial; but survived the storm, during the first part of which he had been absent in his journey to Rome.

St. Pothinus having glorified God by his death in 177, our saint upon his return was chosen the second Bishop of Lyons in the heat of the persecution. Commodus succeeding his father Marcus Aurelius in 180, restored peace to the church. But it was disturbed by a spawn of heresies, particularly of the Gnostics and Valentinians. St. Irenaeus wrote chiefly against these last five books against heresies.

One Blastus, a priest at Rome, formed a schism. He was deposed from the priesthood and St. Irenaeus wrote against him his treatise on schism. The dispute about Easter being renewed Pope Victor threatened to excommunicate the Asiatics; but was prevailed upon to tolerate for some time that practice by a letter of St. Irenaeus. The peace which the church at that time enjoyed afforded our saint leisure to exert his zeal and employ his pen to great advantage. Yet the clamours of the heathens at length moved the new emperor, Severus, to raise a fifth persecution against the church about the year 202. Having been governor of Lyons, and eye-witness to the flourishing state of that church, he seems to have given particular instructions that the Christ-

ians there should be proceeded against with extraordinary severity. Ado, in his chronicle, says that St. Irenaeus suffered martyrdom with an exceeding great multitude. An ancient epitaph inscribed on a pavement in the great church of St. Irenaeus at Lyons says the martyrs who died with him amounted to the number of nineteen thousand. Most place the martyrdom of these saints in 202, the beginning of the persecution; though some defer it to 208, when Severus passed through Lyons in his expedition into Britain.

29 JUNE

St. Peter
PRINCE OF THE APOSTLES
FIRST CENTURY

St. Peter, before his vocation to the apostleship was called Simon. He was son of Jonas and brother of St. Andrew. He originally resided at Bethsaida, a town in Upper Galilee on the banks of the Lake Gennesareth. Peter and Andrew were educated in the laborious trade of fishing. From Bethsaida St. Peter removed to Capharnaum, probably on account of his marriage, for his wife's mother dwelt there. Simon believed in Christ before he saw him; he went with his brother the Jesus, who on that occasion gave him the new name of Cephas, which signifies a rock, and is by us changed into Peter, from the Greek word of the same import. Towards the end of the same year, Jesus saw Simon Peter and Andrew washing their nets and bade them follow him. This invitation they instantly obeyed.

After the passover in 31, Christ chose his twelve apostles in which sacred college the chief place was from the beginning assigned to St. Peter. Christ appeared to him after his resurrection before the rest of the apostles. He gave him a special command to feed his sheep. He promised to commit his whole church to his care. When certain weak disciples deserted Christ, our saviour asked the twelve, 'Will you also go away?' St. Peter answered resolutely, 'Lord, to whom shall we go? Thou hast the words of eternal life.'

Yet this zealous apostle was permitted to fall, that we might learn with him more clearly to discover our own weakness.

Christ was obliged to reproach him that he was not able to watch him one hour. He mingled with the servants of the high priest and other enemies of Christ and renounced all knowledge of him.

St. Peter wrote two canonical epistles. The first seems to have been written between the years 45 and 55. It is chiefly addressed to the converted Jews to confirm them in their faith under their persecutions. His second epistle was written from Rome a little before his death and may be regarded as his spiritual testament. When Nero began to persecute the Christians in 64, they entreated St. Peter to withdraw for a while. The apostle yielded to their importunity; but going out of the gate of the city he met Jesus, or what in a vision appeared in his form, and taking it for a reproof of his cowardice, returned into the city and was put into prison with St. Paul. The two apostles are said to have remained there eight months and it is an ancient tradition that they suffered both together in the same field on the 29th of June. St. Peter, when he was come to the place of execution requested that he might be crucified with his head downwards, alleging that he was not worthy to suffer in the same manner as his divine Master. F. Pagi places the martyrdom in the year 65.

PLATE 33. ST. PETER, 29 JUNE. BUTLER, *LIVES OF THE SAINTS*, TWO-VOLUME ILLUSTRATED 19TH-CENTURY EDITION.

30 JUNE

St. Paul

THE APOSTLE
FIRST CENTURY

Paul's conversion the church commemorates on the 25th of January. After he was baptized he stayed some days at Damascus and preached Christ openly in the synagogue. The Jews laid a plot to take away his life; but the holy convert was let down in a basket over the wall by night. He took this occasion to go to Jerusalem to see St. Peter. The disciples sent him to Tarsus, his native city. He remained there upwards of three years and preached in neighbouring Cilicia and Syria. St. Barnabas went to Tarsus and brought St. Paul to Antioch where they joined their labours. We have in the Acts of the Apostles, a summary account of the missions of St. Paul. Taking with him St. Barnabas in 44, he sailed to Cyprus. There Sergius Paulus, the Roman proconsul, was converted and received baptism.

St. Paul, leaving Cyprus, went by sea to Perge in Pamphilia and from Perge to Antioch, the capital of Pisidia. Many were induced by his discourses to believe in Christ, but the more obstinate Jews drove him out. The apostles preached next at Iconium, and after this at Lystra where the heathens took Barnabas for Juniper, on account of his gravity, and St. Paul for Mercury, because he was chief speaker. They returned to Antioch in Syria after an absence of about three years. During the four following years St. Paul preached over Syria and Judaea and assisted at the first general council held by the apostles at Jerusalem. He then set out to visit the churches he had founded. Whilst he remained at Troas, in a vision a Macedonian seemed to stand before him entreating to come into his country. He took ship and went to Samothracia, Neapolis, and Philippi. The apostle, having laid in this country the foundation of a very eminent church, took leave of the Philippians and arrived at Thessalonica. A tumult at last obliged Paul to quit that town and he made for Athens where he was conducted by a call of the Holy Ghost to Corinth. It was from Corinth that he wrote his two epistles to the Thessalonians, the first of his writings.

He travelled through Galatia, Phrygia and other parts of Asia, from Cappadocia to Ephesus, where he stayed almost three years preaching. He proceeded to Jerusalem in 58, where certain Jews who had opposed him in Asia stirred up that city against him. Felix, governor of the province, detained the apostle in prison two years. Festus succeeded Felix in the government of Judaea and St. Paul was again impeached by the Jews, but appealed to Caesar, which bound him to appear at Rome. He arrived at Rome in the year 61 and, no accusers appearing before him, after two years was set at liberty. Here St. Luke ends his narrative of the travels of St. Paul.

The apostle made several other voyages and returned again to Rome about 64 where he was put in prison. His martyrdom happened in 65, or 66. St. Paul was beheaded; his dignity of a Roman citizen did not allow him to be crucified.

PLATE 34. ST. PAUL, 30 JUNE. BRITISH LIBRARY, KINGS MS 9, F. 34V

PLATE 35. ST. THOMAS, 3 JULY. BODLEIAN LIBRARY, MS LAUD. MISC. 7, F. 165.

3 JULY (21 DECEMBER)

St. Thomas

APOSTLE
FIRST AGE

St. Thomas was a Jew, and probably a Galilean of low origin. He had the happiness to follow Christ, and was made by him an apostle in the year 31.

After our Lord had suffered, was risen from the dead, and on the same day had appeared to his disciples to convince them of the truth of his resurrection, Thomas not being with them on that occasion, refused to believe upon their report that he was truly risen, unless he might see the very prints of the nails and see the wounds in his hands and side. On that day sevennight our Lord presented himself again, and after the usual salutation he turned to Thomas and bid him look upon his hands and put his finger into the hole of his side, and in the prints of the nails. St. Thomas was no sooner convinced of the reality of the mystery, but penetrated with compunction, awe and tender love, he cried out 'My lord and my God.'

After the descent of the Holy Ghost, St. Thomas commissioned Thaddaeus to instruct and baptize Abgar, King of Edessa. As for St. Thomas, Origen informs us that in the distribution made by the twelve, Parthia was particularly assigned to him for his apostolic province, when this nation held the place of the Persian empire and disputed the sovereignty with the Romans. After preaching with good success in Parthia, he did the same all over the East. Sophronius mentions that, by his apostolic labours, he established the faith among the Medes, Persians, Carmanians, Hyrcanians, Bactrians and other nations in those parts.

The modern Indians and Portuguese tell us that St. Thomas preached to the Bracmans, and to the Indians beyond the great island, Taprobana, which some take to be Ceylon, others Sumatra. They add that he suffered martyrdom at Meliapor, in the peninsula on this side the Ganges, on the coast of Coromandel, where his body was discovered with certain marks that he was slain with lances; and that such was the manner of his death is the tradition of all the eastern countries. Eusebius affirms in general that the apostles died by martyrdom. It is certain that his body was carried to the city of Edessa. Where it was honoured in the great church.

Many distant churches in the East ascribe their first foundation to St. Thomas, especially that of Meliapor; but many probably received the faith only from his disciples. The Portuguese, when they came into the east Indies, found there the St. Thomas-Christians, it is said, to the number of fifteen thousand families on the coast of Malabar. On two festivals which they keep in honour of St. Thomas, they resort in great crowds to the place of his burial.

4 JULY (8 JULY)

St. Elizabeth
QUEEN OF PORTUGAL
A.D. 1336

St. Elizabeth was daughter of Peter III, King of Arragon. Her mother Constantia was daughter of Manfred, King of Sicily. Our saint was born in 1271. The young princess was of a most sweet dispositon. At eight years of age she began to fast on vigils and to practise great self-denials. She could bear no other songs that sacred hymns and psalms; and from her childhood said every day the office of the breviary. Her tenderness and compassion for the poor made her even in that tender age to be styled their mother.

At twelve years she was given in marriage to Dionysius, King of Portugal. He allowed her an entire liberty in her devotions and exceedingly admired her extraordinary piety. Our saint planned for herself a regular distribution of her time which she never interrupted unless occasions of duty obliged her to change the order of her daily practices. She rose very early and recited matins, lauds and prime, then she heard mass. Charity to the poor was a distinguishing part of her character. She gave constant orders to have all pilgrims and poor strangers provided for with lodging and necessaries. She visited the sick. She founded in different parts of the kingdom many pious establishment, particularly a hospital near her own palace at Coimbra, a house for penitent women, and a hospital for foundlings. Though King Dionysius was a worldly man, and defiled the sanctity of the nuptial state with abominable lusts, she softened the heart of the king, who kept ever after the fidelity due to his virtuous consort.

St. Elizabeth had by the king two children, Alphonsus and Constantia. This son, when grown up, revolting against his own father, put himself at the head of an army of malcontents. St. Elizabeth exhorted her son to return to his duty, conjuring her husband to forgive him. Certain court flatterers whispering to the king that she was suspected of favouring her son, he banished her to the city of Alanquer. The queen received this disgrace with admirable peace of mind. She would never entertain any correspondence with the malcontents. The king shortly after called her back to court. She reconciled her husband and son, and made peace between Ferdinand of Castile and Alphonsus, his cousin, who disputed the crown; likewise between James, her own brother, and Ferdinand, her son-in-law.

King Dionysius, having reigned forty-five years, fell sick. St. Elizabeth gave him signal testimonies of her love, scarcely leaving his chamber during his illness. He died on the 6th of January, 1325. She attended the funeral procession, and after made a pilgrimage to Compostella; after which she retired to a convent of Clares and made her religious profession. A war being lighted up between her son and her grandson, she resolved to set out to reconcile them; but she arrived ill of a violent fever. She gave up her soul to God on the 4th July, 1336.

7 JULY

St. Palladius
APOSTLE OF THE SCOTS
A.D. 450

The name of Palladius shows this saint to have been a Roman, and most authors agree that he was deacon of the church of Rome. St. Prosper in his chronicle informs us that when Agricola, a noted Pelagian, had corrupted the churches of Britain with the insinuation of that heresy, Pope Calestine, at the instance of Palladius the deacon, in 429 sent thither St. Germanus, Bishop of Auxerre, in quality of his legate, who having ejected the heretics brought back the Britons to the Catholic faith.

It seems not to be doubted that it was the same person of whom St. Prosper again speaks when he afterwards says that in 431 Pope Celestine sent Palladius, the first bishop, to the Scots then believing in Christ, though the number of Christians among them must have been then very small. It is clear from Tertullian and others that the light of the gospel had penetrated among the Picts beyond the Roman territories in Britain, near the times of the apostles. These people, therefore, who had lately begun to receive some tincture of the faith when our saint undertook his mission, were doubtless the Scots who were settled in Ireland.

The Irish writers of the lives of St. Patrick say that St. Palladius had preached in Ireland a little before St. Patrick, but that he was soon banished by the King of Leinster and returned to North Britain, where they tell us he had first opened his mission. It seems not to be doubted but he was sent to the whole nation of the Scots, several colonies of whom had passed from Ireland into North Britain and possessed themselves of that part of the country since called Scotland. After St. Palladius had left Ireland he arrived among the Scots in North Britain, according to St. Prosper, in the year 431. He preached there with great zeal and formed a considerable church. The Scottish historians tell us that the faith was planted in North Britain about the year 200, in the time of King Donald; but they all acknowledge that Palladius was the first bishop in that country and style him their first apostle. The saint died at Fordun, the capital town of the little county of Mernis, fifteen miles from Aberdeen, about the year 450. His relics were preserved with religious respect in the monastery of Fordun. In the year 1409 William Scenes, Archbishop of St. Andrew's, and primate of Scotland, enclosed them in a new shrine enriched with gold and precious stones. Scottish writers and calendars of the Middle Ages, mention St. Servanus and St. Ternan as disciples of St. Palladius, and by him made bishops, the former of Orkney, the latter of the Picts. But from Usher's chronology it appears that they both lived later.

8 JULY

St. Withburge

VIRGIN
A.D. 743

Withburge was the youngest of the four sisters, all saints, daughters of Annas, the holy King of the East-Angles. In her tender years she devoted herself to the divine service, and led an austere life in close solitude for several years at Holkham, an estate of the king her father, near the sea coast in Norfolk where a church, afterwards called Withburgstow, was built. After the death of her father she changed her dwelling to another estate of the crown, called Dereham. This is at present a considerable market town in Norfolk, but was then an obscure retired place. Withburge assembled there many devout virgins, and laid the foundations of a great church and nunnery, but did not live to finish the buildings. Her death happened on the 17th of March, 743.

Her body was interred in the churchyard at Dereham, and fifty-five years after found uncorrupt, and translated into the church. One hundred and seventy-six years after this, in 974, Brithnoth (the first Abbot of Ely, after that house, which had been destroyed by the Danes, was rebuilt), with the consent of King Edgar, removed it to Ely, and deposited it near the bodies of her two sisters. In 1106 the remains of four saints were translated into the new church and laid near the high altar. The bodies of SS. Sexburga and Ermenilda were reduced to dust except the bones. That of St. Audrey was entire, and that of St. Withburge was not only sound, but also fresh, and the limbs perfectly flexible. Herbert, Bishop of Thetford, who in 1094, translated his see to Norwich, and many other persons of distinction were eye-witnesses hereof. This is related by Thomas, monk of Ely in his history of Ely which he wrote the year following, 1107. This author tells us that in the place where St. Withburge was first buried in the churchyard of Dereham, a large fine spring of most clear water gushes forth. It is to this day called St. Withburge's well.

11 JULY (21 MARCH)

St. Benedict

ABBOT, PATRIARCH OF THE WESTERN MONKS
A.D. 543

St. Benedict was a native of Norcia in Umbria and born about the year 480. When he was fit for the higher studies he was sent to Rome and there placed in the public schools. He was not a little shocked at the licentiousness which he observed in some of the Roman youth and therefore left the city and made his way towards the desert mountains of Sublacum, near forty miles from Rome. Near this place the saint met a monk of a neighbouring monastery who gave him the monastic habit and conducted him to a deep narrow cave. In this cavern, now called the Holy Grotto, the young hermit chose his abode. He lived three years in this manner. Certain shepherds discovered the saint near his cave, but at first took him for a wild beast. When they found him to be a servant of God they respected him

PLATE 36. ST. BENEDICT, 11 JULY. BRITISH LIBRARY, EGERTON MS 2125, F. 206V.

exceedingly. From that time he began to be known and many visited him.

The fame of his sanctity being spread abroad, it occasioned several to forsake the world and imitate his penitential manner of life. The desert he soon peopled with monks, for whom he built twelve monasteries, placing in each twelve monks with a superior. St. Benedict's reputation drew the most illustrious personages from Rome and other remote parts to see him. Many prostrated themselves at his feet to beg his blessing, and some placed their sons under his conduct.

Florentius, a priest in the neighbouring country, moved by jealousy, persecuted the saint and aspersed his reputation with slanders. Bennet left Sublacum and repaired to Monte Cassino. Cassino is a small town built on the brow of a high mountain on the top of which stood an old temple of Apollo. The man of God demolished the temple and erected two chapels. This was the origin of the abbey of Monte Cassino, the foundation of which the saint laid in 529. St. Bennet also governed a monastery of nuns, situate near Monte Cassino, and founded an abbey of men at Terracina. Though ignorant of secular learning, he compiled a monastic rule which was afterwards adopted for some time by all the monks of the West. It is principally founded on silence, solitude, prayer, humility and obedience. St. Bennet calls his Order a school in which men learn to serve God; and his life was for his disciples a perfect model. He was enriched with supernatural gifts, even those of miracles and prophesy.

The death of this saint seems to have happened soon after that of his sister, St. Scholastica. He foretold it to his disciples and caused his grave to be opened six days before. When this was done he fell ill of a fever and calmly expired on the 21st of March, probably in 543, having spent fourteen years at Monte Cassino. The greatest part of his relics remains still in that abbey.

12 JULY

St. John

GAULBERT, FOUNDER OF THE ORDER OF
VALLISUMBROSA
A.D. 1073

St. John Gualbert was born at Florence of rich and noble parents. Hugo, his only brother, was murdered; and John determined to revenge the crime by the death of him who had perpetrated it. It happened that riding home to Florence on Good Friday, he met his enemy in so narrow a passage that it was impossible for either of them to avoid the other. John drew his sword and was going to dispatch him. But the other fell upon his knees and with his arms across, besought him by the passion of Jesus Christ to spare his life. The remembrance of Christ, who prayed for his murderers on the cross, exceedingly affected the young nobleman, and he said, 'I not only give you your life, but also my friendship. Pray for me that God may pardon my sin.' They parted, and John went forward on his road till he came to the monastery of St. Minias. Going into the church, he offered up his prayers before a great crucifix, which miraculously bowed its head to him. He cast himself at the feet of the abbot, begging to be admitted to the religious habit. After a few days John cut off his hair and put on a habit which he borrowed.

St. John devoted himself to the exercises of his new state as a true penitent, and was most exact in every religious observance. When the abbot died our saint was entreated by the monks to accept that dignity; but his consent could by no means be extorted. Not long after, he left this house with one companion and went in quest of a closer solitude. He proceeded to an agreeable shady valley called Vallis-Umbrosa, in the diocese of Fiesole and found in that place two hermits, with whom he concerted a project to build themselves a monastery of timber and mud walls. Pope Alexander II in 1070 approved this new Order, together with the rule, in which the saint added certain constitutions to the original rule of St. Benedict. St. John was chosen the first abbot.

St. John was very zealous for poverty and would not allow any monasteries to be built in a costly manner. He left about twelve houses of his Order at his death. Besides monks he received lay brothers, who were exempt from choirs and silence and employed in external offices. This is said to be the first example of such a distinction; but it was soon imitated by other Orders. The holy man at length fell sick of a fever at Passignano and died on the 12th of July, 1073, being seventy-four years old.

[Editorial note: 12 July is also the festival of Veronica, who is said to have wiped the face of Christ with a cloth as he carried his cross to Golgotha. The image of his face was then, according to legend, preserved on the cloth.]

PLATE 37. ST. VERONICA, 12 JULY. BRITISH LIBRARY, EGERTON MS 859, F. 13.

PLATE 38. ST. HENRY, 13 JULY. BUTLER, *LIVES OF THE SAINTS*, TWO-VOLUME ILLUSTRATED 19TH-CENTURY EDITION.

13 JULY

St. Henry

II EMPEROR

A.D. 1204

St. Henry, surnamed the Pious and the Lame, son of Henry, Duke of Bavaria, and of Gisella, daughter of Conrad, King of Burgundy, was born in 972. St. Wolfgang being a prelate the most eminent in all Germany for learning, piety and zeal, our young prince was put under his tuition. The death of his dear master, which happened in 994, was to him a most sensible · affliction. In the following year he succeeded his father in the Duchy of Bavaria and in 1002 he was chosen emperor.

Soon after his accession to the throne he procured a national council of the bishops of all his dominions in order to enforce a strict observance of the holy canons. It was owing to his zeal that many provincial synods were held in several parts of the empire. He was himself present at that of Frankfurt in 1006 and at another of Bamberg in 1011. The protection he owed his subjects engaged him sometimes in wars, in all of which he was successful. In 1014, he was crowned emperor with great solemnity by Pope Benedict VIII.

The idolatrous inhabitants of Poland and Sclavonia had laid waste the diocese of Meersburg. St. Henry marched against those barbarous nations and defeated the infidels. The victorious emperor munificently repaired and restored the episcopal sees of Hildesheim, Magdeburg, Strasburg, Misnia and Meersburg and made all Poland, Bohemia and Moravia tributary to the empire.

The protection of Christendom, and especially of the holy see, obliged St Henry to lead an army to the extremity of Italy, where he vanquished the conquering Saracens, with their allies the Greeks and drove them out of Italy. He came back by Mount Cassino and was honourably received at Rome, but during his stay in that city, by a painful contraction of the sinews in his thigh, became lame, and continued so till his death.

Prayer seemed the chief delight and support of his soul, especially the public office of the church. Though he lived in the world so as to be perfectly disengaged from it in heart and affection, it was his earnest desire entirely to renounce it long before his death, but he was diverted from carrying this project into execution by the advice of Richard, holy abbot. He had married St. Cunegonda, but lived with her in perpetual chastity, to which they had mutually bound themselves by vow. It happened that the empress was falsely accused of incontinency, and St. Henry was somewhat moved by the slander; but she cleared herself by her oath, and by the order trials. Her husband severely condemned himself for his credulity and made her the most ample satisfaction. His health decayed some years before his death, which happened at the castle of Grone, near Halberstadt in 1024, toward the end of the fifty-second year of his life.

14 JULY

St. Camillus

DE LELLIS

A.D. 1614

Camillus de Lellis was born in 1550 at Bacchianico in Abruzzo. He lost his mother in his infancy, and six years after, his father. Camillus, having learned only to read and write, entered himself young in the army, and served first in the Venetian and afterwards in the Neapolitan troops, till in 1574 his company was disbanded. He had contracted so violent a passion for cards and gaming, that he sometimes lost even necessaries, until at length he was reduced to such straits that for a subsistence he was obliged to drive two asses and to work at a building which belonged to the Capuchin friars. A moving exhortation which the guardian of the Capuchins one day made him completed his conversion. He fell on his knees, deplored his past unthinking life and cried to heaven for mercy. This happened in February 1575.

He made an essay of a novitiate both among the Capuchins and the Grey Friars, but could not be admitted to his religious profession among either on account of a running sore in one of his legs which was judged incurable. Therefore, leaving his own country he went to Rome, and there served the sick in St. James's hospital of incurables four years. The administrators having been witnesses to his charity, after some time appointed him director of the hospital.

Camillus grieving to see the sloth of the hired servants in attending the sick, formed a project of associating certain pious persons for that office, took a resolution to prepare himself to receive holy orders and was ordained priest in 1584. Being nominated to serve a little chapel, he quitted the direction of the hospital. Before the close of the same year he laid the foundation of his congregation for serving the sick, and prescribed them certain short rules.

In 1585 his friends hired for him a large house and he ordained that the members of his congregation should bind themselves to serve persons infected with the plague, prisoners and those who lie dying in private houses. Pope Sixtus V confirmed this congregation in 1586 and ordered that it should be governed by a triennial superior. Camillus was the first, and Roger, and Englishman, one of his first companions. In 1588 he was invited to Naples and founded there a new house. Certain galleys that had the plague on board were forbidden to enter the harbour; whereupon these pious 'Servants of the Sick' (the name they took) went on board and attended them. In 1591 Gregory XV erected this congregation into a religious Order.

Camillus was himself afflicted with many infirmities, as a sore in his leg for forty-six years; a rupture for thirty-eight years, which he got by serving the sick; two sores in the sole of one of his feet which gave him great pain, and violent nephritic colics. He founded religious houses at Bologna, Milan, Genoa, Florence, and other places. He died on the 14th of July, 1614.

15 JULY

St. Swithin

OR SWITHUN, BISHOP AND PATRON OF
WINCHESTER
A.D. 862

Wini, the third bishop of the West-Saxons, fixed his see at Winchester, and this church became one of the most flourishing cathedrals of all Britain. St. Swithun received in this church the clerical tonsure and put on the monastic habit in the Old Monastery, which had been founded by King Kynegils.

Being ordained priest he was made provost or dean of the Old Monastery. His learning, piety and prudence moved Egbert, King of the West Saxons to make him his priest. That great prince committed to his care the education of his son, Ethelwolf, and made use of his counsels in the government of his kingdom.

King Egbert reigned thirty-seven years over the West Saxons and nine years over all England, dying in the year 830 or 837. Ethelwolf was advanced to the throne. He governed his kingdom by the prudent advice of Alstan, Bishop of Sherbourne, in temporal affairs and by that of St. Swithun in ecclesiastical matters, especially those which concerned his own soul. Bearing always the greatest reverence to St. Swithun, whom he called his master and teacher, he procured him to be chosen Bishop of Winchester in 852. Though this good bishop was a rich treasure of all virtues, those in which he took most delight were humility and charity to the poor. He built divers churches and repaired others; and made his journeys on foot, and often by night to avoid ostentation.

By his advice King Ethelwolf in a great council of the nation of 854 enacted a new law by which he gave the tenth part of his land throughout the kingdom to the church, exempt and free from all taxation. This charter, to give it a more sacred sanction, he offered on the altar of St. Peter at Rome in the pilgrimage which he made to that city in 855. He likewise procured it to be confirmed by the pope. He extended the Romescot or Peter-pence to his whole kingdom. He reigned two years after his return from Rome, and died in 857.

St. Swithun departed to eternal bliss on the 2nd of July, 862. His body was buried, according to his order, in the churchyard, where his grave might be trodden on by passengers. About one hundred years after, in the days of King Edgar, his relics were taken up by the then Bishop of Winchester and translated into the church in 964. On which occasion Malmesbury affirms that such a number of miraculous cures of all kinds were wrought as was never in the memory of man known to have been in any other place. St. Swithun is commemorated in the Roman Martyrology on the 2nd of July, the day of his death; but his chief festival in England was on the 15th of the same month, the day of the translation of his relics.

18 JULY (6 SEPTEMBER)

St. Pambo

OF NITRIA, ABBOT
A.D. 385

St. Pambo betook himself in his youth to the great St. Antony in the desert and, desiring to be admitted among his disciples, begged he would give him some lessons for his conduct. The great patriarch told him he must take care always to live in a state of penance, and must labour to put a restraint upon his tongue and his appetite. The disciple set himself earnestly to learn the practice of all these lessons. He excelled most other monks in the austerity of his continual fasts. The government of his tongue was no less an object of his watchfulness than that of his appetite. A certain religious brother to whom he had applied for advice began to recite to him the thirty-eighth psalm, 'I said I will take heed to my ways, that I sin not with my tongue'; which words Pambo had no sooner heard but without waiting for the second verse he returned to his cell, saying that was enough for one lesson. St. Antony, who admired the purity of his soul used to say that his fear of God had moved the divine Spirit to take up his resting place in him.

St. Pambo, after he left St. Antony, settled in the desert of Nitria, on a mountain where he had a monastery. St. Melania the Elder, in the visit she made to the holy solitaries who inhabited the deserts of Egypt, coming to St. Pambo's monastery, found the holy abbot sitting at his work making mats. She gave him three hundred pounds weight of silver, desiring him to accept that part of her store for the necessities of the poor among the brethren. St. Pambo, without interrupting his work or looking at her or her present, said to her that God would reward her charity. Then, turning to his disciple he made him take the silver and distribute it among all the brethren who were most needy. Melania continued some time standing, and at length said, 'Father, do you know that here is three hundred pounds weight of silver?' The abbot, without casting his eyes upon the chest of silver, replied, 'Daughter, he or whom you made this offering very well knows how much it weighs without being told.'

St. Pambo said, a little before his death, 'From the time that I came into this desert, and built myself a cell in it, I do not remember that I have ever ate any bread but what I had earned by my own labour, nor that I ever spoke any word of which I afterwards repented; nevertheless, I go to God as one who had not yet begun to serve him.' He died seventy years old, as he was making a basket. Melania took care of his burial, and having obtained this basket, kept it to her dying day.

22 JULY

St. Mary Magdalen
FIRST CENTURY

The illustrious penitent woman mentioned by St. Luke was, by her perfect conversion, an example to all succeeding ages. She is called the Sinner, to express her pre-eminence in guilt. This epithet seems to imply that she led a lewd and disorderly life. The scandal of her debaucheries had rendered her name infamous.

Jesus, not long after he had raised to life the son of a widow at Nain, was invited to dinner by a certain Pharisee called Simon. Our Lord was pleased to accept, chiefly that he might confound the pride of the Pharisees by manifesting the power of his grace in the wonderful conversion of this abandoned sinner. She began her conversion by entering into herself. She did not so much as think of the disgrace to which she exposed herself by appearing before a numerous and honourable assembly. There losing the use of her speech she spoke only by her tears.

Jesus cast on her a favourable eye of mercy. The Pharisee was shocked to see an infamous sinner, well known in that city, admitted by our Lord to stand at his feet. Christ assured this humble sinner that her offences were cancelled and that her lively faith had saved her. Gratitude and devotion having attached her to our Divine Redeemer, she followed him almost wherever he went. She attended him in his sacred passion and stood under the cross on Mount Calvary.

Mary Magdalen forsook not her Redeemer after his death, but remained by his sacred body, was present at its internment, left it only to obey the law of observing the festival, and having rested on the sabbath from sunset on Friday to sunset on Saturday, went to buy spices to embalm our Lord's body. Having made all things ready, in company with other devout women, she set out very early the next morning and arrived at the sepulchre just when the sun was risen. The pious women looked into the sepulchre, and finding the body not there Mary Magdalen ran to inform Peter and the other disciple whom Jesus loved. Not being able to assuage the violence of her grief and of her desire to see her Lord, she stood weeping without the door of sepulchre. She turned about, and saw Jesus himself standing by her, but took him for the gardener. He asked her why she wept and whom she sought. She said to him, 'Sir, if you hast taken him hence, tell me where thou hast laid him, and I will take him away.' Jesus manifested himself to her, saying 'Mary!' Hearing him sweetly call her by her name, and thus knowing him, she said, 'Rabboni', that is, Master. Thus Mary Magdalen, out of whom Jesus had cast several evil spirits, was the first that saw him after his rising from the dead.

It is an ancient popular tradition that St. Mary Magdalen, being expelled by the Jews, put to sea and landed safe at Marseilles.

23 JULY (8 OCTOBER)

St. Bridget
WIDOW
A.D. 1373

St. Birgit, more commonly called Bridget or Brigit, was daughter of Birger, legislator of Upland, and of Ingeburgis, a lady descended from the kings of the Goths, who died soon after the birth of our saint, which happened in 1304. Bridget was brought up by her aunt. In obedience to her father, when she was only sixteen years old, she married Ulpho, Prince of Nericia, who was himself only eighteen. The couple had eight children, four boys and four girls.

To break all worldly ties they made a pilgrimage to Compostella. In their return Upho fell sick and died soon after in 1344. Bridget being by his death entirely at liberty to pursue her inclinations, renounced the rank of princess. Her husband's estates she divided among her children and from that day seemed to forget that she had been in the world. About the time of her husband's death in 1344 she built the monastery of Wastein in the diocese of Lincopen, in which she placed sixty nuns, and · in a separate enclosure friars to the number of thirteen priests, four deacons and eight lay brothers. She prescribed them the rule of St. Augustine, with certain particular constitutions. In this institute, the men are subject to the prioress of the nuns in temporals, but in spirituals the women are under the jurisdiction of the friars.

St. Bridget had spent two years in her monastery at Wastein when she undertook a pilgrimage to Rome. For the last thirty years of her life she was accustomed to go every day to confession, and she communicated several times every week. Nothing is more famous in the life of St. Bridget than the many revelations with which she was favoured by God. Her ardent love of Jesus Christ moved her to make a painful pilgrimage to visit the holy places in Palestine. In her journey she visited the most renowned churches in Italy and Sicily.

Being returned safe to Rome, she lived there a year longer, but during that interval was afflicted with grievous distempers, under which she suffered the most excruciating pains with heroic patience. Having given her last instructions to her son Birger, and her daughter Catherine, who were with her, she was laid on sackcloth, received the last sacraments and died on the 23rd of July 1373, being seventy-one years old.

24 JULY

St. Lupus
BISHOP OF TROYES
A.D. 478

St. Lupus was born of a noble family at Toul and being learned and eloquent pleaded at the bar for some years with great reputation. He married Pimeniola, a sister of St. Hilary of Arles. After six years they parted by mutual consent, and made a vow of perpetual continency. Lupus betook himself to the abbey of Lérins, then governed by St. Honoratus. After the first year, when St. Honoratus was made Bishop of Arles, he went to Macon in Burgundy to dispose of an estate he had left

PLATE 39. ST. MARY MAGDALEN, 22 JULY. BUTLER, *LIVES OF THE SAINTS*, TWO-VOLUME ILLUSTRATED 19TH-CENTURY EDITION

there, in charitable uses. He was preparing to return to Lérins when he was met by the deputies of the church of Troyes, which had chosen him bishop.

About the latter end of the fourth century, Pelagius, a British monk, and Celestius, a Scot, broached their heresy in Africa, Italy and the East, denying the corruption of human nature by original sin, and the necessity of divine grace. One Agricola had spread this poison in Britain. The Catholics addressed themselves to their neighbours, the bishops of Gaul, begging their assistance to check the growing evil. An assembly of bishops probably held at Arles in 529 deputed St. Germanus of Auxerre and St. Lupus of Troyes to go over to oppose this mischief. The two holy pastors accepted the commission and entirely banished the heresy by their prayers, preaching and miracles.

St. Lupus, after his return, set himself with fresh vigour to reform the manners of his own flock. God at that time afflicted the western empire with grievous calamities, and Attila with a numberless army of Huns overran Gaul. Rheims, Cambray,

Besançon, Auxerre and Langres had already felt the effects of his fury, and Troyes was the next place he threatened. The holy bishop went out to meet the barbarian at the head of his army and asked him who he was. 'I am', said Attila, 'the scourge of God.' 'Let us respect whatever comes to us from God,' replied the bishop 'but if you are the scourge with which heaven chastises us, remember you are to do nothing but what that almighty hand which governs and moves you, permits.' Atilla, struck with these words, promised to spare the city. Attila was met by Aetius, the Roman general, and defeated. In his retreat he sent for St. Lupus and caused him to accompany him as far as the Rhine, imagining that the presence of so great a servant of God would be a safeguard to himself and his army; and sending him back he recommended himself to his prayers. This action of the good bishop was misconstrued and he was obliged to leave Troyes for two years. He spent that time in retirement. When his charity and patience had at length overcome the malice of men, he went back to his church, which he governed fifty-two years, dying in 479.

PLATE 40. ST. JAMES THE GREAT, 25 JULY. BODLEIAN LIBRARY, MS. ADD. A 185, F. 59V.

25 JULY

James the Great

APOSTLE
FIRST CENTURY.

St. James, the brother of St. John Evangelist, son of Zebedee, was called the Great to distinguish him from the other apostle of the same name, surnamed the Less, because he was the younger. St. James the Great seems to have been born about twelve years before Christ and many years older than his brother, John.

St. James was by birth a Galilean and by profession a fisherman with his father and brother, living probably at Bethsaida. Jesus, walking by the lake of Genesareth, saw St. Peter and St. Andrew fishing, and he called them to come after him, promising to make them fishers of men. Going on a little farther he saw two other brothers, James and John in a ship with their father, mending their nets, and he also called them; who forthwith left their nets and their father and followed him.

In the year 31 James was present at the cure of St. Peter's mother-in-law and at the raising of the daughter of Jairus from the dead. This same year Jesus formed the college of his apostles into which he adopted St. James and his brother St. John. He gave these two the surname of Boanerges, or Sons of Thunder, probably to denote their active zeal. Christ distinguished St. Peter, St. James and St. John by many special favours. They alone were admitted to be spectators first of his transfiguration and afterwards of his agony in the garden.

How St. James was employed in preaching and promoting the gospel after Christ's Ascension, we have no account from the writers of the first ages of Christianity. It appears that he left Judaea some time after the martyrdom of St. Stephen, and was returned again ten years after, when he suffered martyrdom. Though the apostles, during the first twelve years preached generally in the neighbourhood of Judaea, St. James might in that interval have made a voyage to Spain. That he preached there is constantly affirmed by the tradition of that church, mentioned by St. Isidore, the Breviary of Toledo and others.

Agrippa, the grandson of Herod, being very fond of pleasing the Jewish nation, when he came to Jerusalem to keep the passover in the year 43, began to persecute the Christians, and the first who fell a victim to his popular zeal, was St. James the Great, whom he caused to be apprehended and beheaded there a little before Easter. The body of the apostle was interred at Jerusalem, but not long after carried by his disciples into Spain. The sacred relics were discovered in the beginning of the ninth century and translated to Compostella. This place was first called St. Jacobum Apostolum, which words have been contracted into the name Compostella. It is famous for the extraordinary concourse of pilgrims that resort thither to visit the body of St. James which is kept with great respect in the stately cathedral.

26 JULY

St. Anne

MOTHER OF THE BLESSED VIRGIN

The Hebrew word Anne signifies gracious. St. Joachim and St. Anne, the parents of the Blessed Virgin Mary, are justly honoured in the church, and their virtue is highly extolled by St. John Damascen. The Emperor Justinian I built a church at Constantinople in honour of St. Anne about the year 550. Her body was brought from Palestine to Constantinople in 710, whence some portion of her relics have been dispersed in the West.

God has been pleased by sensible effects to testify how much he is honoured by the devotion of the faithful to this saint, who was the great model of virtue to all engaged in the married state, and charged with the education of children. It was a sublime dignity and a great honour for this saint to give to a lost world the advocate of mercy, and to be parent of the mother of God. But it was a far greater happiness to be, under God, the greatest instrument of her virtue, and to be spiritually her mother by a holy education in perfect innocence and sanctity. St. Anne, being herself a vessel of grace, not by name only, but by the possession of that rich treasure, was chosen by God to form his most beloved spouse to perfect virtue; and her pious care of this illustrious daughter was the greatest means of her own sanctification and her glory in the church of God to the end of ages. It is a lesson to all parents whose principal duty is the holy education of their children.

By this they glorify their Creator, perpetuate his honour on earth to future ages, and sanctify their souls.

27 JULY

St. Pantaleon

MARTYR
A.D. 303

Pantaleon was physician to the Emperor Galerius Maximianus, and a Christian, but fell by a temptation which is sometimes more dangerous than the severest trials or the fiercest torments; for bad example, if not shunned, insensibly weakens, and at length destroys the strongest virtue. Pantaleon being perpetually obsessed by it in an impious idolatrous court, and deceived by often hearing the false maxims of the world applauded, was unhappily seduced into an apostasy. But a zealous Christian called Hermolaus, by his prudent admonitions awakened his conscience to a sense of his guilt, and brought him again into the fold of the church.

The penitent ardently wished to expiate his crime by martyrdom; and, to prepare himself for the conflict, when Diocletian's bloody persecution broke out at Nicomedia in 303, he distributed all his possessions among the poor. Not long after this action he was taken up, and in his house were also apprehended Hermolaus, Hermippus and Hermocrates.

After suffering many torments they were all condemned to lose their heads. St. Pantaleon suffered the day after the rest. He is ranked by the Greeks among the great martyrs. His relics were translated to Constantinople, and there kept with great honour, as St. John Damascen informs us. The greatest part of them are now shown in the abbey of St. Denys near Paris, but his head at Lyons.

Physicians honour St. Pantaleon as their chief patron after St. Luke.

PLATE 41. ST. ANNE, 26 JULY. BUTLER, *LIVES OF THE SAINTS*, TWO-VOLUME ILLUSTRATED 19TH-CENTURY EDITION.

PLATE 42. ST. MARTHA, 29 JULY. BRITISH LIBRARY, ADD. MS 18851, F. 417.

29 JULY

St. Martha

VIRGIN

FIRST CENTURY

Martha was sister to Mary and Lazarus, and lived with them at Bethania, a small town two miles distant from Jerusalem, a little beyond Mount Olivet. Our blessed Redeemer had made his residence in Galilee till in the third year of his ministry he preached chiefly in Judaea, during which interval he frequented the house of these three disciples. Martha seemed to have been the eldest, and to have had the chief care and direction of the household.

It appears from the history of the resurrection of Lazarus that their family was of principal note in the country. In the first visit with which Jesus honoured them, St. Luke tells us that St. Martha showed great solicitude to entertain and serve him. She forgot the privilege of her rank and would not leave so great an honour to servants only, but was herself very busy in preparing every thing for so great a guest. Mary sat all the while at our

Saviour's feet. Martha, sweetly complaining to him, desired him to bid Mary to rise up and help her. Our Lord was well pleased with the devotion wherewith Martha waited on him; yet he commended more the quiet repose with which Mary attended only to the spiritual improvement of her soul. 'Martha, Martha,' said he, 'thou art careful and troubled about many things; but one thing is necessary.'

Another instance which shows how dear this family was to our Saviour is the raising of Lazarus to life. When he fell sick, the sisters sent to inform Christ, who was then absent in Galilee. When he arrived at Bethania, Martha went first out to meet and welcome him; and then called her sister Mary.

Christ was again at Bethania, at the house of Simon the Leper, six days before his passion. Lazarus was one of the guests, Martha waited at table; and Mary poured a box of costly ointments on our Lord's feet, which she wiped with the hair of her head.

St. Martha seems to have been one of those holy women who attended Christ during his passion and stood under his cross. After his ascension, she came to Marseilles, and ended her life in Provence, where her body was found at Tarascon, soon after the discovery of that of St. Mary Magdalen.

31 JULY

St. Ignatius

OF LOYOLA, FOUNDER OF THE SOCIETY OF
JESUS
A.D. 1556

St. Ignatius was born in 1491 in the castle of Loyola, in Guipuscoa. His father was head of one of the most noble families of that country. He was bred under the care of Antony, Duke of Najara, who led him to the army. Francis I, King of France, sent a great army into Spain, which laid siege to Pampeluna. Ignatius had been left there to encourage the garrison, and a shot from a cannon shivered his right leg. He remained lame his whole life after. During the cure of his knee he was confined to bed and a book of the lives of our Saviour and the saints was brought him. Ignatius, being cured, went to Montserrat, a great abbey of Benedictine monks. Three leagues from Montserrat is a village called Manresa with a convent of Dominicans who took him in. He there wrote his *Spiritual Exercises*. After a stay of ten months he took shipping at Barcelona and went to Jerusalem. He returned to Europe in 1524.

The saint, after studying two years at Barcelona went to the university of Alcala. Some accused him of heresy, but he was justified by the inquisitors. Recovering his liberty, he travelled to Paris in February, 1528. He spent two years in perfecting himself in the Latin tongue, then went through a course of philosophy. Laynez, Salmeron, and Alphonso, all Spaniards, associated themselves to the saint and made all together a vow to renounce the world, to go to preach the gospel in Palestine. Ignatius arrived at Venice about 1536 and his nine companions from Paris met him there in 1537. They were ordained. The Venetians having declared war against the Turks, their pilgrimage was rendered impracticable. Ignatius went to Rome, called his companions and proposed to them his design of forming themselves into a religious order, which should possess no real estates or revenues, either in particular or in common. Pope Paul III approved it, under the title of 'The Society of Jesus' by a bull dated the 27th of September, 1540.

In 1546 the Jesuits first opened their schools in Europe. The seminary of Goa in Asia was committed to the Jesuits the preceding year. Among the rules which St. Ignatius gave to the masters he principally inculcated the lessons of humility, modesty and devotion. St. Francis Borgia in 1551 gave a considerable sum towards building the Roman college for the Jesuits. Ignatius made it a strict rule that every one should study to speak correctly the language of the country where he lives; for, without being perfect in the vulgar tongue, no one can be qualified to preach or perform many other functions.

St. Ignatius was general of the Society fifteen years, but was in the end so worn out with infirmities that he procured an assistant in that office. He calmly gave up his happy soul into the hands of his Creator on the last day of July 1556, the sixty-fifth of his age.

2 AUGUST (16 DECEMBER)

St. Eusebius

BISHOP OF VERCELLI
A.D. 371

St. Eusebius was born in Sardinia, where his father is said to have died for the faith. His mother, being left a widow, carried him and a daughter, both in their infancy, to Rome. Eusebius was ordained lector by St. Sylvester. We do not know by what accident he was called to Vercelli, a city now in Piedmont. He served that church with such applause, that the episcopal chair becoming vacant, he was unanimously chosen to fill it. He is the first bishop of Vercelli whose name we know. St. Ambrose assures us that he was the first who in the West united the monastic life with the clerical, living himself and making his clergy live almost in the same manner as the monks in the East did in the desert.

In 354 Pope Liberius deputed St. Eusebius to beg leave of Emperor Constantius to assemble a free council, which met at Milan in 355. Eusebius seeing all things would be carried on by violence through the power of the Arians, though the Catholic prelates were more numerous, refused to go until he was pressed by Liberius. When he was come to Milan, the Arians excluded him for the first ten days. When he was admitted he laid the Nicene Creed on the table and insisted on all signing that rule of faith before the cause of St. Athanasius should be brought to a hearing. The emperor sent for St. Eusebius, St. Dionysius and Lucifer of Cagliari, and press them to condemn Athanasius. They insisted upon his innocence, and that he could not be condemned without being heard. The prince thought once of putting them to death, but was content to banish them. Our saint was sent to Scythopolis in Palestine, there to be treated at the discretion of the Arian bishop, Patrophilus.

St. Eusebius was lodged first with Count Joseph and was comforted by the visits of holy men and of deputies of his church at Vercelli. But Joseph died and the Arians insulted the saint, dragged him through the streets and shut him up in a little chamber. After he remained four days without eating, the Arians sent him back to his lodgings. Twenty-five days afterwards they came again, armed with clubs and dragged him again into a little dungeon. His sufferings were aggravated every day till the place of his exile was changed to Cappodocia, and some time afterwards Upper Thebais in Egypt. Constantius being dead toward the end of 361, Julian gave leave to all banished prelates to return. St. Eusebius came to Alexandria to concert measures with St. Athanasius for applying proper remedies to the evils of the church. He was present in the council there in 362. From Alexandria he went to Antioch and travelled over the East. In Italy St. Hilary of Poitiers and St. Eusebius met and were employed in exposing the Arians. St. Jerome places the death of the latter in 371.

PLATE 43. ST. IGNATIUS LOYOLA, 31 JULY. BUTLER, *LIVES OF THE SAINTS*, TWO-VOLUME ILLUSTRATED 19TH-CENTURY EDITION.

7 AUGUST

St. Cajetan
OF THIENNA
A.D. 1547

St. Cajetan was son of Gaspar, Lord of Thienna in the territory of Vicenza in Lombardy, and was born in 1480. He distinguished himself in the study of divinity; likewise in the civil and canon laws, in which faculty he took the degree of doctor with great applause at Padua.

To devote himself perfectly to the divine service he embraced an ecclesiastical state; and, out of his own patrimony, built and founded a parochial chapel at Rampazzo, for the benefit of many who lived at a considerable distance from the parish church. After this he went to Rome, hoping to lead an obscure life, which it was impossible for him to do in his own country. Nevertheless Pope Julius II compelled him to accept the office of protonotary. Being much delighted with the end proposed by the confraternity called the love of God, he enrolled in it. Upon the death of Julius II he resigned his public employment and returned to Vicenza. There he entered the confraternity of St Jerome which was instituted upon the plan of that of the love of God in Rome, but which consisted only of men in the lowest stations of life. This gave great offence to his worldly friends, who thought it a blemish to the honour of his family. He persisted, however, and sought out the most distressed sick and poor over the whole town and served them with his own hands.

In obedience to the advice of his confessor, John of Crema, a Dominican friar, the saint removed to Venice and pursued his former manner of life. By the advice of the same director Cajetan left Venice to return to Rome to the confraternity of the love of God. A plan was concerted among the associates for instituting an order of regular clergy upon the model of the lives of the apostles. The first authors of this design were St. Cajetan, Caraffa, Archbishop of Theate, Paul Consigliari and Boniface de Colle. The Order was approved in 1524 and Caraffa was chosen the first general. As he still retained the title of Archbishop of Theate, these clerks were called Theatins. The zeal of these holy men drew many to their community. They lived at first in a house in Rome.

The army of the Emperor Charles V took Rome by assault in 1527. The house of the Theatins was rifled and St. Cajetan tortured to extort from him a treasure which he had not. He and his companions repaired to Venice and St. Cajetan was chosen general. At the end of the three years of his office, our saint was sent to Verona, and shortly after to Naples to found a convent of his order in that city. In 1537 he went back to Venice, being made general a second time; but after his three years were expired, he returned to Naples and governed the house of his Order till his death on the 7th of August, 1547.

8 AUGUST (4 AUGUST)

St. Dominic
FOUNDER OF THE FRIAR PREACHERS
A.D. 1221

St. Dominic was born in 1170 at Calaruega in old Castille. He was of the illustrious house of the Guzmans. His uncle, the holy archpriest of Gumiel, was his first preceptor. The saint at fourteen was sent to the public schools of Palentia. Azebedo, being made bishop of Osma, in 1198 invited St. Dominic to accept a canonry, being then twenty-eight years old. Alphonsus IX, King of Castille, chose the Bishop of Osma to go into La Marche to negotiate a match between the daughter of the earl of that country and his son. The bishop took Dominic with him. On their way they passed through Languedoc which was then filled with the heresy of the Albingenses. He in whose house they lodged at Toulouse was tainted with it. St. Dominic pierced to the heart with compassion for his soul, in that one night made him a convert. The treaty of marriage being concluded the ambassadors went to Rome to ask of Pope Innocent III leave to labour among the Albingenses. His holiness gave leave to stay two years in Languedoc. They arrived at Montpellier towards the end of the year 1205, where they met several Cistercian abbots who were commissioned by the pope to oppose the heresies. The archbishop and Dominic proposed to employ persuasion rather than terror.

The first conference of the missionaries with the heretics was held near Montpellier and several conversions were wrought. St. Dominic founded the nunnery of our Lady of Prouille, near Fanjaux in 1206, which is regarded to this day as the mother-house of all the nuns of this order. St Dominic had spent ten years in preaching in Languedoc when in 1215 he founded his religious order of Preaching Friars, the plan of which he had meditated some time before. Sixteen of his fellow missionaries came readily into his project. To establish it the founder was obliged to go to Rome whither he accompanied Fulco, the Bishop of Toulouse. The pope approved the new order by word of mouth, bidding the founder draw up the constitutions and lay them before him. After a mature consultation with his sixteen colleagues he made choice of the rule of the canons of St. Austin. St. Dominic went to Rome in 1217 and the pope gave him the Church of St Sixtus. Several nuns lived in Rome without keeping enclosure and St. Dominic, in order to remove several difficulties, offered to these nuns his own monastery of St. Sixtus, and he undertook to build for his friars a new convent at St. Sabina.

In 1218 he took a journey from Rome and founded a famous convent at Segovia and another at Madrid. He returned to Toulouse and from thence went to Paris, and having founded convents at Avignon, Asti and Bergamo arrived at Bologna in 1219, which city he made from that time his ordinary residence. In 1220 Honorious II commanded him to be styled general. He expired on the 6th of August, 1221.

PLATE 44. ST. DOMINIC, 8 AUGUST. BUTLER, *LIVES OF THE SAINTS*, TWO-VOLUME ILLUSTRATED 19TH-CENTURY EDITION.

St. Oswald

KING AND MARTYR
SEVENTH CENTURY

Ethelfrid, who ruled the kingdom of the Northumbers being slain in battle in 617, his sons Eanfrid, Oswald and Oswi took refuge among the Scots where they were instructed in the Christian faith. In the meantime Edwin reigned; but in 633 was killed fighting against Penda the Mercian and Cadwalla, King of the Britons. Upon this revolution the three sons of Ethelfrid returned from Scotland, and Eanfrid obtained the kingdom of the Deira, whilst Osric was chosen king of Bernicia. Both these princes were slain by Cadwalla. Hereupon Oswald was called to the crown. At that time Cadwalla ravaged all the Northumbrian provinces. Oswald assembled what troops he was able and marched against his mighty enemy. Being come near the enemy's camp, the evening before the engagement, the pious king caused a great wooden cross to be made. When it was fixed, St. Oswald cried out 'Let us now kneel down and jointly pray to God that he would defend us from our enemy; for he knows that we fight in a just war.' All the soldiers did as he commanded.

Almighty God was pleased to bless the king's faith by granting him and his small army a complete victory over Cadwalla, who was killed in battle. St. Oswald immediately set himself to restore good order throughout his dominions and to plant in them the faith of Christ. He entreated the king and bishops of Scotland to send him a bishop and assistants by whose preaching the people might be grounded in the Christian religion and receive baptism. Aidan, a native of Ireland, was chosen for the arduous undertaking. The king bestowed on Aidan the isle of Lindisfarne for his episcopal see and was so edified with his leaning that before the bishop could speak English, he would be himself his interpreter.

Oswald filled his dominions with churches and monasteries. The kingdom of Northumberland was then extended as far as Edinburgh and so great was his power that Adamnan in the life of St. Columba styles him Emperor of Britain. When St. Oswald had reigned eight years in great prosperity, Penda, the barbarous pagan King of Mercia, who nine years before had slain the pious King Edwin, found means again to raise a great army and invade the Christian dominions of our holy king. St. Oswald met him with an inferior force, and was killed in the battle that was fought between them. When he saw himself surrounded with the arms of his enemies he offered his prayer for the souls of his soldiers. He was slain in the thirty-eighth year of his age, of our Lord 642, on the 5th of August, in a place called Maserfield. The inhuman tyrant caused the saint's head and arms to be struck off and fixed on poles; but St. Oswald's brother and succesor, Oswi, took them away the year following and carried the arms to his own royal palace and sent the head to Lindisfarne.

St. Laurence

MARTYR
A.D. 258

St. Xystus, then archdeacon of Rome, took Laurence under his protection. St. Xystus being raised to the pontificate in 257, he ordained Laurence deacon. The Emperor Valerian, in 257 published his bloody edicts against the church. That by cutting off the shepherds he might disperse the flocks, he commanded all bishops, priests and deacons to be put to death without delay. The holy pope was apprehended the year following. As he was led to execution, his deacon, St. Laurence followed him weeping, and being inflamed with a desire to die for Christ, burst into complaint. The holy pope was moved to compassion and answered 'I do not leave you, my son. You shall follow me in three days.' He added a charge to distribute immediately among the poor the treasure of the church lest it should fall into the hands of the persecutors.

Laurence set out immediately to seek all the poor widows and orphans and gave among them all the money which he had; he even sold the sacred vessels to increase the sum. The church of Rome was then possessed of considerable riches. It had likewise very rich ornaments and vessels. The prefect of Rome was informed of these riches and was extremely desirous to secure them. With this view he sent for St. Laurence and said to him, 'You often complain that we treat you with cruelty but no tortures are here thought of. I am told that according to your doctrine you must render to Caesar the things that belong to him. Give us therefore the money and be rich in words.' St. Laurence replied, 'The church is indeed rich. I will show you a valuable part; but allow me a little time to set everything in order.' The prefect granted him three days' respite. During this interval Laurence went all over the city, seeking out the poor who were supported by the church. On the third day he gathered together a great number of them, then he went to the prefect, invited him to come and see the treasure of the church and conducted him to the place. The earthly-minded man cried out in a transport of rage, 'Do you thus mock me?' Then he caused a great gridiron to be made ready and live coals almost extinguished to be thrown under it, that the martyr might be slowly burnt. Laurence was stripped, extended and bound with chains upon his iron bed over a slow fire which broiled his flesh little by little. Such was the tranquillity which he enjoyed that having suffered a long time he turned to the judge and said, 'Let my body be turned; one side is broiled enough.' When the executioner had turned him, he said 'It is dressed enough, you may eat'. The martyr continued in earnest prayer, imploring the divine mercy for the conversion of the city, and having finished his prayer, gave up the ghost. It appears that his feast has been kept since the fifth age.

PLATE 45. ST. LAURENCE, 10 AUGUST. BODLEIAN LIBRARY, MS. ADD. A 185, F. 62.

11 AUGUST

St. Susanna

VIRGIN AND MARTYR

THIRD AGE

Susanna was nobly born in Rome, and is said to have been niece to Pope Caius. Having made a vow of virginity, she refused to marry; on which account she was impeached as a Christian, and suffered with heroic constancy a cruel martyrdom. No genuine acts of her life are now extant: but she is commemorated in many ancient Martyrologies, and the famous church which is at present served by Cistercian monks has borne her name ever since the fifth century, when it was one of the titles of the parishes of Rome. St. Susanna suffered towards the beginning of Diocletian's reign, about the year 295.

[Editorial note: Susanna's name is often linked with that of another Roman martyr, Tiburtius, although they appear to have nothing in common apart from the fact that their names both appear on the same day in the marytrology. It is not known whether they suffered in the same year or even under the same wave of persecution.]

PLATE 46. ST. SUSANNAH, 11 AUGUST. BUTLER, *LIVES OF THE SAINTS*, TWO-VOLUME ILLUSTRATED 19TH-CENTURY EDITION.

11 AUGUST (12 AUGUST)

St. Clare

A.D. 1253

St. Clare was daughter to a noble knight who had three daughters. She was born in 1193 at Assisium, [Assisi], a city in Italy. Her parents began to talk to her very early of marriage, which gave her a great affliction, for it was her most ardent desire to have no other spouse but Jesus Christ. Hearing the great reputation of St. Francis, she found means to be conducted to him, and begged his advice. He spoke to her on the love of God in such a manner as warmed her tender breast and she formed the resolution of renouncing the world. St. Francis appointed Palm Sunday for the day on which she should come to him. On that day, Clare, dressed in her most sumptuous apparel, went with her mother and family to the divine office. She attended the procession, but the evening following, being the 18th of March, 1212, she made her escape and went a mile out of the town to where St. Francis lived with his little community. She put off her fine clothes and St. Francis cut off her hair. The holy father not having yet any nunnery, placed her for the present in the Benedictine nunnery of St. Paul, being then eighteen years of age. The Poor Clares date from this epoch the foundation of their Order.

No sooner was this action made public but the world conspired to condemn it, and her friends and relations came in a body to draw her out of her retreat. Clare resisted their violence and, uncovering her head to show her hair cut, said that Christ had called her to his service. St Francis soon after moved her to another nunnery. There her sister Agnes joined her in her undertaking. She was soon after joined by her mother and several ladies of her kindred. St. Clare founded within a few years monasteries at Perugia, Arezzo, Padua, Venice, Mantua, Bologna, Milan, Siena, Pisa, also at many principal towns in Germany.

St. Clare and her community practised austerities which till then had scarce ever been known among the tender sex. Whilst others asked riches, Clare presented her humble request to Pope Innocent IV that he would confirm to her Order the singular privilege of holy poverty, which he did in 1251.

She was afflicted with continual diseases and pains for eight and twenty years, yet was always joyful, allowing herself no other indulgence than a little straw to lie on. St. Clare bore her sicknesses without so much as speaking of them, and seeing all her spiritual children weep, comforted them and gave them her blessing, calling herself the little plant of her holy father St. Francis. The passion of Christ, at her request, was read to her in her agony, and she sweetly expired on the 11th of August, 1253, in the forty-second year of her religious profession, and the sixtieth year of her age. She was buried on the day following, on which the church keeps her festival.

PLATE 47. ST. CLARE, 11 AUGUST. BRITISH LIBRARY, YATES THOMPSON MS 29, F. 62.

13 AUGUST

St. Hippolytus
MARTYR
A.D. 252

One of the most illustrious martyrs who suffered in the reign of Gallus was St. Hippolytus, one of the twenty-five priests of Rome to have been deceived by Novatian and Novatus, and to have been engaged in their schism; but this fault he expiated by his public repentance and a glorious martyrdom.

He was apprehended and interrogated on the rack in Rome; but the prefect of the city, having filled it with Christian blood, went to Ostia to extend the persecution, and ordered our saint and several other Christians who were then in prison at Rome to be conducted thither after him.

St. Hippolytus being brought out of prison, many of those who had been under his care came to beg his last advice and blessing; and he vehemently exhorted them to preserve the unity of the church. After he had thus undeceived his flock he was conducted to Ostia. The prefect ascended his tribunal, surrounded with his executioners and various instruments of torture. The confessors were ranged before him, and by their emaciated faces the length of their hair, and the filth with which they were covered, showed how much they had suffered by their long imprisonment. The judge, finding that he was not able to prevail with any of them by torments, at length condemned them all to be put to death. Some he caused to be beheaded, other to be crucified, others burnt, and some to be put out to sea in rotten vessels which immediately foundered. When the venerable old man Hippolytus was in his turn brought to him loaded with chains, a crowd of young people cried out to the judge that he was a chief among the Christians and ought to be put to death by some new and remarkable kind of punishment.

Out of the country, where untamed horses were kept, they took a pair of the most furious and unruly they could meet with, and tied a long rope between them to which they fastened the martyr's feet. Then they provoked the horses to run away by loud cries, whipping and pricking them. The last words which the martyr was heard to say as they started, were 'Lord, they tear my body, receive thou my soul.' The horses dragged him away furiously into the woods, through brooks, and over ditches, briers and rocks. The ground, the thorns, trees and stones were sprinkled with his blood which the faithful that followed him at a distance weeping respectfully sucked up from every place with sponges, and they gathered together all the mangled parts of his flesh and limbs, which lay scattered all about. They brought these precious relics to Rome, and buried them in the subterraneous caverns called catacombs.

16 AUGUST (2 SEPTEMBER)

St. Stephen
KING OF HUNGARY
A.D. 1038

Geysa, the fourth duke of the Hungarians, was baptized together with his wife Sarloth. Sarloth, being some time after with child, was assured in a dream that she bore in her womb a son who should complete the work she and her husband had begun. The child was born in 977 and was christened Stephen. Geysa died in 997 and Stephen took the reins of government in his hands.

His first care was to settle a firm peace with all the neighbouring nations. This being done he turned his thoughts wholly to root out idolatry. The zealous prince founded the archbishopric of Gran and ten bishoprics and sent the new elected Bishop of Colcotz to Rome to obtain of Pope Sylvester II confirmation of these foundations and to beseech his holiness to confer upon him the title of king. Sylvester was disposed to grant his request and prepared a rich crown to send him with his blessing. His holiness delivered this crown to his ambassador and confirmed all the religious foundations which our holy prince had made. St. Stephen went to meet his ambassador upon his return, listened standing with great respect to the pope's bulls and fell on his knees as often as the name of his holiness was repeated.

St. Stephen took to wife Gisela, sister to St. Henry, King of Germany. He abolished many barbarous and superstitious customs and repressed blasphemy, murder, theft and other crimes. His excellent code of laws is inscribed to his son, Duke Emeric. In fifty-five chapters the pious legislator has comprised the wisest regulations of the state. The protection of his people engaged him sometimes in war, wherein he was always victorious.

Sickness deprived St. Stephen of all his children. St. Emeric, the eldest, was carried off the last. He had then begun to sustain a great part of the burden of the state and to be assistant to his father. Though brave and expert in war, Stephen had always been a lover of peace: but from this time he took a resolution to spill no blood in war, in which he earnestly begged the interposition of divine Providence. After the death of St. Henry, his successor invaded Hungary with a powerful army in 1030, and advanced so far that St. Stephen was compelled to lead out his army against him, though still trusting in God that the effusion of blood would be prevented. All things seemed to be disposed for battle when to the surprise of all men, the emperor on a sudden turned his back with his army without having executed any thing, and marched home into Germany.

St. Stephen laboured three years under painful distempers. During this time four palatins entered into a conspiracy to take his life. One of them got into the king's chamber but, seeing himself discovered, threw himself at the feet of his sovereign and obtained his pardon. The saint expired on the 15th of August in 1038.

17 AUGUST (16 AUGUST)

St. Hyacinth
CONFESSOR
A.D. 1257

St. Hyacinth, whom the Church historians call the apostle of the North, was of the ancient house of the counts of Oldrovnans in Silesia. He was born in 1185 in the diocese of Breslaw, and studied at Cracow, Prague and Bologna, in which last university he took the degree of doctor of the laws and divinity. Returning to the Bishop of Cracow, that prelate gave him a prebend in his cathedral and employed him as his assistant. The bishop abdicating his dignity, Yvo of Konski was placed in that see, and went to Rome with his two nephews, Hyacinth and Ceslas. St. Dominic was then at Rome, this happening in the year 1218, and Hyacinth received the habit at the hands of Dominic, in March. His made his solemn vows by a dispensation after a novitiate of about six months only; and Hyacinth, then thirty-three years old was appointed superior of their mission. The missionaries passed through the Venetian territories, entered Upper Carinthia, and St. Hyacinth founded a convent.

In Poland they were received with extraordinary marks of joy. At Cracow the first sermons of St. Hyacinth were attended with incredible success and in a short time the public vices which reigned in that capital were banished. He founded a convent of his Order in Cracow, another at Sendomir and a third at Plocsko in Moravia. Having preached through the principal cities of Poland, he undertook to carry the gospel into the vast and savage countries of the North. He banished in many places superstition, vice and idolatry and built convents in Prussia, Pomerania and other countries lying near the Baltic.

The saint left to preach in Denmark, Swedeland, Gothia and Norway. He everywhere founded monasteries and left disciples to preserve and extend them. After the aforesaid missions, he went into Lesser Russia, where he made a long stay and induced the prince and great multitudes to abjure the Greek schism and unite themselves to the Catholic church. From thence he penetrated as far as the Black Sea. Returning towards the north, he entered the great dukedom of Muscovy where he found the Duke Voldimir inflexible in his errors; however he obtained permission to preach to the Catholics. He no sooner began to announce the gospel, but Mahometans, heathens and schismatics flocked to hear him and in great multitudes became docile to the truth.

The saint returned to Cracow in 1231. After two years he made the visitation of his convents among the Danes, Swedes, Prussians, Muscovites and other nations and penetrated among the Tartars. Though Great Tartary be a vast tract of land, St. Hyacinth travelled quite through it, penetrating into Thibet and into Catay, the most northern province of China. After having travelled above four thousand leagues he arrived at Cracow in 1257, which was the seventy-second and last year of his life. He died on the 14th of August.

18 AUGUST

St. Helen
EMPRESS
A.D. 328

We are assured by the unanimous tradition of our English historians that this holy empress was a native of our island. Leland says Helen was the only daughter of King Coilus who first built the walls round Colchester. Constantius, at that time only a private officer in the army, had the happiness to make her his first wife, and had by her Constantine, his eldest son, who as all agree had his first education under her watchful eye.

To understand the sequel of this history, it is necessary to take a view of the empire at the time. The two brothers, Carinus in the West and Numerianus in the East, being become detestable to their subjects, the supreme dignity was devolved upon Diocletian. To oppose Carinus in the West Diocletian declared Maximiam Herculeus Caesar, and the better to secure themselves and carry on their wars, they associated to themselves in 293 two other emperors of inferior rank. Diocletian chose Galerius and Herculeus pitched upon Constantius. Herculeus reserved to himself Italy, Spain and Africa. Constantius had Gaul and Britain, and by the articles of this association, was obliged to divorce Helen and to marry Theodora, the daughter-in-law of Maximian.

Constantine, from his first accession to the throne forbade the Christians to be molested on account of their religion. Fluctuating what deity to invoke before his battle with Maxentius he was inspired to address the true God. From that time he published edicts in favour of the Christian faith, built churches, and distributed alms among the poor. It appears from Eusebius that St. Helen was not converted to the faith with her son, till after his miraculous victory; but so perfect was her conversion that she embraced all the practices of Christian perfection.

Constantine having become master of the East, wrote to the Bishop of Jersualem concerning the building of a church upon Mount Calvary. St. Helen though fourscore years of age, took the charge on herself to see this pious work executed, desiring at the same time, to discover the sacred cross. Eusebius speaks not directly of her discovery of the cross but describes the two magnificent churches which the empress built, one on Mount Calvary, the other of Mount Olivet. She beautified the city of Drepanaun in Bithynia, in honour of St. Lucian, so that Constantine caused that city to be called Helenopolis.

At last this pious princess returned to Rome and, perceiving her last hour to approach, gave her son excellent instructions how to govern his empire. She expired in August, 328, or according to some 326.

20 AUGUST

St. Bernard
ABBOT
A.D. 1153

St Bernard was born in 1091 at Fontaines, a castle near Dijon and a lordship belonging to his father. He was sent to Chatillon on the Seine to pursue a course of studies in a college of secular priests. He was nineteen when his mother died. Bernard was then returned to Fontaines and now become his own master. Affrighted at the snares of the world he began to think of retiring to Cîteaux and embracing the severe Cistercian institute. His brothers and friends endeavoured to dissuade him, but he so pleaded his cause as to draw them all over to join him.

Cîteaux had been founded fifteen years, and was at that time governed by St. Stephen. Bernard made his profession in the hands of St. Stephen with his companions in 1114 and set out with extraordinary ardour in his monastic exercises. He was a great lover of poverty in his habit, cell, and all other things. The number of monks being grown too great at Cîteaux, Hugh, Earl of Troyes, offered a spot of ground in his estates whereon to found a monastery; and the superior, seeing the progress Bernard had made in a spiritual life, appointed him abbot, and ordered him to go with twelve monks, among whom were his brothers, to found a new house in Champagne. The reputation of this house in a short time became so great that the number of monks amounted to one hundred and thirty, and the country gave it the name of Clara-Vallis, now commonly called Clairvaux.

St. Bernard founded in 1118 the abbey of Three Fountains, in Challons, that of Fontenay in Autun and that of Tarouca in Portugal. Being obliged to take a journey to Paris in 1122, he preached to the students who were candidates for holy orders; many of whom accompanied him back to Clairvaux. He was several times chosen Bishop of Langres and Challons, and Archbishop of Genoa, Milan and Rheims; but so strenuously opposed the motion that the popes were unwilling to offer violence to his humility. The remarkable conversions of innumerable princes and prelates wrought by St. Bernard are too long to be inserted. The saint saw himself obliged also to maintain the purity of the Catholic faith. He heard of no innovator in doctrine with whom he did not enter the lists.

He founded before his death one hundred and sixty other monasteries; and their number was so much increased after his death that before the dissolution of monasteries in Britain and the northern kingdoms, eight hundred abbeys were subject to Clairvaux. Pope Eugenius III coming into France in 1147, held there several councils to promote a second crusade and commissioned St. Bernard to preach the holy war. This the abbot executed with incredible success in France and Germany.

In the beginning of the year 1153 St. Bernard fell into a decay, and yielded up his soul to God on the 20th of August.

23 AUGUST (30 AUGUST)

St. Rose
OF LIMA, VIRGIN
A.D. 1617

Rose was of Spanish extraction, born at Lima, the capital of Peru, in 1586. She was christened Isabel; but the figure and colour of her face in the cradle seeming to resemble a beautiful rose, the name of Rose was given her. From her infancy her patience in suffering and her love of mortification were extraordinary, and whilst yet a child, she ate no fruit, and fasted three days a week, allowing herself on them only bread and water, and no other days taking only unsavoury herbs and pulse. When she was grown up, her garden was planted only with bitter herbs, and interspersed with figures of crosses.

One day her mother having put on her head a garland of flowers, she secretly stuck in it a pin, which pricked her so deep, that the maid at night could not take off the garland without some difficulty. Hearing others frequently commend her beauty, and fearing lest it should be an occasion of temptation to any one, whenever she was to go abroad to any public place, she used, the night before, to rub her face and hands with the bark and powder of Indian pepper in order to disfigure her skin with little blotches and swellings.

Her parents by the vicissitude of worldly affairs, fell from a state of opulence into great distress, and Rose was taken into the family of the treasurer Gonsalvo, by that gentleman's pious lady; and by working there all day in the garden, and late at night with her needle, she relieved them in their necessities. She probably would never have entertained any thoughts of another state if she had not found herself importuned by her friends to marry. To rid herself of such troublesome solicitations she enrolled herself in the Third Order of St. Dominic. Her love of solitude made her choose for her dwelling a little lonely cell. Extraordinary fasts, hair cloths, studded iron chains, which she wore about her waist and other austerities were the inventions of her spirit of mortification and penance. She wore upon her head a thin circle of silver, studded on the inside with little sharp pricks or nails, which wounded her head, in imitation of a crown of thorns. God favoured the fervour of her charity with many extraordinary graces; and Christ once in a vision called her soul his spouse.

She suffered, during fifteen years, grievous persecutions from her friends and others; and, what were much more severe trials, interior desolation, and dreadful agonies of spiritual anguish. The devil also assaulted her with violent temptations, filling her head with filthy phantoms. But God afterwards recompensed her fidelity and constancy in this life with extraordinary caresses. Under long and most painful sicknesses it was her prayer 'Lord, increase my sufferings, and with them increase thy love in my heart.' She happily passed to eternal bliss on the 24th of August, 1617, being thirty-one years old.

PLATE 48. ST. BERNARD, 20 AUGUST. BUTLER, *LIVES OF THE SAINTS*, TWO-VOLUME ILLUSTRATED 19TH-CENTURY EDITION.

PLATE 49. ST. ROSE, 23 AUGUST. BUTLER, *LIVES OF THE SAINTS*, TWO-VOLUME ILLUSTRATED 19TH-CENTURY EDITION.

24 AUGUST

St. Bartholomew

APOSTLE
FIRST CENTURY

The name given to this apostle is not his proper, but patronymical name, and imports the son of Tholomew. St. Bartholomew was chosen by Christ to be one of his twelve apostles. He was with them witness of our Lord's glorious resurrection, is mentioned among the other disciples who were met together in prayer after Christ's Ascension, and he received the Holy Ghost with the rest.

St. Bartholomew carried the gospel through the most barbarous countries of the East, penetrating into the remoter Indies, as Eusebius and other ancient writers testify. By the names of Indies the ancients sometimes mean only Arabia and Persia; but here they speak of proper India, for they make mention of the Brachmans of that country. Eusebius relates that St. Pantaenus about the beginning of the third century going into the Indies found there some who still retained the knowledge of Christ and showed him a copy of St. Matthew's gospel, which they assured him that St. Bartholomew had brought into those parts when he planted the faith among them. This apostle returned again into the north-west parts of Asia; and met St. Philip at Hierapolis in Phrygia. Hence he travelled into Lycaonia, where St. Chrysostom affirms that he instructed the people in the faith; but we know not even the names of many of the countries to which he preached.

St. Bartholomew's last removal was into Great Armenia, where, preaching in a place obstinately addicted to the worship of idols, he was crowned with a glorious martyrdom, as St. Gregory of Tours mentions. The modern Greek historians say that he was condemned by the governor of Albanopolis to be crucified. Others affirm that he was flayed alive, which might well enough consist with his crucifixion, this double punishment being in use among the Persians, the next neighbours to the Armenians.

The relics of St. Bartholomew were conveyed to Rome in 983, as Baronius relates. Ever since that time they lie deposited in a porphyry monument under the high altar in the famous church of St. Bartholomew, in the isle of the Tiber. An arm of this apostle's body was sent a present to St. Edward the Confessor, and by him bestowed upon the cathedral church of Canterbury. The feast of St. Bartholomew is marked on the 24 of August in the West, but among the Greeks on the 11th of June.

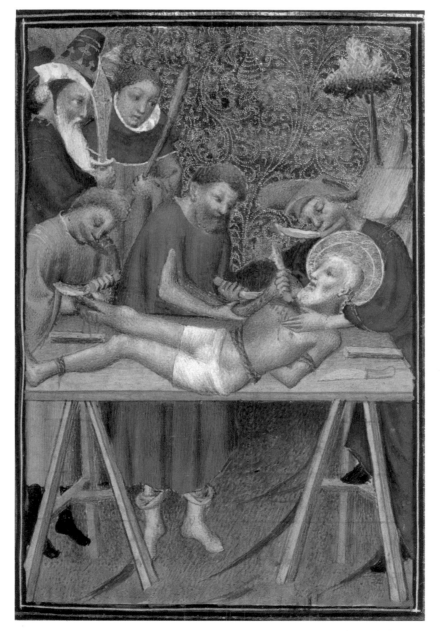

PLATE 50. ST. BARTHOLOMEW, 24 AUGUST. BRITISH LIBRARY, HARLEY MS 2897, F. 379.

25 AUGUST

St. Lewis (Louis)
KING OF FRANCE
A.D. 1270

This great king was the son of Lewis VIII and was born at Poissy, in the diocese of Chartres, on the 25th of April, 1215. His mother was Blanche, daughter to Alphonsus of Castile. Lewis VIII died on the 7th of November, 1226. Blanche was declared regent for her son who was then only twelve years old. To prevent seditions, she hastened the ceremony of his coronation, which was performed at Rheims. The whole time of the king's minority was disturbed by rebels; but the regent, by alliances and courage, dissipated their cabals.

Lewis never thought himself so happy as when he enjoyed the conversation of religious men. When some people said that he spent too much time in his devotions, he answered that if he employed that time in hunting, gaming or plays they would not take so exact an account. He was extremely ingenious in practising self-denials without being taken notice of, exact in holding councils and indefatigable in applying himself to the regulation of his kingdom. King Lewis, before being inured to government, took the reins into his own hands in 1236, but continued to show the greatest deference to his mother. He erected the abbey of Royaumont, founded the Chartreuse at Paris and built many other religious places and hospitals. Baldwin II, Emperor of Constantinople made St. Lewis a present of the holy crown of thorns. In 1241 he received a large piece of the true cross and built that which is now called, from these relics, the Holy Chapel.

In 1230 he, by severe laws, forbade all manner of usury. He set himself to protect vassals from the oppression of the lords. In his wars to reduce rebels he caused the damages which innocent persons had received even by his enemy's forces to be inquired into and restitution to be made. For the holy war, the king set sail in 1248 towards Cyprus. After having waited eight months in Cyprus the fleet arrived before the mouths of the Nile and took possession of Damiata. In 1250 the Christian army was worsted and surrendered themselves prisoners. The sultan demanded the city of Damiata for the king's ransom and a truce was concluded for ten years. After comforting the Christians in Palestine and visiting the holy places, Lewis embarked at Acre in 1254 and after a voyage of ten weeks came to Paris after an absence of almost six years.

Lewis again took the cross on 1267; but before he set out he put the finishing hand to the establishment of the house of Sorbon and made his will. The king embarked with his army upon the 1st of July, 1270 and proceeded towards Africa. The French waited for the arrival of the King of Sicily to lay siege to Tunis, but King Lewis and his eldest son were seized with a distemper, and Lewis breathed his last on the 25th of August, 1270.

27 AUGUST (4 MAY)

St. Monica
WIDOW
A.D. 387

Monica was born in 332 in a pious family, and early instructed in the fear of God. As soon as marriageable she was disposed of to one Patricius, a citizen of Tagaste, a man of honour but an idolater. She had by him two sons, Austin (Augustine) and Navigius, and one daughter. She tolerated the injuries done by him to her marriage-bed in such manner as never to make him the least reproach on that subject. One of the happy fruits Monica reaped from her patience was her husband's conversion to Christ; who thereupon became chaste and faithful; he died the year after he had been baptized.

Her exercises of piety did not hinder her attention in watching over the education of her children, in which God gave her great occasion of merit and suffering, particularly in Austin who was born in November, 354. Patricius died about 371. Austin, who was then seventeen, still continued his studies at Carthage, where in 373 he was seduced by the Manichees and drawn into that heresy. Monica grieved for his spiritual death. She engaged learned prelates to speak to him. Austin was twenty-nine years old when he determined to go to Rome with a view to teach rhetoric. She endeavoured to divert him from such a design, fearing it might delay his conversion; and followed him to the sea-side resolving either to bring him back or to bear him company into Italy. But while she passed the night in a chapel of St. Cyprian in the neighbourhood he secretly set out. Next morning, coming to the sea-side and finding him gone, she was seized with grief.

Upon his arrival at Rome he fell dangerously sick; and he attributes his recovery to the prayers of his mother. From Rome he went to Milan in 384, and being convinced by St. Ambrose of the errors of his sect, renounced that heresy. Monica followed him. Finding him at Milan she redoubled her prayers to obtain his thorough conversion. She respected St. Ambrose as the spiritual physician of his soul and had the joy to see St. Austin perfectly converted in August 386.

St. Austin was baptized at Easter in 387 with some of his friends. St. Monica took as much care of them all as if they had been her children. They all set out together for Africa, but lost Monica on the road, who fell sick at Ostia, where they were about to embark. Conversing there with her son Austin, she said to him 'The only thing for which I desired to live was that I might see you a Catholic. God has done much more, in that I see you now entirely devoted to his service. What further business have I then here?' On the ninth day of her illness in the year 387 she died. Her body was translated from Ostia to Rome in 1430 and remains there in the church of St. Austin.

LUDOVICUS RKX

PLATE 51. ST. LOUIS, 25 AUGUST, BUTLER, *LIVES OF THE SAINTS*, TWO-VOLUME ILLUSTRATED 19TH-CENTURY EDITION.

28 AUGUST

St. Augustine

BISHOP AND DOCTOR OF THE CHURCH
A.D. 430

Augustine was born on the 13th of November, 354, at Tagaste a small town of Numidia in Africa, not far from Hippo. His father was an idolater but by the care of his pious mother he was instructed in the Christian religion. Our saint had the misfortune to fall in his youth into vice and spiritual miseries, of which he himself has drawn a portrait in his *Confessions*. Austin went to Carthage towards the end of the year 370 and soon after fell into the sect of the Manichees, in which he continued between eight and nine years. He opened a school of rhetoric and began to dislike the stories related by the Manichees concerning the system of the world, but not knowing where to find any thing better, determined to remain content till he should fall upon something that should appear more satisfactory. He resolved to go to Rome, and when deputies were sent from Milan requiring some able master of rhetoric, made suit to be the man.

At Milan St. Ambrose gave him particular marks of respect and Austin frequently attended his sermons. In the search of truth he was still perplexed about the origin of evil and found great difficulty in conceiving God to be a pure spirit. He received great light by reading the works of Plato, but finding nothing in them about man's redemption, he betook himself to read the New Testament, especially the writings of St. Paul.

The conversion of St. Austin happened in the year 386 and he was baptized by St. Ambrose in 387. Freed from all anxiety concerning his past life he resolved to return into Africa and landed at Carthage about September 388. He retired to his house in the country with certain devout friends. The religious Order of the hermits of St. Austin dates its foundation from this epoch. When he was ordained priest and removed to Hippo he founded there a new monastery. Knowing that instruction was the principal duty of the pastoral charge he never interrupted the course of his sermons, and we have near four hundred extant. He was consecrated bishop in 395.

He wrote his *Confessions* about the year 397; and when Rome was plundered by Alaric the Goth in 410, and the Pagans renewed their blasphemies against the Christian religion, St. Austin began his great work of *The City of God*, though he only finished it in 426. The holy doctor set himself to oppose heresy by his words and writings. To the chief errors of the Pelagian heresy regarding original sin and divine grace he maintained the contrary truths of the Catholic faith in two books *On The Predestination of the Saints* and *On the Gift of Perseverance*. He died on the 28th of August, 430. This saint was not only the oracle of his own times, but of the principal of the Latin fathers that came after him.

31 AUGUST

St. Aidan

BISHOP OF LINDISFARNE
A.D. 651

When King Oswald desired the bishops of Scotland to send him a person to preach the faith to his Anglo-Saxon pagan subjects, and plant the church among them, the first person who came

PLATE 52. ST. AUGUSTINE OF HIPPO, 28 AUGUST. BRITISH LIBRARY, KINGS MS 9, F. 47V.

was of a rough temper, and being soon forced to return home, he laid the fault on the indocile dispositions of the English. Hereupon the Scottish clergy called a synod to deliberate what was best to be done. Aidan, who was present, told the prelate that the fault lay rather on him who had been too harsh and severe to an ignorant people, who ought first to be fed with the milk of milder doctrine, till they should be able to digest more solid food. At this discourse the whole assembly turned their eyes upon him as one endued with prudence and he was appointed to the arduous mission.

Aidan was a native of Ireland and a monk of the great monastery which his countryman St. Columba had founded. He was most graciously received by King Oswald, who bestowed on him for his episcopal seat the isle of Lindisfarne. Of his humility and piety Bede gives an edifying account. By his actions he showed that he neither sought nor loved the good things of this world; the presents which were made him by the king, or by other rich men, he distributed among the poor, or expended in redeeming captives. He rarely would go to the king's table, and never without taking with him one or two of his clergy, and always after a short repast made haste away to read or pray in the church, or in his cell. From his example even the laity took the custom of fasting till none, that is, till three in the afternoon, on all Wednesdays and Fridays, except during the fifty days of the Easter time.

Aidan fixed his see at Lindisfarne, and founded a monastery there in the year of our Lord 635, the hundred and eighty-eighth after the coming of the English Saxons into Britain, the thirty-ninth after the arrival of St. Augustine, and the second of the reign of King Oswald. From this monastery all the churches of the northern part of the kingdom of the Northumbers, from the Tyne to the Firth of Edinburgh, had their beginning, as had some also of those who inhabited the southern part of the same kingdom from the Tyne to the Humber. The see of York had been vacant thirty years, ever since St. Paulinus left it; so that Aidan governed all the churches of the Northumbers for seventeen years, till his happy death, which happened on the 31st of August, in 651, in the royal villa, Bebbord. He was first buried in the cemetery in Lindisfarne; but when the new church of St. Peter was built there, his body was translated into it and deposited on the right hand of the altar.

1 SEPTEMBER

St. Giles
ABBOT
ABOUT THE END OF THE SEVENTH CENTURY

This saint, whose name has been held in great veneration for several ages in France and England, is said to have been an Athenian by birth, and of noble extraction. His extraordinary piety and learning drew the admiration of the world in such a manner that it was impossible for him to enjoy in his own country that obscurity and retirement which was the chief object of his desires on earth. Therefore, leaving his own country, he sailed to France and chose a hermitage, first in the open deserts near the mouth of the river Rhône, afterwards nigh the river Gard, and lastly in a forest in the diocese of Nîmes.

He passed many years in this close solitude, using no other subsistence than wild herbs or roots, and water, conversing only with God, and living rather like an angel than a man, so perfectly was he disengaged from earthly cares. His historian relates that he was for some time nourished with the milk of a hind in the forest, and that a certain prince discovered him in hunting in those woods, by pursuing the chase of that hind to his hermitage, where the beast had sought for shelter at his feet.

The reputation of the sanctity of his holy hermit was much increased by many miracles which he wrought, and which rendered his name famous throughout all of France. Some, by mistake, have confused this saint with one Giles, whom St. Caesarius made abbot of a monastery near the walls of Arles and whom he sent to Rome in 514, to Pope Symmachus, to obtain of him a confirmation of the privileges of the church of Arles. But the Bollandists prove very well in a long learned dissertation, that the great St. Giles lived only in the end of the seventh and beginning of the eight century, not in the sixth.

St. Giles was highly esteemed by the French king; but could not be prevailed upon to forsake his solitude. He, however, admitted several disciples, and settled excellent discipline in the monastery of which he was the founder, and which, in succeeding ages, became a flourishing abbey of the Benedictine Order, though it has been long since converted into a collegiate church of canons. A considerable town was built about it, called St. Giles, which was famous in the wars of the Albigenses.

PLATE 53. ST. GILES, 1 SEPTEMBER. BRITISH LIBRARY, ADD. MS 29704, F. 138.

3 SEPTEMBER (12 MARCH)

St. Gregory the Great

POPE

A.D. 604

St. Gregory, from his illustrious actions surnamed the Great, was born at Rome about the year 540. Gordianus, his father, enjoyed the dignity of a senator. Our saint was only thirty-four years old when in 574 he was made praetor, or chief magistrate, of Rome. After the death of his father he built and endowed six monasteries in Sicily, and founded a seventh in his own house in Rome, the monastery of St Andrew. The first abbot was Hilarion, the second Valentinus, under whom Gregory himself took the monastic habit in 575.

It was before his advancement to the see of Rome, or even to the government of his monastery, that he first projected the conversion of the English. Gregory happened one day to walk through the market and here taking notice that certain youths of fine features were exposed to sale, he inquired what countrymen they were and was answered that they came from Britain. He asked if the people of that country were Christians and was told they were still heathens. Not long after, Pope Pelagius II sent him to Constantinople in quality of Nuncio. He wrote in that city his thirty-five books of *Morals upon Job*. Pope Pelagius

recalled Gregory in 584 and made him his secretary. He still continued to govern his monastery.

Pope Pelagius dying of the great pestilence in 590, the clergy, senate and Roman people unanimously agreed to choose St. Gregory for their bishop, although he opposed his election with all his power. In the mean time the plague continued to rage at Rome and St. Gregory took occasion to exhort the people to repentance. He appointed a solemn litany or procession in seven companies who were to march from different churches, singing Kyrie Eleison as they went.

He was consecrated on the 3rd of September, 590. His zeal for the glory of God moved him to reform the church music. Preaching he regarded as the indispensable function of every pastor. His forty homilies on the Gospels show that he spoke in a plain style but with eloquence. This great pope always remembered that he was the common father of the poor. He was most liberal in redeeming captives taken by the Lombards. He showed great moderation to the schismatics of Istria and to the Jews. It is incredible how much he wrote.

This holy pope laboured many years under a great weakness of his breast and stomach. God called him to himself on the 12th of March in the year 604, about the sixty-fourth of his age. Both Greeks and Latins honour his name. The Council of Clif under Archbishop Cuthbert in 747 commanded his feast to be observed a holiday in all the monasteries in England, which the Council of Oxford in 1222 extended to the whole kingdom. this law subsisted till the change of religion.

PLATE 54. ST. GREGORY THE GREAT, 3 SEPTEMBER. BODLEIAN LIBRARY, MS. ADD. A 185, F. 28.

5 SEPTEMBER

St. Laurence Justinian

FIRST PATRIARCH OF VENICE

A.D. 1455

St. Laurence was born at Venice in 1380. In the nineteenth year of his age he addressed himself for advice to a learned priest called Marino Querini, his uncle by his mother's side and a canon in the austere congregation of St. George in Alga, established in a little isle which bears that name situate a mile from the city of Venice. The prudent director, understanding that he was inclined to a religious state, advised him first to make a trial of his strength by inuring himself to the habitual practice of austerities. Laurence readily obeyed. The ardour of his resolution showed in the extreme severity with which he treated his body and the continual application of his mind to religion. His mother endeavoured to divert him and contrived an honourable match to be made him. The saint fled secretly to the monastery of St. George and was admitted to the religious habit.

St. Laurence was promoted to the priesthood and, much against his inclination, was chosen general of his Order, which he governed with singular prudence. He reformed its discipline in such a manner as to be afterwards regarded as its founder. He would receive very few into his Order, and these thoroughly tried. The saint never ceased to preach to the magistrates and senators in times of war and all public calamities, that, to obtain the divine mercy, they ought to become sensible that they were nothing.

Pope Eugenius IV being acquainted with the virtue of our saint, obliged him to quit his cloister and nominated him to the see of Venice in 1433. The holy man employed all manner of entreaties to prevent his elevation, but to no effect. Such was his aversion to pomp and show that he took possession of his church so privately that his own friends knew nothing till the ceremony was over. Though he was bishop of so distinguished a see, his household consisted only of five persons; he had no plate, making use only of earthen ware; he lay on a scanty straw bed and wore no clothes but his ordinary purple cassock. He founded fifteen religious houses and a great number of churches, and he increased the number of parishes in Venice from twenty to thirty. He gave alms more willingly in bread and clothes than in money, which might be ill spent. He employed pious matrons to find out and relieve the bashful poor.

Eugenius's successor, Nicholas V, in 1451 transferred the patriarchal dignity to the see of Venice, and the installation of the new patriarch was celebrated with great joy by the whole city. St. Laurence, after this exaltation, considered himself bound by a new tie in labouring for the souls committed to his care. He was seventy-four when he wrote his last work entitled *The Degrees of Perfection*. He calmly expired on the 8th of January, 1455. His festival is kept on the day he was consecrated bishop.

7 SEPTEMBER

St. Cloud

A.D. 560

St. Cloud was son of Clodomir, King of Orleans, the eldest son of St. Clotilda, and was born in 522. He was scarce three years old when his father was killed in Burgundy, but his grandmother brought him and his two brothers up at Paris and loved them extremely. Their ambitious uncles divided the kingdom of Orleans betwixt them and stabbed with their own hands the two elder of their nephews. Cloud by a special providence, was saved from the massacre, and cut off his hair with his own hands, by that ceremony renouncing the world and devoting himself entirely to a monastic state. He had many opportunities of recovering his father's kingdom, but young as he was he saw that all that appears most dazzling in worldly greatness is no better than smoke, and that a Christian gains infinitely more by losing then by possessing it. This victory over himself the prince gained, and constantly maintained by humility, patience, assiduous prayer and holy contemplation. By this means he enjoyed in a little cell a peace which was never interrupted by scenes of ambition or vanity.

After some time he removed from his first abode to put himself under the discipline of St. Severinus, a holy recluse who lived near Paris, from whose hands he received the monastic habit. Under this experienced master, the fervent novice made great progress in Christian perfection; but the neighbourhood of Paris being a trouble to him who desired nothing so much as to live unknown to the world, he withdrew secretly to Provence, where he passed several years.

Seeing he gained nothing by the remoteness of his solitude, after his hermitage was once made public by many resorting to him, he at length returned to Paris and was received with the greatest joy imaginable. At the earnest request of the people he was ordained priest by Eusebius, Bishop of Paris, in 551, and served that church some time. He afterwards retired to Nogent, on the Seine, now called St. Cloud, two leagues below Paris, where he built a monastery dependent on the church at Paris. In this monastery he assembled many pious men, who fled out of the world for fear of losing their souls in it. St. Cloud was regarded by them as their superior. All his inheritance he bestowed on churches, or distributed among the poor; the village of Nogent he settled on the see of Paris, as is mentioned in the letters patent by which this place was erected into a duchy and peerage.

St. Cloud was indefatigable in instructing the people of the neighbouring country and piously ended his days at Nogent about the year 560.

8 SEPTEMBER

The Nativity of the Blessed Virgin

The birth of the Blessed Virgin Mary announced joy and the near approach of salvation to the lost world: therefore is this festival celebrated by the church with praise and thanksgiving. Mary was brought forth into the world, not like other children of Adam, infected with the contagion of sin, but pure, holy and glorious. She is both a mother and a spotless virgin. This is the prerogative of Mary alone. The ancient prophets spoke of it as the distinguishing mark of the Mother of the Messiah. 'The Lord himself shall give you a sign,' said Isaias: 'Behold, a Virgin shall conceive, and bear a son, and his name shall be called Emmanuel.' The title of virgin must here mean one who remained such when a mother; for this circumstance is mentioned as a stupendous miracle.

The perpetual virginity of the Mother of God has been denied by several heretics. Ebion and Cerinthus had the insolence to advance that she had other children before Jesus: but this impious error is condemned by all who receive the holy Gospels. In the fourth age Elvidius and soon after him Jovinian, pretended that she had other children after Christ. Against these errors the Catholic church has always maintained that she was a Virgin before, in and after his birth.

To study the lessons in the life of Mary, to praise God for the graces which he had conferred on her, and to recommend our necessities to so powerful an advocate, we celebrate festivals in her honour. This of her nativity has been kept in the church with great solemnity above a thousand years. The Roman Order mentions the homilies and litanies which were appointed by Pope Sergius in 688 to be read upon it. The Greeks, the Copths in Egypt, and the other Christian churches in the East keep this feast.

The festival of the Holy Name of the Virgin Mary, on the Sunday within the octave of her nativity, was appointed by Pope Innocent XI. What gave occasion to the institution of this feast was a solemn thanksgiving for the relief of Vienna, when it was besieged by the Turks, in 1683.

10 SEPTEMBER

St. Nicholas
OF TOLENTINO
A.D. 1306

This saint received his surname from the town which was his residence for the most considerable part of his life, and in which he died. He was a native of St. Angelo, a town near Fermo, in the Marca of Ancona, and was born about the year 1245. His parents were a mean condition in the world, and he was reputed the fruit of their prayers and a pilgrimage to the shrine of St. Nicholas of Bari, in which his mother, who was then stricken in years, had earnestly begged of God a son who should faithfully serve him. At his baptism he received the name of his patron.

He was yet a young student when for his extraordinary merit he was preferred to a canonry in our saviour's church. This situation was extremely agreeable to his inclination, as by it he was always employed in the divine service. But he aspired to a state which would allow him to consecrate his whole time and thoughts directly to God, without interruptions or avocations. Whilst he was in this dispoition, a sermon preached by an Augustine friar on the vanity of the world, determined him absolutely to quit the world and to embrace the order of that holy preacher. This he executed without loss of time, entering himself a religious man in the convent of that Order of Tolentino, a small town in the ecclesiastical state. He made his profession before he had completed the eighteenth year of his age.

He was sent successively to several convents of his Order; in that of Cingole he was ordained priest by the Bishop of Osimo. From which time, if he seemed an angel in his other actions, he appeared like a seraph at the altar. Devout persons strove every day to assist at his mass, as at a sacrifice offered by the hands of a saint.

The last thirty years of his life, he resided at Tolentino. He preached almost every day, and his sermons were also signalized by remarkable conversions. His exhortations, whether in the confessional or in giving catechism, were always such as reached to the heart and left lasting impressions on those that heard him. What time could be spared from these charitable functions he spent in prayer and contemplation. He was favoured with visions and wrought several miraculous cures. For the exercise of his virtue he was long afflicted with divers painful distempers. His death happened on the 10th of September, in 1306.

13 SEPTEMBER (27 JANUARY)

St. John Chrysostom
FATHER OF THE CHURCH
A.D. 407

This doctor, on account of his eloquence, obtained soon after his death the surname of Chrysostom or Golden Mouth. About the year 344 Antioch was ennobled by his birth. His mother Anthusa provided her son the ablest masters in every branch of literature. John studied under the most famous orator of that age and he for some time pleaded at the bar. In that employment he was drawn into the diversions of the world, when God opened his eyes. He determined to carry his resolution of renouncing the world into execution. He fasted every day and spent the great part of his time in prayer and meditation on the holy scriptures.

St. Meletius, Bishop of Antioch, called the ascetic to the service of the church, and ordained him reader. Not long after, hearing that the bishops of the province deliberated to raise him to the episcopal dignity, he withdrew and lay hid till the vacant sees were filled. John, being then twenty-six, wrote six incomparable books *Of the Priesthood*. Four years after, in 374, he retired into the mountains near Antioch among certain anchorets. St. Chrysostom passed four years under the conduct of a Syrian monk, and afterwards two years in a cave as a hermit. The dampness of this abode brought on him a dangerous distemper and he was obliged to return into the city. He was ordained in 386 and had been twelve years priest when

PLATE 55. NATIVITY OF THE BLESSED VIRGIN MARY. 8 SEPTEMBER. BUTLER, *LIVES OF THE SAINTS*, TWO-VOLUME ILLUSTRATED 19TH-CENTURY EDITION.

the Archbishop of Constantinople dying, the Emperor Arcadius resolved to procure the election of our saint to the patriarchate of that city. John was consecrated in 398. He erected numerous hospitals, took in hand the reformation of his clergy, and converted idolaters and heretics.

John preached a sermon against vanity of women, which was pretended by some to have been levelled at the empress. Knowing that Theophilus, Patriarch of Alexandria, was no friend to the saint, the empress sent to desire his presence at Constantinople in order to depose him. He obeyed the summons, landed in June 303 with several Egyptian bishops and got together a cabal of the saint's enemies, calling themselves the synod at the Oak. The saint held a legal council in the city and refused to appear before that at the Oak. The cabal proceeded to a sentence of deposition, and the emperor issued an order for his banishment.

He was conducted into Bithynia, but Cucusus was pitched upon for the place of his banishment, a poor town in Armenia. His impious enemies, seeing the whole Christian world defend him, procured an order from the emperor that he should be removed to Pytius near Colchis. Two officers were ordered to convey him thither, with a promise of promotion if by hard usage he should die in their hands. They often travelled amidst scorching heats. In the most violent rains they forced him out of doors. When they arrived at Comana Pontica, St. John was very sick and died on the 14th of September, 407.

16 SEPTEMBER

St. Ninian

BISHOP

A.D. 432

This saint, who became the apostle of the southern Picts, was son to a prince among the Cumbrian Britons, who inhabited Cumberland and Galloway. From his cradle it seemed his only delights were to visit churches, to discourse on heavenly things, and to be employed in exercises of devotion and piety. Whilst others take so much pains in their education to advance themselves in the world, our noble youth thought nothing difficult and no labour great that he might improve his soul in the practice of religion. With this view, he bid adieu to the world, and forsaking court, friends and country, undertook a long journey to Rome. In that city he spent many years, applying himself with his whole heart to the study of the sacred sciences.

In this race he ran, as it were, with the strides of a giant. A compassion for his native country, which had received the grace of faith more slowly and imperfectly than the southern provinces of Britain, engaged him at length to return home, to impart to his countrymen a share of that blessing in which their happiness consisted, and which was the sole end of their being. Those few had already received some tincture of the faith, he taught to set a due value on so great a treasure. He brought the idolaters of that province into the paths of eternal life, softened the fierce temper of Tudovald, King of the Picts, and built a church of stone at Whithern, now in Galloway; and as the northern Britons had never before seen any such building of stone, the town, according to Bede and Malmesbury, took from this edifice its name (importing a white house, in Latin, *candida casa*), since changed into Whithern. The saint fixed here his episcopal see, and dedicated the church in honour of St.

Martin, whose tomb he probably had devoutly visited in his journey through France.

He converted from idolatry the Cumbrians, and all the provinces of the southern Picts, as far as Mount Grampus. The church of Whithern became a seminary of apostolic men and many glorious saints. St. Ninian died on the 16th of September in 432. He was illustrious for many miracles, and his relics were kept with veneration, till the change of religion, in the church which bears his name at Whithern.

17 SEPTEMBER

St. Lambert

MARTYR, MISHOP OF MAESTRICHT AND PATRON OF LIÈGE

A.D. 709

St. Landebert, called in latter ages Lambert, was a native of Maestricht, and born of a noble and wealthy family, who had been Christians for many descents. His father caused him to be instructed in sacred learning, and recommended him to St Theodard to perfect his education. This holy bishop in 669 resolved to go to King Childeric II to obtain an order of that prince for the restitution of the possessions of his church which had been usurped by certain powerful persons; but was assassinated upon the road. St. Lambert was chosen to succeed him, with the consent of King Childeric.

Childeric, a debauched and cruel prince, was slain by a conspiracy of noblemen in 673. This revolution affected St. Lambert merely because he had been favoured by Childeric. He was expelled from his see and retired to the monastery of Stavelo with only two of his domestics; and during the seven years that he continued there, he obeyed the rule as strictly as the youngest novice could have done.

Whilst St. Lambert enjoyed the tranquility of retirement, he wept to see the greatest part of the churches of France laid waste. When Theodoric reascended the throne, Pepin of Herstal set himself to repair the evils, expelled the usurping bishops intruded into many sees, and, among many other exiled prelates, restored St. Lambert to the see of Maestricht. The holy pastor returned to his flock animated with redoubled fervour. Finding there still remained many pagans in Taxandria, a province in Brabant, he applied himself to convert them to the faith, softened their barbarous temper by his patience, regenerated them in the holy water of baptism, and destroyed many temples and idols. He frequently visited and conferred with St. Willibrord, the apostle of Friesland.

Pepin, who resided at his castle of Herstal near Liège, lived for some years in a scandalous adultery with a concubine, by whom he had Charles Martel. St. Lambert reproved the parties with so much earnestness that some say certain friends of the lady thence took occasion to conspire against his life. Others assign the following occasion of his death: two brothers by the violences and plunders of the church of Maestricht were become insupportable. At this certain relations of St. Lambert were so exasperated that they slew the two brothers. Dodo, a kinsman of the two young men, resolved to revenge their death upon the innocent bishop and attacked him with a body of armed men at Liège. The troop of enemies entering the house, put to the sword all they met, and one of them throwing a dart at the bishop, slew him. This unjust death happened on the 17th of September, 709.

PLATE 56. ST. JOHN CHRYSOSTOM, 13 SEPTEMBER. BUTLER, *LIVES OF THE SAINTS*, TWO-VOLUME ILLUSTRATED 19TH-CENTURY EDITION.

18 SEPTEMBER

St. Joseph
OF CUPERTINO
A.D. 1663

Joseph was born the 17th of June, 1603, at Cupertino, a small village between Brindisi and Otranto. He was bound apprentice to a shoemaker, which trade he applied himself to for some time. When he was seventeen, he presented himself to be received amongst the Conventual Franciscans, where he had two uncles to distinction in the Order. He was nevertheless refused because he had not made his studies. All he could obtain was to be received among the Capuchins in quality of lay brother; but after eight months he was dismissed as unequal to the duties of the Order. Far from being discouraged he persisted in his resolution of embracing a religious state. At length the Franciscans received him into their convent of Grotella near Cupertino. The saint having finished his novitiate was received as lay brother amongst the Oblates of the Third Order.

Joseph begged to go through a second novitiate. Being ordained priest in 1628, he celebrated his first mass with inexpressible sentiments of faith, love and respect. After having received the priesthood he passed five years without tasting bread or wine, during which time he lived only on herbs and dried fruits. His fast in Lent was so rigorous that for seven years he took no nourishment but on Thursdays and Sundays.

A report being spread that he had frequent raptures and that many miracles were wrought by him, the people followed him in crowds as he was travelling through the province of Bari. A certain vicar general was offended at it and carried his complaints to the inquisitors at Naples. Joseph was ordered to appear, but declared innocent and dismissed. The inquisitor sent him to Rome to his general, who received him with harshness and ordered him to retire to the convent of Assisi. He arrived at Assisi in 1639 and remained there thirteen years. At first he suffered many trials. His superior called him a hypocrite and treated him with great rigour. On the other hand God seemed to have abandoned him, which cast him into so deep a melancholy that he scarce dare lift his eyes. His general being informed of his situation, called him to Rome, and having kept him there three weeks, he sent him back to Assisi. The saint, on his way to Rome, experienced a return of those consolations which had been withdrawn from him.

His miracles were not less remarkable than the other favours he received from God. Many sick owed their recovery to his prayers. The saint, falling sick of a fever at Osimo, the 10th of August, 1663, foretold that his last hour was near at hand. He died the 18th of September, 1663, at the age of sixty years.

21 SEPTEMBER

St. Matthew
APOSTLE AND EVANGELIST
FIRST CENTURY

Matthew seems to have been a Galilean by birth, and was by profession a publican, or gatherer of taxes for the Romans.

Among the Jews these publicans were more infamous and odious because this nation looked upon them as conspiring with the Romans to entail slavery upon their countrymen. Hence the Jews universally abhorred them, regarded their estates as the fortunes of thieves, banished them from all religious worship and shunned them in all affairs of civil society and commerce. It is certain that St. Matthew was a Jew, though a publican. His office is said to have particularly consisted in gathering customs of commodities that came by the lake Genasareth, and a toll which passengers paid that came by water.

Jesus having lately cured a famous paralytic, walked on the banks of the lake. Here he espied Matthew sitting in his custom-house, whom he called to come and follow him. The man was rich, enjoyed a very lucrative post, and perfectly understood what an exchange he made of wealth for poverty. But he left all his interests and relations to become our Lord's disciple. St. Matthew, upon his conversion, to show that he was not discontented at his change, but looked upon it as his greatest happiness, entertained our Lord and his disciples at a great dinner in his house whither he invited his friends, doubtless hoping that by our Saviour's divine conversation they also might be converted. The Pharisees carped at this conduct of Christ, in eating with publicans and sinners. Our divine Saviour answered their malicious secret suggestions that he came for the sick, not for the sound and healthy, and he put them in mind that God prefers acts of mercy and charity, especially in reclaiming sinners before ritual observances.

The vocation of St. Matthew happened in the second year of the public ministry of Christ, who soon after forming the college of his apostles, adopted him into that holy family. Eusebius and St. Epiphanius tell us that after our Lord's Ascension St Matthew preached several years in Judaea and the neighbouring countries until the dispersion of the apostles; and that a little before it he wrote his gospel, or short history of our blessed redeemer, at the entreaty of the Jewish converts. That he compiled it before the dispersion appears, not only because it was written before the other gospels, but also because St. Bartholomew took a copy of it with him into India, and left it there.

St. Matthew, after having made a great harvest of souls in Judaea, went to preach the faith to the barbarous nations of the East. He was a person much devoted to heavenly contemplation and led an austere life. St. Ambrose says that God opened to him the country of the Persians. Rufinus and Scorates tell us that he carried the gospel into Ethiopia, meaning probably the eastern and southern parts of Asia. St. Paulinus mentions that he ended his course in Parthia. His relics were long ago brought into the West.

22 SEPTEMBER

St. Maurice
AND HIS COMPANIONS, MARTYRS
A.D. 226

The Thebean legion was one of those which were sent by Diocletian out of the east to compose his army for his expedition into Gaul. Maximiam, in crossing the Alps, made a halt with his army that the soldiers might repose themselves. They were then arrived at Octodurum, a city on the Rhône above the lake of Geneva. Here Maximiam issued an order that the whole

PLATE 57. ST. MATTHEW, 21 SEPTEMBER. BUTLER, *LIVES OF THE SAINTS,* **TWO-VOLUME ILLUSTRATED 19TH-CENTURY EDITION.**

army should join in offering sacrifices to the gods for the success of their expedition. The Thebean legion hereupon withdrew itself and encamped near Agaunum, now called St. Maurice, three leagues from Octodurum. The emperor sent them repeated orders to return to the camp and join in the sacrifices; and, upon their constant and unanimous refusal, he commanded them to be decimated. Thus every tenth man was put to death, according as the lot fell; the rest exhorting one another all the while to perseverance.

After the first decimation a second was commanded, unless the soldiers obeyed the orders given; but they cried out that they would rather suffer all extremities than do any thing contrary to their religion. They were principally encouraged by three of their officers, Maurice, Exuperius and Candidus.

The emperor sent fresh threats that if they persisted in their disobedience not a man among them should escape death. The legion answered him by a dutiful remonstrance, the substance of which was as follows: 'We are your soldiers, but are servants of the true God. We owe you military service and obedience; but we cannot renounce Him who is our Creator and Master. You command us to punish the Christians: behold, we are all such. We have arms in our hands, but we do not resist, because we had rather die innocent than live by any sin.'

This legion consisted of about six thousand six hundred men. Maximian commanded his whole army to surround them and cut them to pieces. They made no resistance, but dropping their arms, suffered themseles to be butchered like innocent sheep The ground was covered with their bodies, and streams of blood flowed on every side.

These martyrs were styled by Fortunatus 'the Happy Legion'. Their festival is mentioned on this day in the Martyrologies of St. Jerome, Bede, and others.

22 SEPTEMBER (18 SEPTEMBER)

St. Thomas

OF VILLANOVA, ARCHBISHOP OF VALENCIA
A.D. 1555

St. Thomas was born at Fuenlana in Castile in 1488; but received his surname from Villanova de los Infantes, a town where he had his education. His parents were also originally of Villanova. At the age of fifteen he was sent to the university of Alcala. After eleven years he was made professor of philosophy in that city, being twenty-six years old. His father had built him a house against his return home; but this the saint converted into a hospital. After he had taught two years at Alcala he was invited to the same employment at Salamanca, where he taught moral philosophy two years. After the most mature deliberation he determined to enter himself among the Hermits of St. Augustine. He took the habit in a house of that institute at Salamanca in 1518. He was promoted to priestly orders in 1520, employed in preaching, and taught a course of divinity in the school of the Augustinians. He was afterwards prior at Salamanca, Burgos and Valladolid, was twice provincial of Andalusia, and once of Castile.

George, uncle to the emperor, resigning some time after the archbishopric of Valencia, ordered his secretary to draw up a placit, or letter of recommendation for Thomas to sign in favour of a certain religious man. Finding that the secretary had put down the name of F. Thomas of Villanova, he asked the reason. The secretary answered that he thought he had heard his name but would rectify the mistake. 'By no means,' said the emperor, 'this has happened by a particular providence of God.'

PLATE 58. ST. MAURICE, 22 SEPTEMBER. BRITISH LIBRARY, ADD. MS 18851, F. 461.

So he signed the placit for Thomas. Pope Paul II sent the bull for his consecration and that ceremony was performed at Valladolid. The saint set out very early next morning for Valencia on foot. The chapter made him a present of four thousand ducats towards furnishing his house; but he immediately sent the money to the hospital. When pressed to put himself into a dress suitable to his dignity, his answer was that he had made a vow of poverty. There came to his door every day about five hundred poor people and each of them received an alms. When, in 1550, a pirate had plundered a town in his diocese the archbishop immediately sent four thousand ducats and cloth worth much more to furnish the inhabitants with necessaries and to ransom the captives.

He was taken ill of a quinsy, on the 29th of August. Having commanded all the money in his possession to be distributed among the poor, he ordered his goods to be given to the rector of his college, except the bed on which he lay. He gave this bed to the jailer for the use of prisoners, but borrowed it of him till he should expire. On the 8th of September he rendered his soul into the hands of God in the sixty-seventh year of his age, of our Lord 1555.

23 SEPTEMBER

St. Thecla

VIRGIN AND MARTYR
FIRST CENTURY

St. Thecla, who is styled by the Greeks the protomartyr of her sex, was a native of Isauria, or Lycaonia. St. Ambrose and other fathers mention that St. Paul by his preaching converted her to the faith at Iconium, probably about the year 45, and that his discourses kindled in her breast of love of virginity. Upon this change she broke off a treaty of marriage which had been set on foot by her parents with a rich, comely and amiable young nobleman.

St. Chrysostom lets us know that her parents, perceiving an alteration in her conduct, without being acquainted with the motive, plied her with the strongest arguments, mixed with commands, threats and reprimands, to engage her to finish the affair of her marriage to their satisfaction. Her servants entreated her with tears, her friends and neighbours exhorted her, and the authority and threats of the civil magistrate were employed to bring her to the desired compliance.

The young nobleman to whom she was engaged thought of nothing but how to be revenged of her, from whom he pretended he had received a grievous affront. He delivered her into the hands of the magistrates and urged such articles against her that she was condemned to be torn in pieces by wild beasts. Nevertheless her resolution was invincible. She was exposed naked in the amphitheatre in the midst of lions, pards and tigers. But the lions on a sudden forgetting their natural ferocity, walked gently up to the holy virgin, and laying themselves at her feet, licked them. At length they meekly retired like lambs.

She was at another time delivered from the power of fire, and preserved without hurt in the midst of flames. A very ancient Martyrology which bears the name of St. Jerome mentions that Rome was the place where God extinguished the flames to preserve the life of this holy virgin. She attended St. Paul in several of his apostolical journeys. Her sufferings justly purch-

ased her the title of martyr, though Bede in his Martyrology tells us that she died in peace. The latter part of her life she spent in devout retirement in Isauria, where she died, and was buried at Seleucia, the metropolis of that country.

[Editorial note: the cult of St. Thecla was suppressed in the Roman Church in 1969.]

24 SEPTEMBER

St. Gerard

BISHOP OF CHONAD, MARTYR
A.D. 1046

St. Gerard, the apostle of a large district in Hungary, was a Venetian, and born about the beginning of the eleventh century. He renounced early the enjoyments of the world, forsaking family and estate to consecrate himself to the service of God in a monastery.

After some years, with the leave of his superiors, he undertook a pilgrimage to the holy sepulchre at Jerusalem. Passing through Hungary, he became known to St. Stephen who with great earnestness persuaded him that God had only inspired him with the design of that pilgrimage that he might assist the souls in that country. Gerard, however, would by no means consent to stay at court, but built a little hermitage at Beel, where he passed seven years with one companion in constant fasting and prayer. The king drew Gerard out of his solitude and the saint preached the gospel with wonderful success. Not long after the good prince nominated him to the see of Chonad, a city eight leagues from Temeswar. Two-thirds of the city were idolaters; yet the saint in less than a year made them all Christians. His labours were crowned with almost equal success in all others parts of the diocese.

St. Stephen seconded the zeal of the good bishop as long as he lived. But that prince's nephew and successor, Peter, a debauched and cruel prince, declared himself the persecutor of our saint, and was expelled by his own subjects in 1042, and Abas a nobleman of a savage disposition, was placed on the throne. St. Stephen had established a custom that the crown should be presented to the king by some bishop. Abas gave notice to St. Gerard to come to court to perform that ceremony. The saint refused. Two years after, the very persons who had placed Abas on the throne turned against him and cut off his head on the scaffold. Peter was recalled; but two years after banished a second time. The crown was then offered to Andrew, cousin to St Stephen, upon condition that he should restore idolatry and extirpate the Christian religion. Hereupon Gerard and three other bishops set out to divert the new king from this sacrilegious engagement.

When the four bishops were going to cross the Danube, they were set upon by a party of soldiers under the command of Duke Vatha, the most obstinate patron of idolatry. They attacked St. Gerard first with a shower of stones, and, exasperated at his meekness, overturned his chariot and dragged him on the ground. Whilst in their hands, the saint raised himself on his knees, and prayed, with the protomartyr St. Stephen, 'Lord, lay not this to their charge; for they known not what they do.' He had scarce spoke these words when he was run through the body with a lance and expired. St. Gerard's martyrdom happened on the 24th of September, 1046.

PLATE 59. ST. COSMAS AND ST. DAMIAN, 26 SEPTEMBER. BRITISH
LIBRARY, ADD. MS 18851, F. 462.

26 SEPTEMBER

SS. Cosmas and Damian
MARTYRS
ABOUT THE YEAR 303

Saints Cosmas and Damian were brothers and born in Arabia,
but studied the sciences in Syria and became eminent for their
skill in physic. Being Christians, and full of that holy temper of
charity in which the spirit of our divine religion consists, they
practised their profession with great application and wonderful
success; but never took any gratification or fee.

They lived at Aegae or Egaea in Cilicia, and were remarkable both for the love and respect which the people bore them on
account of the good offices which they received from their
charity, and for their zeal for the Christian faith, which they
took every opportunity their profession gave them to propagate.

When the persecution of Diocletian began to rage, it was
impossible for persons of so distinguished a character to lie
concealed. They were therefore apprehended by the order of
Lysias, governor of Cilicia, and after various torments, were
beheaded for the faith. Their bodies were carried into Syria and
buried at Cyrus. Theodoret, who was bishop of that city in the
fifth century, mentions that their relics were then deposited in a
church there, which bore their names.

The Emperor Justinian, who began his reign in 527, out of a
religious regard for the treasure of these precious relics,
enlarged and strongly fortified this city of Cyrus, and finding a
ruinous church at Constantinople, built in honour of these
martyrs, as is said, in the reign of Theodosius the Younger,
raised a stately edifice in its room, as a monument of his
gratitude for the recovery of his health in a dangerous fit of
sickness, through their intercession, as Procopius relates.

27 SEPTEMBER

St. Vincent of Paul
FOUNDER OF THE LAZARITES, OR FATHERS OF
THE MISSION
A.D. 1660

Vincent was a native of Poui, a village in Gascony. His parents
occupied a small farm. His father was determined to procure
him an education and placed him under the care of the
Cordeliers or Franciscan friars at Acqs. In 1596 he went to
Toulouse where he was promoted to the priesthood in 1600,
having received the tonsure and minor orders before he left
Acqs. The saint went to Marseilles in 1605 to receive a legacy
left him by a friend. Intending to return to Marseilles he set out
in a boat from Marseilles but was met in the way by African
pirates. The Christians were soon obliged to surrender; the
Mahometans cut the captain in pieces, put the rest in chains and
sailed for Barbary. In Tunis Vincent was bought by a fisherman
who soon sold him again to an old physician. In 1606 he was
sold to a renegade Christian who came from Nice. Sincerely
repenting of his apostasy, he agreed with Vincent to make their
escape together. They crossed the Mediterranean in a small boat
and landed safe near Marseilles in 1607.

After a short stay in Rome Vincent returned to Paris where he
became preceptor to the children of Emmanuel de Gondy,
Count of Joigny. His lady, the countess entreated Vincent to
preach in the church of Folleville in 1617. He did so and such
crowds flocked to make general confessions that he was obliged
to call in the Jesuits to his assistance. The congregation of the
mission dates its first institution from this time. St. Vincent left
the house of the countess in 1617 and formed a little community
in the parish of Chatillon. The good countess gave him sixteen

PLATE 60. ST. VINCENT DE PAUL, 27 SEPTEMBER. BUTLER, *LIVES OF THE SAINTS*, TWO-VOLUME ILLUSTRATED 19TH-CENTURY EDITION.

thousand livres to found a perpetual mission among the common people. All things being agreed, St. Vincent took possession of this house in April, 1625. He drew up for it certain rules which were approved by Pope Urban VIII in 1632. In 1633 the canons of St. Victor gave this new institute the Priory of St. Lazarus, and from it the fathers were often called Lazarites. They are a congregation of secular priests who devote themselves to labour, the conversion of sinners and training up clergymen for the ministry.

St. Vincent established many other confraternities as that called Of Charity to attend all sick persons; and one called Of the Dames of the Cross, for the education of young girls. He directed the foundation of several great hospitals, as in Paris that of foundlings; at Marseïlles the stately hospital for the galley-slaves. He assisted King Lewis XIII at his death and was in the highest favour with the queen regent who nominated him a member of the young king's council and consulted him in all ecclesiastical affairs, which office he discharged ten years.

He calmly expired in his chair on the 27th of September, 1660 and was buried in the church of St. Lazarus in Paris.

28 SEPTEMBER

St. Wenceslas

DUKE OF BOHEMIA
A.D. 938

St. Wenceslas was son of Uratislas, Duke of Bohemia, and grandson of the blessed Ludmilla. His father was a valiant and good prince; but his mother was a pagan, not less cruel than haughty, nor less perfidious than impious. Ludmilla obtained that the education of Wenceslas might be entrusted to her, and in this task she was assisted by Paul, her chaplain. At a convenient age he was sent to a college at Budweis, above sixty miles from Prague.

He was yet young when his father dying, his mother Drahomira assumed the title of regent and seized on the government. She gave a free loose to her rage against the Christians (which she had concealed whilst her husband lived). Ludmilla, full of concern for the interest of religion, which she and her consort had established with so much difficulty, showed Wenceslas the necessity of taking the reins of the government into his own hands. The young duke obeyed, and the Bohemians testified their approbation of his conduct; but to prevent disputes between him and his younger brother, they divided the country between them.

Wenceslas directed all his views to the establishment of peace, justice and religion in his dominions, and by the advice of Ludmilla chose able and zealous Christian ministers. Drahomira never ceased to conjure up all the furies of hell against him. Looking upon Ludmilla as the first mover of all counsels in favour of the Christian religion, she laid a plot to take away her life. The assassins found her prostrate in prayer before the altar in her domestic chapel strangled her with her own veil. This complicated crime was very sensible to Wenceslas.

The severity with which the saint checked oppressions and certain other disorders in the nobility made some throw themselves in the faction of his unnatural mother, who concerted measures with her other son, Boleslas, to take him off. A son being born to Boleslas, that prince and his mother invited the good duke to favour them with his company at the

PLATE 61. ST. WENCESLAS, 28 SEPTEMBER. BRITISH LIBRARY, ADD. MS 18851, F. 463V.

rejoicings. St Wenceslas went without the least suspicion of treachery, and was received with all imaginable marks of kindness. This they did the better to cover their hellish design. The entertainment was splendid, but nothing could make the saint neglect his usual devotions. At midnight he went to offer his customary prayers in the church. Boleslas, at the instigation of Drahomira, followed him thither, and when his attendants had wounded him, he dispatched him with his own hand, running him through with a lance. The martyrdom of the holy duke happened on the 28th of September, in 938.

30 SEPTEMBER

St. Jerome
DOCTOR OF THE CHURCH
A.D. 420

St Jerome was born at Sdrigni, near Aquileia. His father took great care to have his son instructed at home, and afterwards sent him to Rome. St. Jerome had there for tutor the famous pagan grammarian Donatus. He became master of the Latin and Greek tongues and made such progress in oratory that he for some time pleaded at the bar; but he forgot the sentiments of piety which had been instilled into him in his infancy, and was full of worldly views. Being arrived at man's estate he resolved upon travelling and made a tour through Gaul. He arrived at Triers not long before the year 370 and it was in this city that his heart was converted to God.

St. Jerome shut himself up in the monastery at Aquileia for some time. Experience convinced him that neither his own country nor Rome were fit places for a life of solitude and he resolved to withdraw into some distant country. Being arrived at Antioch, St. Jerome made some stay in that city to attend the lectures of Apollinaris, then went into a desert between Syria and Arabia where he spent four years in studies. A great schism divided the church of Antioch. The monks in the desert warmly took part in this unhappy division and were for compelling St. Jerome to declare to which side he adhered. Teased by these importunities he left his wilderness and went to Antioch. A little before he left he wrote two letters to consult St. Damasus, who had been raised to the papal throne. St. Jerome received the order of priesthood before the end of 377, to which he only consented on condition that he should not be obliged to serve in the functions of his ministry. Soon after, he went into Palestine to perfect himself in the Hebrew tongue.

About the year 380 our saint went to Constantinople, there to

PLATE 62. ST. JEROME, 30 SEPTEMBER. BODLEIAN LIBRARY, MS LITURG. 401, F. 198V.

study the scriptures under St. Gregory Nazianen. Not long after, he was called to Rome where Pope Damusus detained St. Jerome and employed him as his secretary. Our holy doctor soon gained a universal esteem on account of his learning. He was charged with the conduct of many devout ladies, as SS Marcella, Paula and many others. After having stayed about three years at Rome, St. Jerome resolved to return into the east. He visited the chief monasteries of Egypt, after which he retired to Bethlehem. St. Paula, who had followed him, built for him a monastery. Nothing has rendered the name of St. Jerome so famous as his critical labours on the holy scriptures. Pope Damasus commissioned St. Jerome to revise and correct the Latin version of the gospels. He afterwards did the same with the rest of the New Testament. His new translation of the Old Testament, writ in Hebrew, was a more difficult undertaking. He died in the year 420, on the 30th of September.

2 OCTOBER

THE FEAST OF THE HOLY ANGEL-GUARDIANS

The providence of God vouchsafes to employ superior beings in the execution of his will in various dispensations towards other inferior creatures. It is clear, in the holy scriptures, that those blessed spirits which we call angels (as much as to say God's messenger) receive this very name from their office, in being employed by him in executing his commissions in our favour and defence.

That particular angels are appointed and commanded by God to watch over each particular person among his servants, that is all the just or such as are in the state of grace, is an article of the Catholic faith of which no ecclesiastical writer in any age ever entertained the least doubt. The psalmist assures us, 'He hath given his angels charge over thee, to keep thee in all thy ways.' So certain was the belief of a guardian angel being assigned to every one that when St. Peter was miraculously delivered out of prison, the disciples who, upon his coming to them, could not at first believe it to be him, said 'It is his angel.'

That St. Michael was the protector of the Jewish nation, or of the people of God, and that countries or collective bodies of man have their tutelar angels, is clear from holy scripture. The devils with implacable envy and malice, study to compass our eternal ruin. God is pleased to oppose to their efforts his good angels, by making them our defenders. The good angels, out of the same zeal with which they continue their war against these wicked spirits, come to our relief.

A second motive which exceedingly endears us to their protection is their compassion and charity for us. They consider that we are shortly to be their companions in eternal bliss. They see the miseries of sin into which we are fallen, the dangers which surround us, and the infinite evils under which we groan.

PLATE 63. GUARDIAN ANGEL, 2 OCTOBER. BRITISH LIBRARY, ADD. MS 15114, F. 48V.

PLATE 64. ST. FRANCIS, 4 OCTOBER. BUTLER, *LIVES OF THE SAINTS*, TWO-VOLUME ILLUSTRATED 19TH-CENTURY EDITION.

We must not only respect but gratefully and devoutly love and honour our tutelar spirit. He is a faithful guardian, a true friend, a watchful shepherd and a powerful protector. He invisibly performs for us the offices which that angel who led the Jews into the promised land did for them. 'In God,' says St. Bernard, 'let us affectionately love the angels.' We likewise ought to place a confidence in the protection of our good angel. To deserve his protection we must above all things fly sin. 'As smoke chases away bees, and stench doves, so the ordure of sin driveth away the angel, the keeper of life,' says St. Basil.

4 OCTOBER

St. Francis

OF ASSISI, FOUNDER OF THE FRIAR MINORS
A.D. 1226

The blessed St. Francis was born at Assisi in Umbria in 1181. His father was a merchant. Francis, whilst he yet lived in the world, was meek, patient, and liberal to the poor. He often visited hospitals, served the sick and kissed the ulcers of lepers.

One day, as he was praying in the church of St. Damian without Assisi, before a crucifix, he seemed to hear a voice coming from it which said three times, 'Francis, go and repair my house, which thou seest falling.' The saint seeing that the church was old, thought our Lord commanded him to repair it. He therefore took a horse-load of cloth out of his father's warehouse and sold it. The priest of St. Damian's would not take the money. His father insisted that Francis should either return home or renounce all his share in his inheritance. The son cheerfully went with his father before the bishop, stripped himself of all his clothes and renounced the world. The bishop covered him with his cloak. This happened in 1206.

Francis went out, singing the divine praises along the highways. For the building of St. Damian's he himself carried stones and saw that church put in good repair. He exhorted people to penance with such energy that his words pierced the hearts of his hearers. Many began to admire the virtue of this great servant of God and some desired to be his companions and disciples. The saint gave his habit to them on the 16th of August 1209, which is called the foundation of this Order.

In his rule, he exhorts his brethren to manual labour, but to receive for it things necessary for life, not money. He bids them not to be ashamed to beg alms and forbids them to preach any place without the bishop's licence. He carried his rule to Rome to obtain the pope's approbation and was ordained deacon. In less than three years his order was multiplied to sixty monasteries.

Ten years after the first institution of his Order, in 1219, St. Francis held the famous general chapter of Matts. Having journeyed to Palestine and Spain he returned in 1215, and Count Orlando of Catona bestowed on him a solitude on Mount Alverno where he built a convent and church for the Firar Minors. In 1224 St. Francis retired into a most secret place in Mount Alverno, and on the 15th of September he saw, as it were, the figure of a man crucified. After a secret conversation the vision disappearing, the marks of nails began to appear in his hands and feet. St. Francis endeavoured to conceal this singular favour of heaven from the eyes of men, but notwithstanding these precautions, these miraculous wounds were seen by

great multitudes after his death. During the two years he survived after this vision he was much afflicted with sickness. He yielded up his soul on the 4th of October, 1226.

5 OCTOBER (15 JANUARY)

St. Maurus

ABBOT
A.D. 584

Among the several noblemen who placed their sons under the care of St. Benedict, to be brought up in piety and learning, Equitius, one of that rank, left with him his son Maurus, then but twelve years old, in 522. The youth surpassed all his fellow monks in the discharge of monastic duties, and when he was grown up, St. Benedict made him his coadjutor in the government of Sublaco. Maurus, by his singleness of heart and profound humility, was a model of perfection to all the brethren, and was favoured by God with the gift of miracles. St. Placidus, a fellow monk, going one day to fetch water, fell into the lake and was carried the distance of a bow-shot from the bank. St. Benedict saw this in spirit in his cell, and bid Maurus run and draw him out. Maurus obeyed; walked upon the waters without perceiving it, and dragged out Placidus by the hair, without sinking in the least himself. He attributed the miracle to the prayers of St. Benedict, but the holy abbot to the obedience of the disciple. Soon after that holy patriarch had retired to Cassino, he called Maurus thither, in the year 528.

St. Maurus, coming to France in 543, founded the great abbey of Glanfeuil, now called St. Maur-sur-Loire, which he governed several years. In 581 he resigned the abbacy to Bertulf, and passed the remainder of his life in close solitude. After two years he fell sick of a fever, with a pain in his side; he received the sacraments lying on sackcloth before the altar of St. Martin, and in the same posture expired on the 15th of January, in the year 584. He was buried on the right side of the altar in the same church and is named in the ancient French litany composed by Alcuin. For fear of the Normans, in the ninth century his body was translated to several places; lastly, in 868 to St. Peter's des Fosses, than a Benedictine abbey, near Paris.

Our ancestors had a particular veneration for St. Maurus under the Norman kings, and the noble family of Seymour (from the French *Saint Maur*) borrow from his its name.

[Editorial note: modern scholars believe that the Maurus who saved St. Placidus and the Maurus who became abbot of Glanfeuil are not in fact the same man. The feast of St. Placidus, who is said to have been killed by pirates about the year 546, is celebrated on the same day.]

6 OCTOBER

St. Bruno

FOUNDER OF THE CARTHUSIAN MONKS
A.D. 1101

St. Bruno was born at Cologne about the year 1030. His parents placed him very young in the college of the clergy of St.

PLATE 65. ST. BRUNO, 6 SEPTEMBER. BUTLER, *LIVES OF THE SAINTS*, TWO-VOLUME ILLUSTRATED 19TH-CENTURY EDITION.

Cunibert's church, where he gave extraordinary proofs of his learning, insomuch that St. Anno, Bishop of Cologne, preferred him to a canonry in that church. He was yet young when he left Cologne and went to Rheims for his studies, where he excelled chiefly in philosophy and theology. The Archbishop of Rheims in 1056 made Bruno scholasticus, to which dignity belonged the direction of all the great schools of the diocese. He taught a considerable time in the church of Rheims. The Archbishop dying in 1067, Manasses by open simony got possession of that church and oppressed it. The pope's legate summoned Manasses to appear at a council in 1077. St. Bruno and two others accused him in this council. The usurper, exasperated against the three canons, caused their houses to be plundered and sold their prebends. The canons took refuge in the castle of the Count of Rouci till August 1078.

Before this time St. Bruno had concerted the project of his retreat; and when the church of Rheims was ready to choose him archbishop in place of Manasses, who had then been convicted and deposed, he resigned his benefice and persuaded some of his friends to accompany him into solitude. He seems first to have retired to Reciac, a fortified town in Champagne. After some time he went to Cologne, and some time after to Saisse-Fontaine in the diocese of Langres.

In this solitude he addressed himself for advice to St. Robert of Molesme, who exhorted him to apply to Hugh, Bishop of Grenoble, being informed that in the diocese there were woods, rocks and deserts most suitable to his desire of perfect solitude. St. Bruno and six companions arrived at Grenoble about midsummer, 1084. St. Hugh received them with open arms and assigned them Chartreuse for their retreat. Bruno and his companions immediately built an oratory there and very small cells. Such was the original Order of the Carthusians. Peter the Venerable writes of them, 'Their dress is meaner than that of other monks. They fast almost perpetually. Their constant occupation is praying, reading and manual labour, which consists chiefly in transcribing books.' This manner of life they follow without any written rule. St. Bruno had not governed this congregation six years when Pope Urban II sent him an order to repair to Rome that he might assist him in the government of the church. He set out in 1089. The pope had too great a value for such a friend to grant his request of returning to the Chartreuse but at length consented that he might retire. The saint found a convenient solitude in Squillaci, where he settled in 1090 with some new disciples whom he had gained in Rome. He resigned his soul to God on the 6th of October, 1101.

7 OCTOBER

St. Osith

ABOUT THE YEAR 870

St. Osith was born at Quarendon, and was daughter of Frewald, a Mercian prince, and niece to Editha, to whom belonged the town and manor of Ailesbury, where she was brought up with her pious aunt. Osith was married young to a king of the East Angles; but the same day obtained his consent to live always a virgin. That king confirming her in her religious purpose, bestowed on her the manor of Chick, in which she built a monastery. She had governed this house many years with great sanctity, when she was crowned with martyr-

dom in the inroads of Hinguar and Hubba, the barbarous Danish leaders, being beheaded for her constancy in her faith and virtue, about the year 870. For fear of Danish pirates, her body after some time was removed to Ailesbury, and remained there forty-six years; after which it was brought back to Chick, or Chich, in Essex, near Colchester, which place was for some time called St. Osithe's. A great abbey of regular canons was erected under her invocation, which continued to the dissolution famous for the relics and honoured with many miracles.

[Editorial note: St. Osith was the subject of many legends during the Middle Ages, including one story which told how she carried her own severed head, after it had been cut off, for a distance of three miles to the church where she was buried. In addition to her chief shrine at Chich, there was a secondary shrine at Aylesbury at which people continued to pray until 1502. It may well be that there were in fact two Osiths, one of Chich and another of Aylesbury, which were combined into a single figure.]

9 OCTOBER

St. Dionysius

(DENIS) OF PARIS, AND HIS COMPANIONS, MARTYRS
A.D. 272

Of all the Roman missionaries sent into Gaul St. Dionysius carried the faith the furthest into the country, fixing his see at Paris, and by him and his disciples the see of Chartres, Senlis and Meaux were erected. We are assured in the acts of the martyrdom of St. Dionysius that this zealous bishop built a church at Paris, and converted great numbers to the faith.

He seems to have suffered in the persecution of Valerian in 272, though some moderns defer his death to the beginning of the reign of Maximian Herculeus, who resided chiefly in Gaul from the year 286 to 292. The western Martyrologists inform us that after a long and cruel imprisonment he was beheaded for the faith together with Rusticus, a priest, and Eleutherius, a deacon. The Acts add that the bodies of the martyrs were thrown into the river Seine, but taken up and honourably interred by a Christian lady named Catalla not far from the place where they had been beheaded. The Christians soon after built a chapel over their tomb.

In 469, through the pious exhortations of St. Genevieve, a church was raised upon the ruins of this chapel, which was a place of great devotion, much restorted to by pilgrims. By a donation of Clotaire II it appears that here was then a religious community governed by an abbot. Dagobert, who died in 638, founded the great abbey in this place in which he was interred, and which has been for many ages the usual burial place of the French kings. Pepin and his son Charlemagne were principal benefactors to this monastery, which was magnificently rebuilt by Abbot Suger. The relics of SS. Dionysius, Rusticus and Eleutherius are kept here in three silver shrines. St. Dionysius of France is commonly called St. Denis, from the French Denys.

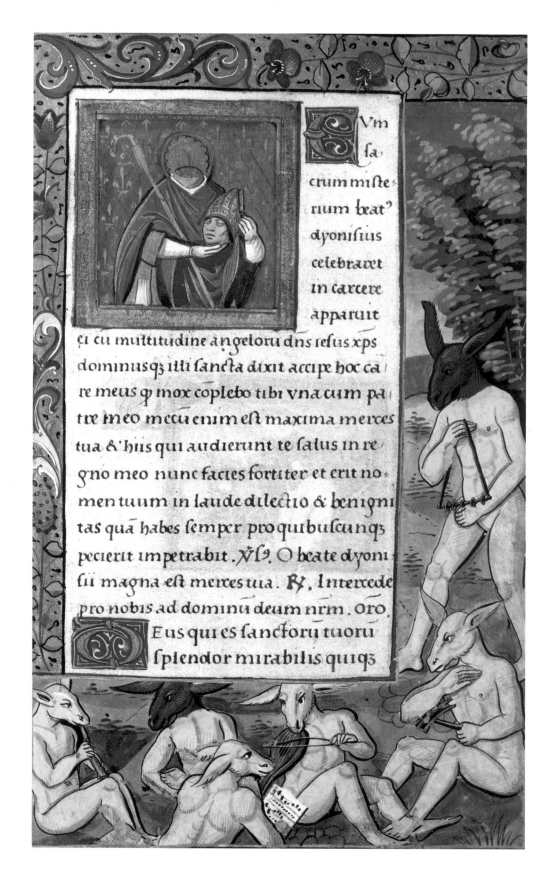

Vm fa-
crum mifte-
rium beat⁹
dyonifius
celebraret
in carcere
apparuit
ei cu multitudine angeloru dns iefus xps
dominusq; illi fancta dixit accipe hoc care meus qp mox coplebo tibi vna cum pa-
tre meo mecu enim eft maxima merces
tua & hiis qui audierunt te falus in re-
gno meo nunc facies fortiter et erit no-
men tuum in laude dilectio & benigni-
tas qua habes femper pro quibufcunq;
pecierit impetrabit. Vf9. O beate dyoni-
fii magna eft merces tua. Ry. Intercede
pro nobis ad dominu deum nrm. Oro.
Eus qui es fanctoru tuoru
fplendor mirabilis quiq;

PLATE 66. ST. DENIS OF PARIS, 9 OCTOBER. BODLEIAN LIBRARY, MS DOUCE 276, F. 124.

12 OCTOBER

St. Wilfrid

BISHOP OF YORK
A.D. 709

St. Wilfrid was born in Northumberland towards the year 634. At fourteen he was sent to Lindisfarne. A desire of improvement put him upon a project of travelling into France and Italy. At Lyons he was detained a whole year by St. Delphinus, archbishop of that city, who offered him his niece in marriage. But the saint continued steadfast in the resolution he had taken to devote himself to God. At Rome, the holy pope St. Martin gave him his blessing. After this Wilfrid left Rome, and returned to Lyons where he received the tonsure from St. Delphinus.

Alcfrid, son of King Oswi, being informed that Wilfrid had been instructed in the discipline of the Roman church, sent for him, and conjured him to instruct him and his people. This St. Wilfrid consented to and the prince gave him land at Rippon to found a monastery upon. Agilbert, Bishop of the West Saxons, said that a person of such merit ought to be promoted to a bishop and ordained him priest in 663. Alcfrid sent Wilfrid to France to receive consecration, but Wilfrid being absent a long time Oswi caused Chad to be ordained bishop. On his return to England Wilfrid retired to Rippon. St. Theodorus, Archbishop of Canterbury, found the election of St. Chad to have been irregular and put St. Wilfrid in possession of the see of York in 669. The monastic state was a principal object of St. Wilfrid's care; and this he settled among the Midland and Northern English.

King Egfrid had taken to wife St. Audrey, who preferring a religious life St. Wilfrid consented to give her the veil. This action provoked the king and a project was set on foot for dividing his bishopric. Wilfrid appealed to the pope and embarked for Rome. Being driven by contrary winds upon the coast of Friesland he converted and baptized many there. He arrived at Rome in 679. A synod decreed that in the British church one archbishop should ordain the other bishops; but that none of the bishops should presume to meddle with the rights of any other. When Wilfrid arrived in England he repaired to the kingdom of the South Saxons, where he resided in the peninsula of Selsey, till upon the death of Egfrid he was called back into Northumberland. After his restoration his vigilancy and zeal raised new storms against him and he retired to Mercia. Finding his enemies were soliciting a sentence of deposition against him he appealed a second time to Rome. Pope John VI honourably acquitted the saint and sent letters charging Archbishop Brithwald to call a synod to do him justice. His restitution was agreed to and Wilfrid took possession of the diocese of Hexham, but chiefly resided at Rippon. He died at Oundle on the 24th of April, 709. The 12th of October, the day of his translation, became his principal festival.

13 OCTOBER

St. Edward
KING AND CONFESSOR
A.D. 1066

This prince was son of King Ethelred II, by his second wife Emma, daughter to Richard I, and sister to Richard II, the third and fourth Dukes of Normandy. Though educated in the palace of the Duke of Normandy he was always an enemy to vanity, pleasure and pride. His character from his youth was the aggregate of all Christian and moral virtues.

With the joy of the whole kingdom he was anointed and crowned in Easter day in 1042, being about forty years old. Though he ascended the throne in the most difficult times of distraction and commotions, yet never was any reign more happy. The very Danes that were settled in England loved, respected and feared his name. The only war the saint ever undertook was to restore Malcolm, King of Scotland, to which a glorious victory immediately put an end. At home, Earl Godwin and some other ambitious spirits complained that he kept several Normans about his person. But the king brought them to reason or obliged them to leave his dominions without bloodshed.

Being placed upon the throne, he was entreated both by his nobility and people to take a royal consort. Earl Godwin, whose power and wealth seemed to raise him above the level of his fellow subjects, moved every engine to make the choice fall upon his daughter Edgitha, a lady totally unlike her father,

being most remarkably virtuous and abstemious. Edward hoped she would be easily engaged to become his wife upon condition always to live in holy virginity, it not being in his power otherwise to marry, he having consecrated himself to God by a vow of perpetual chastity. She readily assented so that, being joined together in holy wedlock, they always lived as brother and sister.

The laws framed by St. Edward were the fruit of his wisdom, and that of his counsellors. In them punishments were very mild; scarce any crimes were capital and fines were certain, not inflicted at the pleasure of judges.

St. Edward resided sometimes at Winchester, sometimes at Windsor, or at London. Christmas being one of the chief feasts on which the nobility waited on the king, St. Edward chose that solemnity for the dedication of the new church at Westminster. The king signed the charter of the foundation and of the immunities and privileges granted to this church. Being taken ill before the ceremony of dedication was over, he continued to assist at it to the end. He then betook himself to his bed, and prepared himself for his passage to eternity. In his last moments seeing his nobles all bathed in tears round his bed, and his affectionate and virtuous queen sobbing more vehemently than the rest, commending her to her brother Harold and certain other lords, he declared he left her a virgin. He calmly expired on the 5th January, in 1066, having reigned twenty-three years, in the sixty-fourth year of his age.

14 OCTOBER

St. Calixtus
OR CALLISTUS, POPE AND MARTYR
A.D. 222

The name of St. Callistus is rendered famous by the ancient cemetery which he beautified and which, for the great number of martyrs whose bodies were there deposited, was the most celebrated of all those about Rome. He was a Roman by birth and succeeded St. Zephirin in the pontificate in 217 or 218. Antoninus Carcalla, who had been the most barbarous oppressor of the people, having been massacred by a conspiracy raised by Macrinus, who assumed the purple in 217, the empire was threatened on every side with commotions. Julia Moesa, sister to Caracalla's mother, had two daughters, Sohemia and Julia Mammaea. The latter was mother of Alexander Severus, the former of Bassianus, who being priest of the sun was surnamed Heliogabalus, who prevailed for money with the army in Syria to proclaim his emperor; and Macrinus was defeated and slain in 219.

Heliogabalus, for his unnatural lusts, prodigality and gluttony, was one of the most detestable tyrants that Rome ever produced. He reigned only three years, being assassinated on the 11th of March 222. His cousin Alexander was for his clemency, modesty and prudence one of the best of princes. He had in his private chapel the images of Christ, Abraham and Orpheus, and learned of his mother to have a great esteem for the Christians. It reflects great honour on our pope that this wise emperor used always to admire with what caution the choice was made of persons that were promoted to the priesthood, whose example he often proposed to his officers and to the people, to be imitated in the election of civil magistrates. It was in his peaceable reign that the Christians first began to build

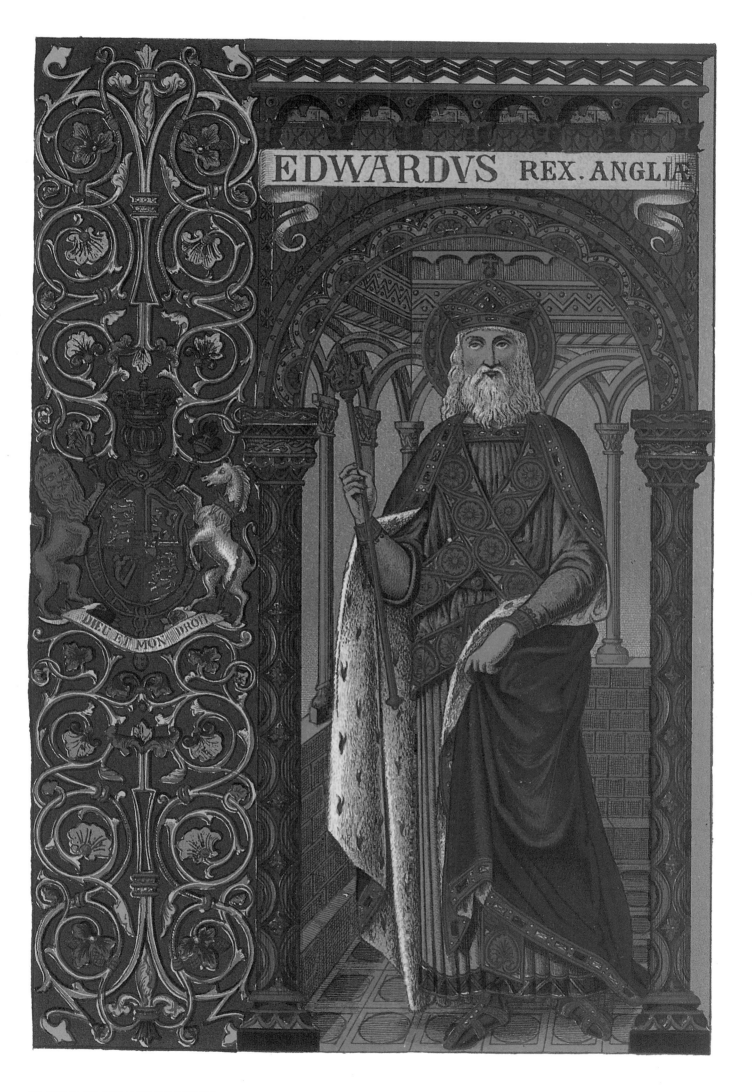

EDWARDVS REX. ANGLIÆ

PLATE 67. ST. EDWARD CONFESSOR, 13 SEPTEMBER. BUTLER, *LIVES OF THE SAINTS*, TWO-VOLUME ILLUSTRATED 19TH-CENTURY EDITION.

churches, which were demolished in the succeeding persecution.

To the debaucheries of Heliogabalus St. Callistus opposed fasting and tears. His apostolic labours were recompensed with the crown of martyrdom on the 12th of October, 222. The Liberian calendar testifies that he was buried on the 14th of this month three miles from Rome.

[Editorial note: Callistus is said to have been a slave whose master gave him a large sum of money to invest. Callistus lost the money and was sentenced to the treadmill. Although others among his creditors managed to get him released he was rearrested and sent to work in the mines of Sardinia. Eventually he was freed and returned to Rome where he entered the priesthood.]

15 OCTOBER

St. Teresa

A.D. 1582

St. Teresa was born at Avila, in Old Castile, on the 28th of March, 1515. Her father was of a good family and had three children by a first wife, and nine by a second, mother to our saint, who died when Teresa was twelve. About that time a certain cousin, a worldly young woman, began to visit her and wrought such a change in Teresa that forgetting her former devotions she gradually fell off from her fervour. Her father placed her in a convent, but after a year and a half the saint fell dangerously sick, and her father took her home.

After a violent fever (for she had often bad health) she determined to become a nun. She went privately to the convent of the Carmelite nuns without the walls of Avila, where her great friend sister Jane Suarez lived and made her profession in November, 1534.

St. Teresa, after having exercised herself twenty years in mental prayer, had frequent experience of interior speeches and was everywhere censured and ridiculed as an enthusiast or hypocrite. In 1559 St. Peter of Alcantara, coming to Avila, conversed several days with Teresa and discovered in her the most certain marks of the graces of the Holy Ghost. In her ecstasies revelations were imparted to her. In raptures she was sometimes elevated in the air. She sometimes saw Christ in the bosom of his Father, sometimes the Blessed Virgin and other saints, and frequently angels.

St. Teresa concerted a project of establishing a reform in her Order. Despite violent opposition from her fellow nuns, the nobility, magistrates and people, a married sister of the saint began with her husband to build a new convent at Avila in 1561. The pope's brief for the erection of her new convent was brought thither and towards the end of 1562 the bishop prevailed with the provincial to send Teresa to this new convent, whither she was followed by four fervent nuns from the old house. The general of the Order coming to Avila in 1566, was charmed with the wise regulation of the house and gave St. Teresa authority to found other convents upon the same plan.

St. Teresa declared prayer, silence, retirement and penance to be the four pillars of the spiritual edifice she had raised. She lived to see sixteen nunneries of her Reformed Order founded, and fourteen convents of Carmelite friars. She was returning to Avila, where she was prioress, when she was sent for by the Duchess of Alba. She was at that time very ill. Yet when she arrived at Alba she conversed with the Duchess several hours, then went to her convent in the town. She was seized with a flux, took to her bed, and never rose out of it any more. She expired on the 4th of October 1582, the next day (by the reformation of the calendar) being reckoned the 15th, the day afterwards appointed for her festival.

16 OCTOBER (17 OCTOBER)

St. Hedwiges

DUCHESS OF POLAND

A.D. 1243

The father of this saint was Bertold III, Marquis of Meran, Count of Tyrol and Prince of Carinthia and Istria. She was placed very young in the monastery of Lutzingen, and only taken thence, when twelve years old, to marry Henry, Duke of Silesia. She bore her husband three sons and three daughters. After the birth of her sixth child she engaged her husband to agree to a mutual vow of perpetual continence, from which time they never met but in public places. Her husband faithfully kept this vow for thirty years, during which time he never wore any gold, silver or purple, and never shaved his beard, from which circumstance he was surnamed Henry the Bearded.

The duke, at her persuasion, founded the great monastery of Cistercian nuns at Trebnitz. This building was begun in 1203, and was carried on fifteen years without interruption, during which time all the malefactors in Silesia, instead of other punishments, were condemned to work at it. The monastery was finished and the church dedicated in 1219.

The duchess practised in her palace greater austerities than those of the most rigid monks and exhausted her revenues in relieving the necessitous. Her desire of advancing in perfection put her upon leaving the palace with her husband's consent, and fixing altogether at Trebnitz near the monastery. Often retiring for some days into that house where she complied with all the penitential exercises of the community. She wore the same cloak and tunic summer and winter. She fasted every day except Sundays and great festivals. With going to churches barefoot, her feet were often blistered and left the ground stained with traces of her blood. Her example had so powerful an influence over her husband that he began in some degree to copy her virtues. He died in 1238, and from that time she put on the religious habit at Trebnitz and lived in obedience to her daughter Gertrude who, having made her religious profession in that house when it was first founded, had been chosen abbess.

Three years after the death of her husband she sustained a grievous trial in the loss of her eldest and most beloved son Henry who had succeeded his father. The Tartars having plundered their way through Russia and Bulgaria arrived at Cracow in Poland. Duke Henry assembled his forces at Legnitz and for some time drove the barbarians before him, but was slain. St. Hedwiges herself had retired to the fortress of Chrosne. Upon the news of this disaster, without letting fall a single tear, she said 'I thank you, my God, for having given me such a son. To see him alive was my great joy; yet I feel a still greater pleasure in seeing him united to you in the kingdom of your glory.' God was pleased to put a happy end to her labours by calling her to himself on the 15th of October, 1243.

THERESIA

PLATE 68. ST. TERESA, 15 SEPTEMBER, BUTLER, *LIVES OF THE SAINTS*, TWO-VOLUME ILLUSTRATED 19TH-CENTURY EDITION.

17 OCTOBER (1 FEBRUARY)

St. Ignatius

BISHOP OF ANTIOCH

A.D. 107

St. Ignatius was a zealous convert and an intimate disciple of St. John the Evangelist, as his acts assure us. During the persecution of Domitian, St. Ignatius defended his flock by prayers, fasting and daily preaching the word of God. He rejoiced to peace restored on the death of that emperor; but the governors of several provinces renewed the persecution under Trajan, his successor. That emperor, in the year 106, set out for the East on an expedition against the Parthians and made his entry into Antioch on the 7th of January 107. His first concern was about the worship of the gods, and he resolved to compel the Christians to sacrifice to them or suffer death.

Ignatius suffered himself to be taken and carried before Trajan who sentenced him to be bound and conducted to Rome, to be devoured there by wild beasts for the entertainment of the people. Having prayed for the church, Ignatius put on the chains and was hurried away by a troop of soldiers to be conveyed to Rome. On his arrival at Seleucia, a sea port about sixteen miles from Antioch he was put on board a ship. On

reaching Smyrna, he was suffered to go ashore to salute St. Polycarp, who had been his fellow disciple under St. John, and was met by deputies of several churches who were sent to salute him. From Smyrna St. Ignatius wrote four letters. In that to the church of Ephesus he exhorts the people to be subject in unanimity to their bishop and priests and to assemble as often as possible in public prayer, by which the power of Satan is weakened; to oppose only meekness to anger, humility to boasting and to suffer all injuries without murmuring. He calls the Eucharist the medicine of immortality, the antidote against death. The like instructions he repeats to the churches of Magnesia and of the Trallians. His fourth letter was written to the Christians at Rome to beg that they would not endeavour to obtain of God that the beasts might spare him. He writes, 'Though I am alive at the writing of this, yet my desire is to die. My love is crucified.'

The guards pressed the saint to leave Smyrna, that they might arrive at Rome before the shows were over. They sailed to Troas where he wrote three other letters to the church of Philadelphia, to the Smyrneans and to St. Polycarp. On landing, the faithful of Rome came out to meet him and he was hurried into the amphitheatre. The saint, hearing the lions roar, cried out, 'I am the wheat of the Lord; I must be ground by the teeth of these beasts to be made the pure bread of Christ.' Two fierce lions instantly devoured him, leaving nothing of his body but the larger bones. His martyrdom happened in 107.

18 OCTOBER

St. Luke

THE EVANGELIST

First century

St. Luke was a native of Antioch and acquired a stock of learning in his younger years, which we are told he improved by his travels in some parts of Greece and Egypt. St. Jerome assures us he was very eminent in his profession, and St. Paul, by calling him his most dear physician, seems to indicate that he had not laid it aside. Besides his abilities in physic, he is said to have been very skilful in painting.

St. Luke was a proselyte to the Christian religion, and wrote his gospel from the relations of those 'who from the beginning were eye-witnesses and ministers of the word'. No sooner was he enlightened but he set himself heartily to learn the spirit of his faith and practise its lessons. He became St. Paul's companion in his travels and fellow-labourer in the ministry of the gospel. The first time in his history of the missions of St. Paul he speaks in his own name in the first person, is when that apostle sailed from Troas into Macedon, in the year 51, soon after St. Barnabas had left him. Before this he had doubtless been for some time an assiduous disciple of that great apostle; but from this time he seems never to have left him unless by his order upon commissions for the churches he had planted. In his company he made some stay at Philippi, then travelled with him through all the cities of Greece.

About the year 56 St. Paul sent St. Luke with St. Titus to Corinth with this high commendation, that his praise in the gospel resounded throughout all the chuches. St. Luke attended him to Rome, whither he was sent prisoner from Jerusalem in 61. The apostle remained there two years in chains, but was permitted to live in a house which he hired, though under the

PLATE 70. ST. LUKE, 18 OCTOBER. BODLEIAN LIBRARY, MS. ADD. A 185, F. 15.

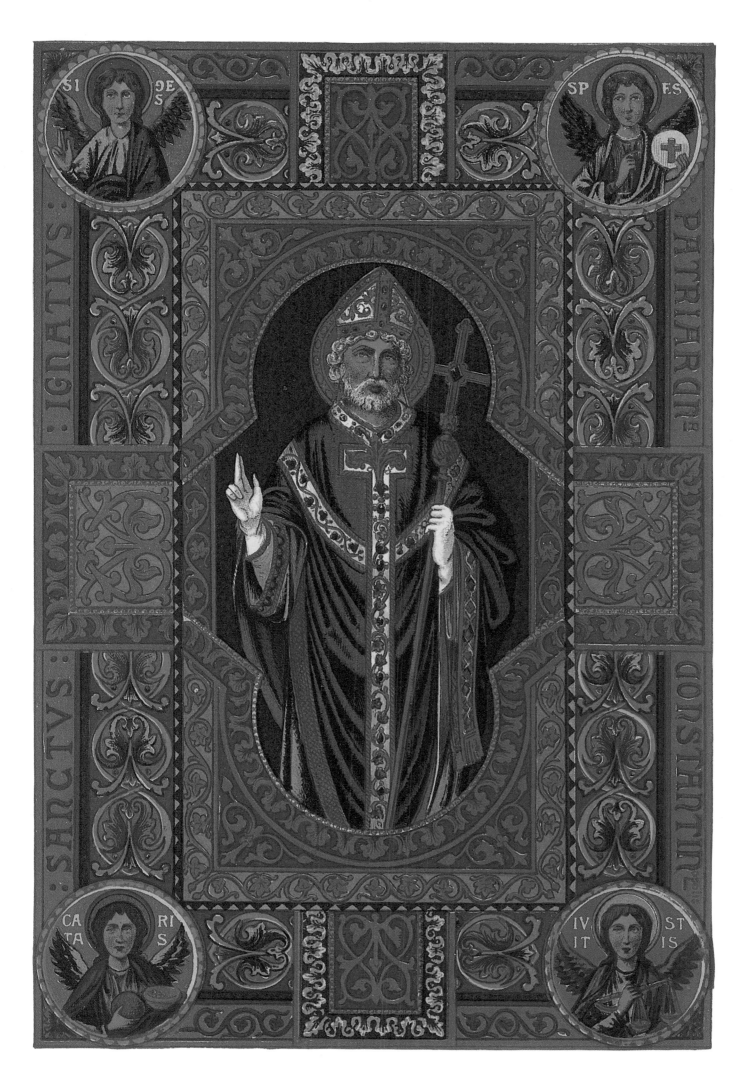

PLATE 69. ST. IGNATIUS OF ANTIOCH, 17 OCTOBER. BUTLER, *LIVES OF THE SAINTS*, TWO-VOLUME ILLUSTRATED 19TH-CENTURY EDITION.

custody of a guard; and there he preached to those who daily restored to hear him. St. Luke was the apostle's faithful assistant and attendant during his confinement, and had the comfort to see him set at liberty in 63.

St. Epiphanius says that after the martyrdom of St. Paul, St. Luke preached in Italy, Gaul, Dalmatia and Macedon. Nicephorus says that he died at Thebes in Boetia, and that his tomb was shown near that place. The modern Greeks tell us he was crucified on an olive tree. The bones of St. Luke were translated from Patras in 357, by order of the Emperor Constantius, and deposited in the Church of the Apostles at Constantinople, together with those of St. Andrew and St. Timothy. Some of his relics are kept in the great monastery on Mount Athos in Greece.

25 OCTOBER

SS. Crispin

AND CRISPINIAN, MARTYRS
A.D. 287

The names of these two glorious martyrs are famous in France. They came from Rome to preach the faith in Gaul towards the middle of the third century, together with St. Quintin and others. Fixing their residence at Soissons, they instructed many in the faith of Christ, which they preached publicly in the day, at seasonable times; and worked with their hands in the night, making shoes, though they are said to have been nobly born, and brothers.

The infidels listened to their instructions and were astonished at the example of their lives, especially of their charity, disinterestedness, heavenly piety and contempt of glory and all earthly things; and the effect was the conversion of many to the Christian faith. The brothers had continued this employment several years, when the Emperor Maximian Herculeus coming into the Belgic Gaul, a complaint was lodged against them. The emperor, perhaps as much to gratify their accusers as to indulge his own superstition, and give way to his savage cruelty, gave order that they should be convened before Rictius Varus, the most implacable enemy of the Christian name, whom he had first made governor of that part of Gaul, and had then advanced to the dignity of prefect.

The martyrs were victorious over this most inhuman judge, by the patience and constancy with which they bore the most cruel torments, and finished their course by the sword about the year 287. They are mentioned in the Martyrologies of St. Jerome, Bede, Florus, Ado, etc. A great church was built at Soissons in their honour in the sixth century, and St. Eligius richly ornamented their sacred shrine.

[Editorial note: there is an improbable English tradition that Crispin and Crispinian escaped from the persecutions in Gaul and came to the town of Faversham in Kent, where there is an altar dedicated to them in the parish church. The house in which they are supposed to have lived and worked was still an object of pilgrimage up the the seventeenth century.]

26 OCTOBER (7 JANUARY)

St. Cedd

BISHOP OF LONDON
A.D. 664

St. Cedd was brother to St. Chad and long served God in the monastery of Lindisfarne. When Peada, the son of Penda, King of Mercia, was appointed by his father king of the midland English, he went to the seat of Oswi, king of the Northumbers, and was there baptized with all his attendants by Finian, Bishop of Lindisfarne. Four priests, St. Cedd, Adda, Betta and Diuma, were sent to preach the gospel to his people, the midland English.

St. Cedd, after labouring there some time with great success, was called from his mission to a new harvest. Sigebert, King of the East Saxons, paying a visit to Oswi, was persuaded by that prince to forsake his idols and was baptized by Bishop Finian. When he returned to his own kingdom, he entreated Oswi to send him some teachers, who might instruct his people in the faith of Christ. Oswi called St. Cedd and sent him with another priest to the East Saxons. When they had travelled over that whole province, and gathered numerous churches to our Lord, St. Cedd returned to Lindisfarne to confer with Bishop Finian, who ordained him bishop of the East Saxons. St. Cedd, going back to his province, pursued the work he had begun, built churches and ordained priests and deacons.

Two monasteries were erected by him in those parts, which seem afterwards to have been destroyed by the Danes and never restored. The first he founded near a city called Ythancester, which was swallowed up by the gradual encroaching of the sea. St. Cedd's other monastery was built at Tilbury. In a journey which he made to his own country, Edilwald, who reigned in Yorkshire, desired him to accept some land to build a monastery. St. Cedd pitched upon a place amidst craggy and remote mountains. Here he resolved first to spend forty days in fasting and prayer, to consecrate the place to God. This monastery, being founded in 658, was called Lestingay. St. Cedd placed in it monks, with a superior from Lindisfarne; but continued to superintend the same and afterwards made several visits thither.

In 664 St. Cedd was present at the synod of Whitby, in which he forsook the Scottish custom, and agreed to receive the canonical observance of the time of Easter. Soon after, a great pestilence breaking out in England, St. Cedd died of it, in his beloved monastery of Lestingay, since destroyed by the Danes, so that its exact situation is not known. Thirty of the saint's religious brethren in Essex, upon the news of his death, came to Lestingay, in the resolution to live and die where their holy father had ended his life. They were willingly received, but were all carried off by the same pestilence, except a little boy, afterwards found not to have been baptized; he being in the process of time advanced to the priesthood, lived to gain many souls to God.

27 OCTOBER

St. Frumentius

APOSTLE OF ETHIOPIA
Fourth age

A certain philosopher named Metrodorus, out of a desire of

seeing the world, made several voyages and travelled into Persia and into farther India, which name the ancients gave to Ethiopia. His success encouraged Meropius, a philosopher of Tyre, to undertake a like voyage. He carried with him two of his nephews, Frumentius and Edesius, with whose education he was entrusted.

In the course of their voyage homewards the vessel touched at a certain port to take in provisions and fresh water. The barbarians of that country stopped the ship, and put the whole crew and all the passengers to the sword, except the two children who were studying their lessons under a tree at some distance. When they were found, they were carried to the king, who resided at Axuma, formerly one of the greatest cities in the East, now a poor village called Accum. The prince was charmed with the wit of the two boys, took especial care of their education, and not long after made Edesius his cupbearer, and Frumentius, who was the elder, his treasurer and secretary of state. They lived in great honour with this prince, who on his death bed thanked them for their services and gave them their liberty.

After his demise the queen, who was left regent for her eldest son, entreated them to remain and assist her in the government of the state. Frumentius had the principal management of affairs, and desiring to promote the faith of Christ in that kingdom, encouraged several Christian merchants who traded there to settle in the country, and by his own fervour and example strongly recommended the true religion to the infidels.

When the young king came to age and took the reins of government into his own hands, the brothers resigned their posts, and though he invited them to stay, Edesius went back to Tyre, where he was afterwards ordained priest. But Frumentius took the route of Alexandria and entreated the archbishop, St. Athanasius, to send some pastor to that country, ripe for a conversion to the faith.

St. Athanasius called a synod of bishops, and by their unamimous advice ordained Frumentius himself bishop of the Ethiopians, judging no one more proper than himself to finish the work which he had begun. Frumentius, vested with this sacred character, went back to Axuma, and gained great numbers to the faith by discourses; for seldom did any nation embrace Christianity with greater ardour, or defend it with greater courage. The Abyssinians honour him as the apostle of the country of the Axumites, which is the most considerable part of their empire.

28 OCTOBER

St. Simon

SURNAMED THE ZEALOT, AND ST. JUDE, APOSTLES

First century

St. Simon is surnamed the Cananean and the Zealot to distinguish him from St. Peter and from St. Simeon. From the first of these surnames some have thought that St. Simon was born at Cana, in Galilee, and certain Greeks pretend that it was at his marriage that our Lord turned the water into wine. Hammond and Grotius think that St. Simon was called the Zealot because he was one of that particular sect among the Jews called Zealots, from a singular zeal they possessed for the honour of God and the purity of religion. A party called Zealots were famous in the

PLATE 71. ST. SIMON AND ST. JUDE, 28 OCTOBER. BODLEIAN LIBRARY, MS LAUD MISC. 7, F. 167V

war of the Jews against the Romans. They were the main instruments in instigating the people to shake off the yoke of subjection.

St. Simon, after his conversion, was zealous for the honour of his Master, and exact in all the duties of the Christian religion. No further mention appears of him in the gospels than that he was adopted by Christ into the college of the Apostles. Some martyrologies place his martyrdom in Persia, and those who mention the manner of his death say he was crucified. St. Peter's Church on the Vatican at Rome, and the Cathedral of Toulouse are said to possess the chief portions of the relics of SS. Simon and Jude.

The apostle St. Jude is distinguished from the Iscariot by the surname of Thaddeus, which signifies praising or confession, also by that of Lebbeus, which is given him in the Greek text of St. Matthew. St. Jude was brother to St. James the Less; likewise of St. Simeon of Jerusalem and of one Joses, who are styled the brethren of our Lord. This apostle's kindred to our Saviour exalted him not so much in his Master's eyes as his contempt of the world and his sufferings for his sake.

It is not known when and by what means he became a disciple of Christ, nothing having been said of him in the gospels before we find him enumerated in the catalogue of the Apostles. After our Lord's ascension and the descent of the Holy Ghost, St. Jude set out to pull down the prince of darkness from his usurped throne. The martyrologies tells us that St. Jude preached especially in Mesopotamia. St. Paulinus says that St. Jude planted the faith in Libya.

This apostle returned to Jerusalem in the year 62 after the martyrdom of his brother St. James, and wrote a general epistle to all the churches of the East, particularly addressing himself to the Jewish converts. St. Peter had wrote to the same two epistles before this and St. Jude sometimes copied certain expressions of St. Peter.

Fortunatus and the western martyrologies tell us that St. Jude suffered martyrdom in Persia. Many Greeks say he was shot to death with arrows; some add whilst he was tied on a cross.

29 OCTOBER

St. Narcissus

BISHOP OF JERUSALEM
Second century

St. Narcissus was born towards the close of the first century, and was almost fourscore years old when he was placed at the head of the church of Jerusalem.

The veneration of all good men for this holy bishop could not shelter him from the malice of the wicked. Three incorrigible sinners, fearing his inflexible severity in the observance of ecclesiastical discipline, laid to his charge a detestable crime. They confirmed their atrocious calumny by dreadful oaths and imprecations; one wish he might perish by fire, another that he might be struck with a leprosy, and the third that he might lose his sight, if what they alleged was not the truth. Notwithstanding these protestations, their accusation did not find credit; and, some time after, the divine vengance pursued the calumniators.

Narcissus, notwithstanding the slander had made no impression on the people to his disadvantage, could not stand the shock of the bold calumny, or rather made it an excuse for leaving Jerusalem and spending some time in solitude, which had long been his wish. He spent several years undiscovered in his retreat, where he enjoyed all the happiness and advantage which a close conversation with God can bestow. That his church might not remain destitute of a pastor, the neighbouring bishops of the province, after some time, placed in its Pius, and after him Germanion, who, dying in a short time, was succeeded by Gordius.

Whilst this last held the see, Narcissus appeared again, like one from the dead. The whole body of the faithful, transported at the recovery of their holy pastor, whose innocence had been most authentically vindicated, conjured him to reassume the administration of the diocese. He acquiesced; but afterwards, bending under the weight of extreme old age, made St. Alexander his coadjutor. St Narcissus continued to serve his flock, and even other churches, by his assiduous prayers and his earnest exhortations to unity and concord, as St. Alexander testifies in his letter to the Arsinoites in Egypt, where he says that Narcissus was at that time about one hundred and sixteen years old.

30 OCTOBER

St. Marcellus

THE CENTURION, MARTYR
A.D. 298

The birthday of the Emperor Maximian Herculeus was celebrated in the year 298, with extraordinary feasting and solemnity. Pompous sacrifices to the Roman gods made a considerable part of this solemnity. Marcellus, a Christian centurion or captain in the legion of Trajan, then posted in Spain, not to defile himself with taking part in those impious abominations, cast away his military belt at the head of his company, declaring aloud that he was a soldier of Jesus Christ, the eternal King. He also threw down his arms and the vine-branch, which was the mark of his post of centurion; for the Roman officers were forbid to strike a soldier with any instrument except a vine-branch, which the centurions usually carried in their hands.

The soldiers informed Anastasius Fortunatus, prefect of the legion, by whose order Marcellus was committed to prison. When the festival was over, the judge ordered Marcellus to be brought before him, and asked him what he meant by his late proceedings. Marcellus said, 'When you celebrated the emperor's festival on the 12th before the calends of August, I said aloud that I was a Christian, and could serve no other than Jesus Christ, the Son of God.' Fortunatus told him that it was not in his power to connive at his rashness, and that he was obliged to lay his case before the Emperor Maximian and Constantius Caesar.

Spain was immediately subject to Constantius, who was at that time Caesar, and most favourable to the Christians; but Marcellus was sent under a strong guard to Aurelian Agricolaus, vicar to the prefect of the praetorium, who was then at Tangier, in Africa. Agricolaus asked him whether he had really done as the judge's letter set forth; and, upon his confessing the fact, the vicar passed sentence of death upon him for desertion and impiety, as he called his action. St. Marcellus was forthwith led to execution and beheaded on the 30th of October. His relics were afterwards translated from Tangier to Leon, in Spain, and are kept in a rich shrine in the chief parish church in that city, of which he is the titular saint.

1 NOVEMBER

ALL SAINTS

The church in this great festival honours all the saints together; first to give thanks to God for the graces of all his elect: secondly to excite ourselves to imitate their virtues: thirdly to implore the divine mercy through this multitude of intercessors.

It is in his saints that God is wonderful above all his other works. For them was this world framed: for their sakes is it preserved and governed. In the revolutions of states and empires, and in the extirpation of conservation of cities and nations, God has his elect chiefly in view. By the secret unerring order of his providence, 'All things work together for good to them.' For their sake will God shorten the evil days in the last period of the world. For the sanctification of one chosen soul he often conducts innumerable second causes and hidden springs. And with what infinite condescension and tenderness does the Lord of all things watch over every one of his elect! With what unspeakable invisible gifts does he adorn them! To how sublime and astonishing a dignity does he exalt them, making them companions of his blessed angels, and co-heirs with his divine Son! Weak and frail men, plunged in the gulf of sin, he, by his oimnipotent arm, and by the most stupendous mercy, has rescued from the slavery of the devil and jaws of hell; has cleansed them from all stains; and by the ornaments of his grace, has rendered them most beautiful and glorious, and

PLATE 72. ALL SAINTS, 1 NOVEMBER. BUTLER, *LIVES OF THE SAINTS*, TWO-VOLUME ILLUSTRATED 19TH-CENTURY EDITION.

with what honour has he crowned them. His grace conducted them by humility, patience, charity, and penance, through ignominies, torments, pains, sorrows, mortifications, and temptations, to joy and bliss, by the cross to their crowns.

These glorious citizens of the heavenly Jerusalem he has chosen out of all the tribes of the children of Israel, and out of all nations, without any distinction, of Greek or barbarian; persons of all ages, showing there is no age which is not ripe or fit for heaven; and out of all states and conditions; in the throne amidst the pomp of wordly grandeur; in the cottage; in the army; in trade; in the magistracy; clergymen; monks, virgins, married persons, widows, slaves and freemen.

God obliges not men in the world to leave their business; on the contrary, he commands them diligently to discharge every branch of their temporal stewardship. The tradesman is bound to attend to his shop, the husbandman to his tillage, the servant to his work, the master to the care of his household and estates. But then, they must always reserve to themselves leisure for spiritual and religious duties.

3 NOVEMBER

St. Malachy
ARCHBISHOP OF ARMAGH
A.D. 1148

In the fifth century Ireland was converted from heathenism to Christianity; but in the ninth century it was infested by barbarians, who, under the name of Normans, ravaged at the same time the maritime districts of France, England and Scotland. It was in this state of the nation that this saint was born. Malachy was a native of Armargh. To learn more perfectly the art of living wholly to God, Malachy put himself under the discipline of a holy recluse named Imar, who led a most austere life in a cell near the great church of Armargh. This step in one of his age astonished the whole city and his friends reproached him. Soon many desired to be his companions. Malachy prevailed upon Imar to admit the most fervent among these petitioners and they formed a considerable community.

Imar and Celsus, Archbishop of Armargh, judged Malachy worthy of holy orders and the prelate obliged him to receive the priesthood when he was twenty-five years old. At the same time the archbishop made him his vicar to preach the word of God and to extirpate evil customs. Malachy renewed the use of the sacraments, especially of confession, of confirmtion, and regular matrimony.

The great Abbey of Benchor lay at that time in a desolate condition, and its revenues were possessed by an uncle of St. Malachy. This uncle resigned it to his nephew and by the care of the saint it became a flourishing seminary. St. Melachy, in the thirteenth year of his age, was chosen Bishop of Connor. After some years the city of Connor was taken and sacked by the King of Ulster; upon which St. Malachy with a hundred a twenty disciples retired into Munster and there built the monastery of Ibrac. Whilst our saint governed this family Archbishop Celsus was taken with that illness of which he died and appointed St. Malachy to be his successor. To obtain the confirmation of many things which he had done, he undertook a journey to Rome in 1139. In his way through France he visited Clairvaux, where he was so edified with the piety he discovered

in St. Bernard and his monks that he desired to join them. Pope Innocent II received him with great honour but would not hear of his petition for spending the remainder of his life at Clairvaux. He made him his legate in Ireland.

St. Malachy was received in Ireland with joy and discharged his office of legate with wonderful zeal, holding synods, abolishing abuses and working many miracles. Innocent II died before the two palls which he had promised could be sent. St. Malachy received a deputation to make a fresh application to the apostolic see. He determined not to cross the Alps without visiting his beloved Clairvaux. But when he arrived there he was seized with a fever and died on the 2nd of November, 1148.

4 NOVEMBER

St. Charles
BORROMEO, CARDINAL, ARCHBISHOP OF MILAN
A.D. 1584

St. Charles Borromeo was son of Gilbert, Count of Arona, and Margaret of Medici, and was born on the 2nd of October 1538, in the castle of Arona, upon the borders of Lake-Major [Maggiore]. Charles learned Latin and humanity at Milan and was afterwards sent to the university of Pavia where he studied the civil and canon law. On account of an impediment in his speech and his love of silence, he was by some esteemed slow, yet made good progress.

His uncle, the Cardinal of Medici, was chosen pope in 1559 and nominated him Archbishop of Milan when he was in the twenty-third year of his age. The pope, however, detained him at Rome, entrusted him with the administration of the ecclesiastical state and made him legate of Bologna, Romaniola and Ancona, and protector of Portugal, the Low Countries and the Catholic cantons of Switzerland.

In November 1562 the saint's elder brother was carried off by a fever. All his friends and the pope pressed him to resign his ecclesiastical dignities; but he was ordained priest before the end of that year. He founded the noble college of the Borromeos at Pavia, for the education of the clergy of Milan. The Council of Trent, which had been often interrupted and resumed, was brought to a conclusion in 1563, owing to the unwearied zeal and prudence of St. Charles Borromeo, who began to enforce the execution of all its decrees for the reformation of discipline.

The saint left Rome in 1565 and was received at Milan with the utmost joy. Soon after, he opened his first provincial council and set about the visitation of his diocese. He sold plate and other effects to the value of thirty thousand crowns and applied the whole sum for the relief of distressed families in the diocese, built seminaries and repaired churches and hospitals. His confessor was Gryffydd Roberts, a Welshman. St. Charles, by six provincial councils and eleven diocesan synods made excellent regulations for the reformation of the manners both of the clergy and people and established schools in which were three thousand and forty catechists and forty thousand and ninety-nine scholars.

In 1568 he took in hand the reformation of the Humiliati, a religious Order of which he was the protector. Having employed every means to annul the regulations which our saint had made, three provosts of that Order entered into a conspiracy to murder the archbishop. Whilst the prelate was at his devotions, an assassin discharged at him a blunderbuss but the shot pierced his clothes and stopped at his skin, leaving only a bruise. In 1575 the plague broke out, and though his vicars entreated him not to expose his life, he did not abandon his flock but for the destitute gave all his furniture, even the straw bed on which he lay.

He died on the night between the 3rd and 4th of November 1584.

5 NOVEMBER

St. Bertille

ABBESS OF CHELLES
A.D. 692

St. Bertille was born of one of the most illustrious families in Soissons, in the reign of Dagobert I. From her infancy she preferred the love of God to that of creatures and as she grew she learned to despise the world and earnestly desired to renounce it. Not daring to discover this inclination to her parents, she first opened herself to St. Ouen, by whom she was encouraged in her resolution.

Her parents conducted her to Jouarre, a great monastery in Brie, founded not long before by Ado, brother of St. Ouen, who took the monastic habit there and established a nunnery in the neighbourhood. St. Bertille was received with great joy and trained up in the strictest practice of monastic perfection. By her submission to all her sisters she seemed every one's servant and in her whole conduct was a model of humility, obedience and devotion. Though she was yet young the care of entertaining strangers, of the sick and of the children that were educated in the monastery was successfully committed to her. In all these employments she had acquitted herself with great charity when she was chosen prioress to assist the abbess.

When St. Bathildes, wife of Clovis II, refounded the abbey of Chelles near the Marne, four leagues from Paris, she desired the abbess to furnish a small colony of the most experienced nuns of Jouarre who might direct the novices. Bertille was sent at the head of this holy company and was appointed the first abbess of Chelles in 646, or thereabouts. The reputation of the sanctity of our saint drew several foreign princesses thither. Among others Bede mentions Hereswith, Queen of the East Angles, who in 646 became a nun at Chelles. Queen Bathildes, after the death of her husband in 655, was left regent of the kingdom during the minority of her son, but as soon as he was of age to govern in 665 she retired thither, took the religious habit from the hands of St. Bertille, and obeyed her as if she had been the last sister in the house.

St. Bertille governed this great monastery for the space of forty-six years with equal vigour and discretion. In her old age, far from abating her fervour, she strove daily to redouble it. In these holy dispositions the saint closed her penitential life in 692.

PLATE 73. ST. LEONARD, 6 NOVEMBER. BRITISH LIBRARY, ADD. MS 54782, F. 39

6 NOVEMBER

St. Leonard

HERMIT
Sixth age

St. Leonard was a French nobleman in the court of Clovis I, and in the flower of his age was converted to the faith by St. Remigius, probably after the battle of Tolbiac. He resolved to lay aside all wordly pursuits, quitted the court, and became a constant disciple of St. Remigius. He preached the faith some time, but finding it very difficult to resist the king's importunities, who would need call him to court, and burning with a desire of giving himself up entirely to the exercises of penance and contemplation, he retired privately into the territory of Orleans, where St. Mesmin governed the monastery of Micy. In this house St. Leonard took the religious habit.

St. Leonard aspiring after a closer solitude, with the leave of St. Mesmin, left his monastery, travelled through Berry, and coming into Limousin, chose for his retirement a forest four leagues from Limoges. Here, in a place called Nobiliac, he built himself an oratory, lived on wild herbs and fruit and had no other witness of his virtues but God alone. His devotion sometimes carried him to neighbouring churches, and some who by his discourses were inflamed with a desire of imitating his manner of life, joined him in his desert and formed a community, which in succeeding times became a flourishing monastery.

The reputation of his sanctity being spread very wide, the king bestowed on him and his fellow hermits a considerable part of the forest where they lived. The saint, even before he had retired to Micy, had been most remarkable for his charity towards captives and prisoners and he obtained of the governors the liberty of many. It is related that some were miraculously delivered from their chains by his prayers, and that the king, out of respect for his eminent sanctity, granted him a special privilege of sometimes setting prisoners at liberty. But the saint's chief aim in this charitable employment was to bring malefactors to a true sense of their sins and to a sincere spirit of compunction. When he had filled up his measure of good works, his labours were crowned with a happy death about the year 559, according to the new Paris breviary.

In honour of the saint his church enjoys still great exemptions from public burdens and exactions. Many other places in France bear his name, and many great churches in England of which he is the titular saint show his name to have been formerly no less famous in England. In a list of holidays published at Worcester in 1240, St. Leonard's festival is ordered to be kept a half-holiday, with an obligation of hearing mass and a prohibition of labour except that of the plough.

7 NOVEMBER

St. Willibrord

FIRST BISHOP OF UTRECHT
A.D. 738

St. Willibrord was born in Northumberland towards the year 658 and placed by his parents before he was seven years old in the monastery of Rippon. Willibrord had made great progress in learning, when, out of a desire for further improvement, in the twentieth year of his age, he went over into Ireland, where he joined St. Egbert and the blessed Wigbert. In their company he spent twelve years in the study of the sacred sciences.

St. Egbert had long entertained a desire of going to preach the gospel in Friesland or Lower Germany. But he was diverted from that design by persons of piety who engaged him to employ his labours in the islands between Ireland and Scotland. His companion, Wigbert, went in the meantime to Friesland and after two years came back without having met with any success. Willibrord, who was then about thirty-one and had been ordained a priest a year before, expressed a great desire to be allowed to undertake this dangerous charge. He was joined by St. Swidbert and ten other English monks in this mission.

Our twelve missionaries landed at the mouth of the Rhine. Pepin the Big, who had lately conquered part of Friesland, received courteously St. Willibrord and his companions. But Willibrord set out for Rome and cast himself at the feet of Pope Sergius, begging his blessing and authority to preach the gospel to idolatrous nations. The pope granted him the most ample licences and gave him a quantity of relics for the consecration of churches. St. Willibrord, under the protection of Pepin, preached the gospel with wonderful success in that part of Friesland that had been conquered by the French; so that after six years Pepin sent the saint to Rome with letters of recommendation that he might be ordained bishop. Pope Sergius ordained him Archbishop of the Friesians.

The holy man stayed only fourteen days in Rome, came back to Utrecht, and chose that city for his residence. In the second year after his consecration he founded in 698 the abbey of Epternac, which he governed to his death. Not content to have planted the faith in the country which the French had conquered he extended his labours in West Friesland, which obeyed Radbod, Prince of the Friesians, who continued an obstinate idolater. The apostle penetrated also into Denmark and purchased thirty young Danish boys, whom he baptized and brought back with him. In his return he was driven by stress of weather upon the pagan island called Fositeland (Heliogoland). One of his company was sacrificed to the superstition of the people and died a martyr.

After the death of Radbod in 719, Willibrord was at full liberty to preach in every part of the country. By the zealous labours of this apostle and his colleagues, the faith was planted in most parts of Holland, Zealand and the Netherlands. He died, according to Pagi, in 739 and was buried at Epternac.

PLATE 74. ST. LEO THE GREAT, 10 NOVEMBER. BUTLER, *LIVES OF THE SAINTS*, TWO-VOLUME ILLUSTRATED 19TH-CENTURY EDITION.

10 NOVEMBER (11 APRIL)

St. Leo

THE GREAT
A.D. 461

St. Leo, surnamed the Great, was descended of a noble Tuscan family, but born at Rome. Being made archdeacon of the church of Rome, he had the chief direction of the most important affairs under Pope Celestine. It happened that Aetius and Albinus, two generals of the Emperor Valentinian, were at variance in Gaul, and no one being so well qualified to compose their differences as Leo, he was sent upon that important commission. During his absence Sixtus III died in 440, and the Roman clergy cast their eyes upon him for their pastor, judging that he was the most worthy to be seated in the first chair of the church. He was invited to Rome by a public embassy, but it was forty days before he could arrive. The joy with which he was received is not to be expressed and he received the episcopal consecration on 29th September, 440. A hundred and one sermons preached by this pope are now extant. His one hundred and forty-one epistles are wholly employed in treating on important subjects of discipline and faith. He brought many infidels to the faith. His signal victories over the Manichees, Arians, Apollinarists, Nestorians, Eutychians, Novatians and Donatists are standing proofs of his zeal.

Many affairs in the churches of the East furnished this great pope with employment. But above all the rest, the rising heresy of Eutyches drew his attention. While the Eastern empire was distracted by heretical factions, the Western was harassed by barbarians. Attila the Hun, enriched with the plunder of many nations and cities, marched against Rome. In the general consternation Leo went to meet Attila in hopes of averting the dangers that threatened his country. Contrary to the expectations of every one, he received the pope with great honour, and through his suggestion, concluded a treaty of peace with the empire on the condition of an annual tribute.

In 455 the friends of Aetius (whose arrogance had given the emperor so much umbrage that he caused him to be assassinated) revenged the death of that general by the murder of Valentinian himself. His wife Eudoxia invited Genseric, the Arian Vandal king from Africa, to come and revenge the murder of her husband. Genseric arrived and found the gates of Rome open to receive him. St. Leo went out to meet him and prevailed with him to restrain his troops from slaughter and burning, and to content himself with the plunder of the city. After the departure of the Vandals, Leo sent priests and alms for the relief of the captives in Africa. He repaired the Basilica and replaced the ornaments of the churches which had been plundered. This great hope, for his humility, mildness, and charity, was reverenced and beloved by emperors, princes and all ranks of people. He filled the holy see twenty-one years, dying on the 10th November, 461.

PLATE 75. ST. MARTIN, 11 NOVEMBER. BODLEIAN LIBRARY, MS. ADD. A 185, F. 63.

11 NOVEMBER

St. Martin
BISHOP OF TOURS
A.D. 397

The great St. Martin was a native of Lower Hungary. St. Gregory of Tours places his birth in 316 or 317. His parents carried him with them in his infancy to Pavia whither they removed. His father was an officer in the army. Though his parents were idolaters, at ten years of age he made his way to the church and desired to be enrolled among the catechumens. An imperial order being issued to oblige the sons of veteran officers to bear arms, at fifteen years of age he was compelled to take the military oath and entered in the cavalry.

Of his compassion and charity St. Sulpicius has recorded the following example. One day, in the midst of a very hard winter he met at the gate of Amiens a poor man almost naked, trembling for cold and begging alms. By his charities to others Martin had nothing left but his arms and clothes; when, drawing his sword, he cut his cloak in two pieces, gave one to the beggar and wrapped himself in the other half.

He received baptism in the eighteenth year of his age, but still continued two years in the army. St. Martin, having quitted the camp, went to St. Hilary who had been made bishop of Poitiers. Martin was very desirous to pay his parents a visit. He converted his mother and many others, but his father remained in his infidelity. In Italy he heard that St. Hilary was banished; upon which news he chose a retreat near Milan where he entered upon a monastic life. Auxentius, the Arian invader of the see of Milan, soon became acquainted with his zeal for the orthodox and drove him out. Understanding in 360 that St. Hilary was returning to his bishopric he accompanied him to Poitiers. St. Hilary gave him a little spot of land two leagues from the city where our saint built a monastery, which seems to have been the first that was erected in Gaul. In the year 371 he was chosen the third Bishop of Tours and consecrated on the 3rd of July.

St. Martin in this new dignity continued the same austerity of life and meanness of dress. He lived at first in a little cell near the church and retired to a monastery which he built two miles from the city, which is the famous abbey of Marmoutier. He had in a short time about fourscore monks. He destroyed many temples of idols and immediately built churches or monasteries.

Whilst St. Martin was employed in making spiritual conquests, the Western empire was shaken with horrible convulsions. Neither St. Ambrose nor St Martin would communicate with Ithacius or those bishops who held communion with him because they sought to put heretics to death. Martin also besought the Emperor Maximus not to spill the blood of the guilty.

St. Martin was above four score years when he died on the 8th of November, probably in 397.

13 NOVEMBER

St. Homobonus
MERCHANT
A.D. 1197

Homobonus was son to a merchant of Cremona, in Lombardy, who gave him this name (which signifies Good Man) at his baptism. He trained him up to his own mercantile business in shopkeeping without any school education. By the advice of his parents Homobonus took to wife a virtuous virgin, who was a prudent and faithful assistant in the government of his household.

Charity to the poor is a distinguishing part of the character of every disciple of Christ and a tribute which the merchant owes to God out of his gains; and this was the favourite virtue of Homobonus. Not content with giving his tenths to the distressed, after the death of his father (of whom he inherited a considerable stock in trade, besides a house in the town and a small villa in the country) he seemed to set no bounds to his alms; he sought out the poor in their cottages, and whilst he cheerfully relieved their corporal necessities, he tenderly exhorted them to repentance and holy life. His wife sometimes complained that by his excessive alms he would soon reduce the family to beggary; but he mildly answered her, that giving to the poor is putting out money to the best interest, for a hundred fold, for payment whereof Christ himself has given us his bond. The author of his life assures us that God often recompensed his charities by miracles in favour of those he relieved, and multiplying his stores.

His abstinence and temperature were not less remarkable than his almsdeeds. The saint spent a considerable part of his time in prayer, so that his shop, his chamber, the street, and every place was to him a place of prayer. It was his custom every night to go to the church of St. Giles a little before midnight, and to assist at matins, which it was then usual for many of the laity to do; and he left not the church till after high mass the next morning. Sundays and holidays he always consecrated entire to his devotions.

On the 13th of November in 1197 he was present at matins, according to his custom, and remained kneeling before the crucifix till mass began. At the *Gloria in excelsis* he stretched out his arms in the figure of a cross, and soon after fell on his face to the ground, which those who saw him thought he had done out of devotion. When he did not stand up at the gospel, they took more notice of him, and some persons coming to his perceived that he had calmly expired. Sicard, Bishop of Cremona, after a rigorous examination of his virtues and miracles, went himself to Rome to solicit his canonization, which Pope Innocent III performed after the necessary scrutinies. The saint's body was taken up in 1356 and translated to the cathedral, but his head remains at the church of St. Giles.

St. Laurence
ARCHBISHOP OF DUBLIN
A.D. 1180

Laurence was youngest son to Maurice O'Toole, a rich and powerful prince in Leinster. He was but ten years old when his father delivered him up a hostage to Dermod, King of Leinster. The barbarous king kept the child in a desert place, where he was treated with great inhumanity; till his father being informed that his son was fallen into a bad state of health, obliged the tyrant to put him in the hands of the Bishop of Glendaloch, by whom he was carefully instructed in the service of God, and at twelve years of age sent back to his father.

Upon the death of the Bishop of Glendaloch, who was at the same time abbot of the monastery, Laurence, though but twenty-five years old, was chosen abbot, and only shunned the episcopal dignity by alleging that the canons require in a bishop thirty years of age. The saint governed his numerous community with admirable prudence, and in a great famine which raged during the first four months of his administration, was the saviour of his country by his boundless charities.

Gregory, the Archbishop of Dublin happening to die about the time that our saint was thirty, he was unanimously chosen to fill that see, and was consecrated in 1162. His first care was to reform the manners of the clergy and to furnish his church with worthy ministers. About the year 1163 he engaged the secular canons of his cathedral to receive the rule of Arouasia. Our saint took himself the religious habit, which he always wore under his pontifical attire and frequently made choice of Glendaloch for his retreats.

St. Laurence was obliged for the affairs of his church to go over to England, in order to make application to Henry II. The third general council of Lateran was held at Rome in 1179. St. Laurence went on from England to Rome and assisted at this council. The pope appointed him legate of the holy see in Ireland. As soon as the saint was returned home he found the whole country afflicted with a terrible famine which continued three years. The saint laid himself under an obligation of feeding every day fifty strangers and three hundred poor of his diocese.

Henry II was offended at Roderic, the Irish monarch, and our saint undertook another journey into England to negotiate a reconciliation between them. Henry would not hear of a peace and set out for Normandy. Laurence followed him to France, and Henry was at length so much moved by his piety that he left the whole negotiation to his discretion. Having discharged his commission, Laurence was obliged by a fever which seized him upon the road to stop his journey. He took up his quarters in the monastery at Eu and there he died on the 14th of November in 1180.

St. Margaret
OF SCOTLAND, QUEEN OF SCOTLAND
A.D. 1093

St. Margaret was little niece to St. Edward the Confessor and granddaughter to Edmund Ironside. Upon the death of the latter in 1017, Cnute the Dane caused himself to be acknowledged guardian to the infant sons of his late colleague, Edward and Edmund. Cnute sent the two princes to the King of Sweden, that they might by him be made away with. The Swede refused to imbrue his hands in their innocent blood and sent them to Solomon, King of Hungary, by whom they were kindly received. Edmund died, but Edward, marrying Agatha, sister to the queen, had by her Edgar, Christina, a nun, and Margaret. When Edward the Confessor was called to the throne in 1041 he invited Edward over from Hungary with his children. At the death of St. Edward many desired to raise Edgar, the lawful Saxon heir, to the English throne; but he was unable to make good his claim by arms and fled the kingdom. The ship in which he put to sea was driven by tempest upon the coast of Scotland, where Malcolm entertained him and his sister in the most courteous manner.

Malcolm was so much taken with the virtues of the Princess Margaret that he most impatiently desired to make her his royal consort. His consent being obtained, she was married, and crowned Queen of Scotland in 1070, being twenty-four years of age. The marriage was solemnized at the king's castle of Dumfermline. Malcolm was rough and unpolished, but neither haughty nor capricious. Margaret softened his temper, cultivated his mind, and inspired him with all Christian virtues.

God blessed this royal couple with a numerous and virtuous offspring, six boys and two daughters. The holy queen remembered that by the rank in which Providence had placed her the whole kingdom was her family. It was her first care to procure zealous pastors to be established in all parts of her dominions. Simony, usury, incestuous marriages and other abuses were banished. Charity to the poor was her darling virtue. Whenever she stirred out of her palace she was surrounded by troops of widows, orphans and other distressed persons; nor did she send any one away without relief. She erected hospitals for poor strangers. 'As to her own eating, it was so sparing that it barely sufficed to maintain life,' says Theodoric. 'In a word, her works were more wonderful than her miracles, though these were not wanting to her.'

Malcolm reigned thirty-three years and died in 1093. This misfortune was to the queen an affliction which only her virtue enabled her to bear with resignation. She lay at the same time on her death-bed. She was loosed from the bonds of her mortal body on the 16th of November, 1093. Her body was interred in the church which she had built in honour of the Holy Trinity at Dumfermline.

<table>
<tr><td>

17 NOVEMBER

St. Hugh
BISHOP OF LINCOLN
A.D. 1200

</td><td>

17 NOVEMBER (19 NOVEMBER)

St. Elizabeth
OF HUNGARY, WIDOW
A.D. 1231

</td></tr>
</table>

St. Hugh was born of a good family in Burgundy in 1140, lost his mother before he was eight years old, and was educated in a convent of regular canons situated near his father's seat. When he was nineteen, the abbot took the saint with him to Chartreuse. The retirement and solitude and the deportment of the monks kindled in Hugh's breast a strong desire of embracing that institute. Nor were the canons his brethren able to dissuade him; so that he secretly went back to Chartreuse and was admitted to the habit. The saint had passed ten years in his private cell when the general procuratorship of the monastery was committed to him: to which weighty charge the reputation of his prudence and sanctity was spread over all France.

King Henry II of England founded the first house of Carthusian monks at Witham in Somersetshire and sent to the great Chartreuse to desire that Hugh might be sent over to take upon him the government of this monastery. After much debating, and though the saint protested that he was most unfit for the charge, he was ordered by the chapter to England. As soon as he landed he went directly to Witham, and by the humility and meekness of his deportment gained the hearts of the most inveterate enemies of that foundation.

The see of Lincoln, having been kept by his majesty some years vacant, he was pleased to give leave to the dean and chapter to choose a pastor, and the election fell upon St. Hugh, who received the consecration 1186. As soon as he was raised to the episcopal chair he employed all the authority which his station gave him in restoring discipline, especially among his clergy. Good part of his time he always bestowed in relieving the necessities of the poor.

Henry II, a prince most impatient of advice, stood in awe of this holy prelate and received his admonitions with seeming deference. The king's foresters exercised an inhuman tyranny, putting to death or maiming any one who had killed a wild beast. A company of these rangers had laid hands on a clerk. St. Hugh excommunicated the head of them, which action Henry took very ill. The bishop demonstrated to him how he had had a regard purely to the service of God, and to the salvation of his majesty's soul, which incurred manifest danger if oppressors of the church were protected. The king was so moved as to remain perfectly satisfied.

Hugh with the same liberty exhorted King Richard I to shun incontinence and defended the immunities of the church in his reign and in that of King John who came to the throne in 1199. St. Hugh was sent ambassador by this latter into France to conclude a peace between the two crowns. In his return he arrived at London and was seized with a fever. He died on the 17th of November 1200.

Elizabeth, daughter to Alexander II, King of Hungary, and his queen, Gertrude, was born in 1207. Herman, Landgrave of Thuringia and Hesse, had a son born about the same time and named Lewis. This prince obtained a promise from the King of Hungary that his daughter should be given in marriage to his new-born son; and the princess, at four years of age, was sent to his court and there brought up. Herman dying when Elizabeth was only nine years old, the government fell into the hands of his widow in the name of her son, till he should be of age.

The saint was in her fourteenth year when Lewis returned home after a long absence, on account of his education. The eminent virtue of Elizabeth gave him the highest esteem for her person and not long after he solemnized his marriage with her. Conrac of Marpurg, a most holy and learned priest was the person whom she chose for her spiritual director. Elizabeth with her pious husband's consent, often rose in the night to pray. The rest of her time, which was not spent in prayer or reading, she devoted to works of charity. The austerity of her life surpassed that of recluses. Her meal frequently consisted only of bread and honey, or the like. She was a great enemy to rich apparel. In attending the sick, she cheerfully washed and cleansed the most filthy sores, and waited on those that were infected with the most loathsome diseases. In 1225, Germany being severely visited by a famine, she exhausted the treasury.

Purely upon motives of religion the landgrave took the cross to accompany the Emperor Frederic Barbarossa in the holy war to Palestine, but as he was going to embark, fell ill of a fever at Otranto and expired. Envy, jealousy and rancour broke loose at once against the virtuous landgravine. It was alleged that the saint had squandered away the public revenue upon the poor and that Henry, young brother to the late landgrave, ought to be advanced to the principality. Henry got possession and turned Elizabeth out of the castle. Reduced to the lowest ebb, she applied to a priest for relief, who received her into his little house. The abbess of Kitzingen, our saint's aunt, hearing of her misfortunes, advised her to repair to her uncle the Bishop of Bamberg. In the mean time the body of her late husband was taken up and carried into Germany. The princess entreated the barons and knights that attended it to use their interest with her brother-in-law to do her justice. This they did and Henry promised to restore to Elizabeth her dower and all the rights of her widowhood.

Her dower she converted to the use of the poor and she spent the last three years of her life in the most fervent devotion, charity and penance. The day of her happy death was the 19th November, in 1231, in the twenty-fourth year of her age.

PLATE 76. ST. ELIZABETH OF HUNGARY, 17 NOVEMBER. BUTLER, *LIVES OF THE SAINTS*, TWO-VOLUME ILLUSTRATED 19TH-CENTURY EDITION.

PLATE 77. ST. EDMUND, 20 NOVEMBER. BRITISH LIBRARY, ADD. MS 29704, F. 160V.

20 NOVEMBER

St. Edmund

KING AND MARTYR
A.D. 870

Though from 802 the kings of the West Saxons were monarchs of all England, yet several kings reigned in certain parts after that time, in some measure subordinate to them. One Offa was King of the East Angles, who resigned his crown to St. Edmund, at that time only fifteen years of age. The saint was crowned on Christmas Day in 855. Religion and piety were the most distinguishing part of her character. Monks and devout persons used to know the psalter without book, that they might recite the psalms at work, in travelling, and on every other occasion. To get it by heart St. Edmund lived in retirement a whole year in his royal tower at Hunstanton in Norfolk.

The holy king had reigned fifteen years when the Danes infested his dominions. Hinguar and Hubba, two brothers, the most barbarous of all the Danish plunderers, landing in England, wintered among the East Angles; then, having made a truce with that nation, they in summer sailed to the north and plundered with fire and sword Northumberland and afterwards Mercia. Out of a lust of rage and cruelty, and the most implacable aversion to the Christian name, they everywhere destroyed the churches and monasteries; and massacred all priests and religious persons. In the great monastery of Coldingham, beyond Berwick, the nuns fearing not death but insults which might be offered to their chastity cut off their noses and upper lips that appearing to the barbarians frightful spectacles of horror they might preserve their virtue from danger; the infidels spared their virtue but put them all to the sword.

In their march, amongst other monasteries, those of Bardney, Crowland, Peterborough, Ely and Huntingdon were levelled with the ground. The barbarians, reeking with blood, poured down upon St. Edmund's dominions, burning Thetford. The first town they met with, and laying waste all before them. The good king raised what forces he could, met the infidels near Thetford and discomfited them. But seeing them soon after reinforced, he disbanded his troops and retired towards his castle of Framlingham in Suffolk. In his flight he was overtaken and conducted to the general's tent. Terms were offered him prejudicial to religion and to his people, which the holy king refused to confirm, declaring that religion was dearer to him than his life. Hinguar caused him to be beaten with cudgels, then to be tied to a tree and torn a long time together with whips. The infidels made him a mark wantonly to shoot at, till his body was covered with arrows like a porcupine. Hinguar at length commanded his head to be struck off. Thus the saint finished his martyrdom on the 20th of November 870. The saint's head was carried off into a wood and thrown into bushes; but miraculously found by a pillar of light.

PLATE 78. ST. CECILY, 22 NOVEMBER. BRITISH LIBRARY, HARLEY MS 2897, F. 440V.

22 NOVEMBER

St. Cecily

A.D. 230

St. Cecily was a native of Rome, of a good family, and educated in the Christian religion. In her youth she by vow consecrated her virginity to God, yet was compelled by her parents to marry a nobleman named Valerian. Him she converted to the faith, and soon after gained to the same his brother Tibertius. The men first suffered martyrdom, being beheaded for the faith. St. Cecily finished her glorious triumph some days after them. Their acts, which are of very small authority, make them contemporary with Pope Urban I, and consequently place their martyrdom about the year 230; others, however, place the triumph of these martyrs between the years 176 and 180.

Mention is made of an ancient church of St. Cecily in Rome in the fifth century. Pope Paschal I began to rebuild it; but was in some pain how he should find the body of the saint, for it was thought that the Lombards had taken it away. One Sunday, as this pope was assisting at matins at St. Peter's, he fell into a slumber, in which he was advertised by St. Cecily herself that the Lombards had in vain sought for her body, and that he should find it; and he accordingly discovered it in the cemetery called by her name, clothed in a robe of gold tissue, with linen cloths at her feet, dipped in her blood. With her body was found that of Valerian, her husband; and the pope caused them to be translated to her church in the city; as also the bodies of Tiburtius and Maximus, martyrs. This translation was made in 821. Pope Paschal founded a monastery in honour of these saints, near the church of St. Cecily, that the monks might perform the office day and night. He adorned that church with great magnificence, and gave to it silver plate to the amount of about nine hundred pounds; and a great many pieces of rich stuffs for veils, and such kinds of ornaments; in one of which was represented the angel crowning St. Cecily, Valerian and Tiburtius.

St. Cecily from her assiduity in singing the divine praises (in which, according to her Acts, she often joined instrumental music with vocal), is regarded as patroness of church music.

23 NOVEMBER

St. Clement

POPE

A.D. 100

St. Clement, the son of Faustinus, a Roman by birth, was of Jewish extraction, for he tells us himself that he was of the race of Jacob. He was converted to the faith by St. Peter or St. Paul and was so constant in his attendance on these apostles, and so active in assisting them in their ministry that St. Jerome and other fathers called him an apostolic man. St. Paul calls him his fellow-labourer, and ranks him among those whose names are written in the book of life.

St. Clement followed St. Paul to Rome, where he also heard St. Peter preach. Tertullian tells us that St. Peter ordained him bishop, by which some understand that he made him a bishop of nations, to preach the gospel in many countries; others that he made him his vicar at Rome, to govern that church during his absence in his frequent missions. After the martyrdom of SS. Peter and Paul, St. Linus was appointed Bishop of Rome, and after eleven years succeeded by St. Cletus. Upon his demise in 89 or 91, St. Clement was placed in the apostolic chair.

At Corinth, an impious and detestable division happened amongst the faithful, and a party rebelled against holy priests and presumed to depose them. It seems to have been soon after the death of Domitian in 96 that St. Clement in the name of the church of Rome wrote to them his excellent epistle, a piece highly extolled in the primitive church as an admirable work. St. Clement begins his letter by conciliating the benevolence of those who were at variance. The saint laments that they were fallen into pride, envy, strife and sedition and exhorts them to lay aside all anger, for Christ is theirs who are humble.

We have a large fragment of a second epistle of St. Clement to the Corinthians. In it our saint exhorts the faithful to despise this world and its false enjoyments, and to have those which are promised us always before our eyes. Besides these letters of St. Clement, two others have been discovered which are addressed to spiritual eunuchs, or virgins.

St. Clement with patience and prudence got through the persecution of Domitian. The tempest increased under Trajan and it was in the year 100 that the third general persecution was raised by him. Rufin, Pope Zosimus and the council of Bazas expressly style St. Clement a martyr. Eusebius tells us that St. Clement departed this life in 100. From this expression some will have it that he died a natural death.

The ancient church of St. Clement in Rome, in which St. Gregory the Great preached several of his homilies, still retains part of his relics. It was repaired by Clement XI, but still shows entire the old structure of Christian churches, divided into three parts. the narthex, the ambo and the sanctuary.

PLATE 79. ST. CLEMENT, 23 NOVEMBER. BRITISH LIBRARY, ADD. MS 18851, F. 494.

PLATE 80. ST. CATHERINE OF ALEXANDRIA, 25 NOVEMBER. BUTLER, *LIVES OF THE SAINTS*, TWO-VOLUME ILLUSTRATED
19TH-CENTURY EDITION.

25 NOVEMBER

St. Catherine

VIRGIN AND MARTYR
SUPPOSEDLY FOURTH CENTURY

St Catherine glorified God by an illustrious confession of the faith at Alexandria under Maximinus II. Her acts are so much adulterated that little use can be made of them. The Emperor Basil in his Greek menology relates that this saint who was of the royal blood and an excellent scholar, confuted a company of the ablest heathen philosophers, whom Maximinus had commanded to enter into a disputation with her, and that being converted by her to the faith, they were all burnt in one fire. He adds that Catherine was at length beheaded. She is said first to have been put upon an engine made of four wheels joined together, and stuck with four sharp pointed spikes, that, when the wheels were moved, her body might be torn to pieces. The acts add that, at the first stirring of the terrible engine, the cords with which the martyr was tied, were broke asunder by the invisible power of an angel, and the engine falling to pieces by the wheels being separated from one another, she was delivered from that death. Hence the name of St. Catherine's wheel.

The body of St. Catherine was discovered by the Christians in Egypt about the eighth century. It was soon after translated to the great monastery on the top of Mount Sinai in Arabia, built by St. Helen. Falconius, Archbishop of San-Severino, speaks of this translation as follows: 'As to what is said, that the body of this saint was conveyed by angels to Mount Sinai, the meaning is that it was carried by the monks of Sinai to their monastery, that they might devoutly enrich their dwelling with such a treasure. – It is well known that the name of an angelical habit was often used for a monastic habit, and that monks, on account of their purity and functions, were anciently called "Angles".' From that time we find more frequent mention made of the festival and relics of St. Catherine. In the eleventh age, Simeon, a monk of Sinai, coming to Rouen to receive an annual alms of Richard, Duke of Normandy, brought with him some of her relics which he left there. The principal part of the mortal remains of this saint is still kept in a marble chest in the church of this monastery on Mount Sinai.

[Editorial note: the cult of St. Catherine of Alexandria was suppressed in the Roman Catholic church in 1969.]

27 NOVEMBER

St. James

SURNAMED INTERCISUS, MARTYR
A.D. 421

St. James was a native of Beth-Lapeta, a city in Persia. When his prince declared war against the Christian religion, this courtier had not the courage to renounce his royal benefactor's friendship; and rather than forfeit his favour, abandoned the worship of the true God, which he before professed. His mother and wife were extremely afflicted at his fall. Upon the death of King Isdegerdes, they wrote to him: 'We were informed that for the sake of the king's favour and for worldly riches, you have forsaken the love of the immortal god. Think where that king now lies, on whose favour you set so high a

value. And know that if you persevere in your crimes, you yourself will fall under that punishment, together with the king your friend. As for our parts, we will have no more commerce with you.'

James was deeply affected by reading this letter. He appeared no more at court; nor did he fear openly to condemn himself. His words were soon carried to the new king, who immediately sent for him. The saint boldly confessed himself a Christian. Vararanes reproached him with ingratitude, enumerating the many favours he had received from his royal father. St James calmly said, 'Where is he at present?' These words exceedingly exasperated the tyrant who threatened that his punishment should not be a speedy death, but lingering torments.

The king called together his ministers and judges in order to deliberate what new cruel death could be invented for the chastisement of so notorious an offender. The council came to a resolution that, unless the pretended criminal renounced, he should be hung on the rack, and his limbs cut off one after another, joint by joint.

The heathens conjured him to dissemble his religion. The martyr answered them, 'This death was very little for the purchase of eternal life.' At the loss of each part the martyr repeated the praises of God. Whilst he lay weltering in his own blood, his thighs were torn from his hips. Lying a naked trunk, and having already lost half his body, he still continued to pray, and praise God with cheerfulness, till a guard, by severing his head from his body, completed his martyrdom. This was executed on the 27th of November in 421. The Christians offered a considerable sum of money for the martyr's relics, but were not allowed to redeem them. However, they afterwards carried them off by stealth. They found them in twenty-eight different pieces.

29 NOVEMBER

St. Saturninus

MARTYR, BISHOP OF TOULOUSE
A.D. 257

St. Saturninus went from Rome by the direction of Pope Fabian about the year 245, to preach the faith of Gaul, where St. Trophimus, the first Bishop of Arles, had some time before gathered a plentiful harvest. In the year 250 St. Saturninus fixed his episcopal see at Toulouse. Fortunatus tells us that he converted a great number of idolaters by his preaching and miracles. This is all the account we have of him till the time of his martyrdom.

The author of his acts, who wrote about fifty years after his death, relates that he assembled his flock in a small church; and that the capitol, which was the chief temple in the city, lay in the way between that church and the saint's habitation. In this temple oracles were given; but the devils were struck dumb by the presence of the saint as he passed that way. The priests spied him one day going by, and seized and dragged him into the temple, declaring that he should either appease the offended deities by offering sacrifice to them, or extirpate the crime with his blood.

Saturninus boldly replied, 'I adore one only God, and to him I am ready to offer a sacrifice of praise. Your gods are devils, and are more delighted with the sacrifice of your souls that with those of your bullocks.' The infidels, incensed at this reply, abused the saint, and after a great variety of indignities, tied his feet to a wild bull, which was brought thither to be sacrificed. The beast being driven from the temple ran violently down the hill, so that the martyr's skull was broken, and his brains dashed out. His happy soul was released from the body by death, and fled to the kingdom of peace and glory, and the bull continued to drag the sacred body, and the limbs and blood were scattered on every side, till the cord breaking, what remained of the trunk was left in the plain without the gates of the city. Two devout women laid the remains on a bier and hid them in a deep ditch to secure them from any further insult, where they lay in a wooden coffin till the reign of Constantine the Great. Then, Hilary, Bishop of Toulouse, built a small chapel over his predecessor's body. Silvius, towards the close of the fourth century, began to build a magnificent church in honour of the martyr which was finished by his successor Exuperius who translated the relics into it. The martyrdom of this saint probably happened in the reign of Valerian, in 257.

30 NOVEMBER

St. Andrew

APOSTLE
FIRST CENTURY

St. Andrew was a native of Bethsaida, a town in Galilee, upon the banks of the lake of Genasareth. He was the son of Jonas, or John, a fisherman of that town, and brother of Simon Peter, but whether elder or younger the holy scriptures have not acquainted us. They had afterwards a house at Capharnaum, where Jesus lodged when he preached in that city.

It is no small proof of the piety of St. Andrew that when St. John Baptist began to preach penance, he was not content with going to hear him as others did, but became his disciple. He was with his master when John, seeing Jesus pass by said 'Behold the Lamb of God'. Andrew and another disciple of the Baptist went after Jesus. Turning back as he walked, and seeing them follow him, he said 'What seek ye?' They said they desired to know where he dwelt; and he bade them come and see.

Andrew, who loved affectionately his brother Simon, called afterwards Peter, could not rest till he had brought him to Christ that he might also know him. The brothers tarried one day with him to hear his divine doctrine, and the next day returned home again. From this time they became Jesus's disciples, not constantly attending upon him but hearing him frequently as their business would permit, and returning to their trade and family affairs again. Jesus wrought his first miracle at Cana and was pleased that these two brothers should be present. Our Saviour, meeting one day Peter and Andrew fishing in the lake, called them to a constant attendance saying that he would make them fishers of men. Whereupon they immediately left their nets to follow him and never went from him again.

After Christ's resurrection St. Andrew preached the gospel in Scythia. Several calendars commemorate the feast of the chair of St. Andrew at Patrae in Achaia. It is agreed that he laid down his life there for Christ. St. Sophronius, St. Gaudentius and St. Austin assure us that he was crucified. The body of St. Andrew was translated to Constantinople in 357 and deposited in the Church of the Apostles which Constantine the Great had built a little before.

It is the common opinion that the cross of St. Andrew was in the form of the letter X, composed of two pieces of timber crossing each other obliquely in the middle. That such crosses were sometimes used is certain; yet no clear proofs are produced as to the form of St. Andrew's cross.

The Scots honour St. Andrew as principal patron of their country, and there historians tell us that a certain abbot called Regulus brought thither from Patrae in 369, or from Constantinople some years later, certain relics of this apostle which he deposited in a church which he built in his honour, with a monastery called Abernethy where now the city of St. Andrew's stands.

1 DECEMBER

St. Eligius

BISHOP OF NOYON
A.D. 659

Eligius was born at Catelat, two leagues north of Limoges, about the year 588. His parents placed him with a goldsmith named Abbo, who was master of the mint at Limoges. Eligius was a youth of uncommon genius, arrived at an eminent skill in his profession, and became known to Bobo, treasurer to Clotaire II at Paris. This king gave the saint an order to make him a magnificent chair of state, took him into his household and made him master of the mint. His great credit at court hindered him not from attending his profession, and he was much delighted in making rich shrines for the relics of saints.

He had not been there long when he formed a resolution of entering a more devout and austere way of life. He gave all his ornaments to the poor and daily fed a great number at his own house. When he knew that a slave was to be sold in any place, he made haste thither and sometimes ransomed fifty or a hundred at a time, especially Saxons.

Clotaire dying in 628, his successor Dagobert frequently consulted the saint preferably to all his council about public affairs, which drew on him the envy of the whole court. But their calumnies served only to enhance Dagobert's veneration for him, though it was never in his power to make him rich, because all that the saint received was immediately employed in raising charitable and religious foundations. The first of these was the abbey of Solignac, which he built two leagues from Limoges, on a piece of ground granted him by the king for that purpose. Dagobert also gave our saint a handsome house at Paris, which he converted into a nunnery.

The sees of Noyon and Tourney, which then comprised Upper Picardy and all the provinces that lie between that country and the mouth of the Rhine, became vacant in 639, and St. Eligius was required to take upon him that arduous charge. King Clovis II, who had succeeded Dagobert, stood in need of such ministers; but St. Eligius obtained a delay of two years to prepare himself, during which time he was ordained priest. In this new dignity, the first year he employed in reforming his clergy. After this he turned his thoughts to the conversion of the infidels among the Flemings. A great part of Flanders was chiefly indebted to St. Eligius for receiving the gospel. He preached in the territories of Antwerp, Ghent and Courtray. Every year at Easter he baptized great numbers whom he had brought to the knowledge of the true god in the twelve preceding months.

The saint having governed his flock nineteen years was favoured with a foresight of his death and foretold it to his disciples. Seeing them weep, he said, 'Grieve not, my children. I have longed for this time and have wished for a releasement.' He expired on the 1st December, 659.

PLATE 81. ST. ANDREW, 30 NOVEMBER. BUTLER, *LIVES OF THE SAINTS*, TWO-VOLUME ILLUSTRATED 19TH-CENTURY EDITION.

PLATE 82. ST. ELIGIUS, 1 DECEMBER. BRITISH LIBRARY, EGERTON MS 859, F. 17.

3 DECEMBER

St. Francis Xavier

APOSTLE OF THE INDIES

A.D. 1552

Francis was born in Navarre at the castle of Xavier in 1506. A propensity to learning determined his parents to send him to Paris in his eighteenth year; where he entered the college of St. Barbara. Having studied philosophy two years, he taught at Beauvais college. St. Ignatius came to Paris in 1528 and entered the college of St. Barbara. This holy man had conceived a desire of forming a society devoted to the salvation of souls. In 1534 St. Ignatius and his six companions, of whom Francis was one, made a vow at Montmartre to visit the Holy Land and unite their labours for the conversion of the infidels. They arrived at Venice in 1537 and waited for an opportunity to embark for Palestine. Xavier was ordained priest and in 1538 was called by St. Ignatius to Rome to deliberate about the foundation of their Order.

The King of Portugal requesting men to be sent to plant the faith in the East Indies, our saint left Rome in March 1540 and arrived in Lisbon about the end of June. He set sail in April 1541, with at least a thousand persons, and they landed at Goa in May 1542. There were not four preachers in all the Indies; nor any without the walls of Goa.

Nothing more sensibly afflicted Francis than the scandalous deportment of the Christians; he therefore thought it best to open his mission with them. The reformation of the whole city of Goa was accomplished in half a year, when the saint embarked in 1542 and sailed to Cape Comorin. He had laboured about fifteen months in the conversion of the Paravas when he was obliged to return to Goa to procure assistants; and some he carried with him to the kingdom of Travancor, where he baptized ten thousand Indians in one month. Having preached in other islands, he made a considerable stay in the Moluccas and in 1548 landed in Ceylon, where he converted great numbers. There he took a resolution to go to Japan, and arrived at Cangoxima in August 1549. After a year he went to Firando, Amanguchi and Meaco. In two towns he narrowly escaped being stoned, but vast multitudes desired to be instructed and baptized. Our saint embarked to return to India in 1551, where he was received with the greatest joy. The missionaries he had dispersed before his departure had spread the gospel on every side.

St. Francis hoped to find means to land secretly in China, although the ports were narrowly guarded. The Portuguese at Sancian, fearing this attempt might be revenged by the Chinese on them, endeavoured to traverse the design. Whilst the voyage was deferred Xavier fell sick and retired into the vessel which was the common hospital of the sick. At last, on the 2nd of December 1552 he died. He was only forty-six years old.

4 DECEMBER

St. Barbara
VIRGIN AND MARTYR
A.D. 306?

This holy virgin and martyr is honoured with particular devotion in the Latin, Greek, Muscovite and Syriac calendars, but her history is obscured by a variety of false acts. Baronius prefers those who tell us that she was a scholar of Origen, and suffered martyrdom at Nicomedia in the reign of Maximinus I, who raised the sixth general persecution in 235. But Joseph Assemani shows the acts which we have in Metaphrastes and Mombritius to be most exact and sincere. By these we are informed that St. Barbara suffered at Heliopolis, in Egypt, about the year 306. This account agrees with the Emperor Basil's Menology, and the Greek Synaxary. Her name was given to an old monastery near Edessa.

[Editorial note: the feast of St. Barbara was suppressed in the Roman calendar of 1969. A legendary account of her life says that she was shut up in a tower by her father so that no man should see her. While her father was away she became a Christian, and enraged by this he reported her to the authorities. A judge ordered her father to kill her, but he was struck by lightning. For this reason St. Barbara came to be seen as the patron of those in danger of sudden death, and more particularly of being struck by lightning, mines or cannon-balls.]

5 DECEMBER

St. Sabas
ABBOT
A.D. 532

St. Sabas was born in Cappadocia, not far from Caesarea, in 439. His father was an officer in the army, and being obliged to go to Alexandria, recommended his son, with the care of his estate, to Hermias, the brother of his wife. This uncle's wife used the child so harshly that, three years after, he went to an uncle called Gregory, brother to his father. Gregory demanded also the administration of his estate, whence great lawsuits and animosities arose between the two uncles. Sabas took offence at these discords and retired to a monastery three miles from Mutalasca.

When Sabas had been ten years in this monastery, being eighteen years old, he went to Jerusalem. He passed the winter in the monastery of Passarion, but his great love of silence and retirement made him prefer the manner of life practised by St. Euthymius. He cast himself at the feet of that holy abbot, who judged him too young for his cluster of separate cells in the desert and therefore recommended him to the monastery below the hill about three miles distant. When he was thirty years of age, he obtained leave of St. Euthymius to spend five days a week in a remote cave. He left his monastery on Sunday evening, carrying with him palm twigs, and came back on Saturday morning with fifty baskets which he had made.

After the death of St. Euthymius a relaxation of discipline crept into that monastery; on which account Sabas retired into a desert towards the East. He chose his dwelling in a cave on the top of a high mountain, at the bottom of which ran the brook Cedron. After he had lived here five years, several resorted to him, desiring to serve God under his direction. He was at first unwilling to consent; but charity overcoming his resistance, he founded a new laura which consisted at first of seventy persons, and a little chapel. He had no priest in his community, and Sallust, Bishop of Jerusalem, compelled Sabas to receive that sacred character at his hands and established him superior-general over all the monks of Palestine who lived in several cells.

The eastern churches were then in great confusion. The emperor Anastasius supported Eutychian heresy and banished many Catholic bishops. The Patriarch Elias sent St Sabas to endeavour to stop this persecution. Sabas was seventy years old when he undertook this journey to Constantinople. He stayed all the winter and often visited the emperor to gain his point. In the ninety-first year of his age, at the request of Peter, patriarch of Jerusalem, he undertook a second journey to Constantinople in favour of the Christians of Palestine, who had been calumniated at court. Justinian, who then occupied the throne, granted him all his requests. Soon after his return to his laura he fell sick, and on the 5th of December 532 he died.

PLATE 83. ST. BARBARA, 4 DECEMBER. BUTLER, *LIVES OF THE SAINTS*, TWO-VOLUME ILLUSTRATED 19TH-CENTURY EDITION.

6 DECEMBER

St. Nicholas

ARCHBISHOP OF MYRA

A.D. 342

All accounts agree that Nicholas was a native of Patara in Lycia, a large province of Asia, in which St. Paul had planted the faith. Myra, the capital, three miles from Patara and from the sea, was an archi-episcopal see. This church falling vacant, the holy abbot Nicholas was chosen archbishop, and in that exalted station became famous by his extraordinary piety and zeal. The Greek histories of his life agree that he suffered imprisonment for the faith, and that he was present at the great council of Nicea and there condemned Arianism. The silence of other authors make many suspect these circumstances.

The history of the translation of his relics places his death in 342. He died at Myra and was buried in his own cathedral. Certain merchants of Bari, a sea port in the kingdom of Naples, sailed in three ships to the coast of Lycia; and watching an opportunity when no Mahometans were near the place, went to the church in which the relics of St. Nicholas were kept, which stood in a desert place and was guarded by a small community of monks. They broke open the marble coffin in which the sacred bones lay and carried them off to their ships. They landed at Bari on the 9th of May, 1087, and the sacred treasure was deposited in the church of St. Stephen. On the first day, thirty persons were cured of various distempers imploring the intercession of St. Nicholas, and from that time the tomb of St. Nicholas of Bari has been famous for pilgrimages. St. Nicholas is esteemed a patron of children.

[Editorial note: although little is known of the life of St. Nicholas, a number of legends grew up around him and these have resulted in his being regarded as patron saint of children, sailors, unmarried girls, and so on. According to one of these stories he miraculously restored to life three boys who had been murdered in a brine-tub. Another tells how he provided dowries for three unmarried girls so that they should not have to enter a life of prostitution.]

PLATE 84. ST. NICHOLAS OF MYRA, 6 DECEMBER. BODLEIAN LIBRARY, MS. ADD. A 185, F. 64.

7 DECEMBER

St. Ambrose

DOCTOR OF THE CHURCH
A.D. 397

Ambrose's father was prefect in Gaul. He was born in the city where his father resided about the year 340. His father dying whilst he was an infant, his mother returned to Rome. He learned the Greek language, became a good poet and orator and pleaded causes with so much reputation that Probus made him governor of Liguria and Aemilia. Auxentius, an Arian, had usurped the see of Milan, and the city was distracted by furious tumults. To prevent open sedition Ambrose thought it the duty of his office to go to the church where the assembly was held, where both Catholics and Arians unanimously proclaimed him Bishop of Milan. He was therefore first baptized, and after due preparation, received the consecration on the 7th of December 374.

St. Ambrose first applied himself to study the scriptures under the instruction of Simplicianus, a learned priest. He purged the diocese of Milan of the Arian heresy. In his discourses he frequently enlarged on the praises of virginity and executed three books *On Virginity* in 377, and wrote his treatise *Of Widows*, to exhort them to perpetual chastity. For Gratian he wrote *On the Faith* which is a confutation of the Arian heresy.

The Emperor Gratian was a zealous Christian; and St. Ambrose prevailed with him to remove the altar of victory out of the senate house. Yet this emperor did not sufficiently attend to business and Maximus, a general who commanded the troops in Britain, assumed the purple and passed with his army into Gaul in 383. Gratian fled and Maximus treated those of Gratian's party with great severity. The Empress Justina dispatched St. Ambrose upon an embassy to Maximus, who concluded with him a treaty. The Emperor Theodosius in the East in 388 declared war against Maximus, defeated him and restored the whole western empire to Valentinian who put himself entirely under the discipline of St. Ambrose.

St. Ambrose held a council in 390, and this was yet sitting when the news of a dreadful massacre committed at Thessalonica was brought. Theodosius was transported with passion and it was resolved that a warrant should be sent to the commander to let loose the soldiers against the city till about seven thousand persons should be put to death. St. Ambrose wrote him a strong letter, exhorting him to penance and the emperor made a public confession of his sin. Our holy bishop made the sacrament of penance a chief part of his pastoral care. Against the Novatian heresy he wrote his two books of Penance. He exhorts the faithful to very frequent communion and recommends to new believers to keep the mysteries secret. St. Augustine, who was baptized by St. Ambrose in 387, must have been present at these discourses which St. Ambrose made to the neophytes.

St. Ambrose died on the 4th of April, 397. He was about fifty-seven years old.

PLATE 85. ST. AMBROSE, 7 DECEMBER. BRITISH LIBRARY. ADD. MS 29704, F. 100V.

9 DECEMBER

The Seven Martyrs at Samosate

THIRD CENTURY

In the year 297 the Emperor Maximian, returning victorious from the defeat of the Persian army, celebrated the quinquennial games at Samosata, upon the banks of the Euphrates. He commanded all the inhabitants to repair to the temple of Fortune to assist at the solemn sacrifices to the gods. Hipparchus and Philotheus, persons of birth and fortune in the city, had some time before embraced the Christian faith. In a secret closet in the house of Hipparchus they made an image of the cross, before which they adored the Lord Jesus seven times a day. Five friends, much younger in years, named James, Paragrus, Habibus, Romanus and Lollianus, found them in this private chamber praying and asked them why they prayed at home when by the emperor's command all persons were commanded to go to the temple of Fortune to pray. They answered that they adored the Maker of the World. After much discourse together, the five young men declared they desired to be baptized.

On the third day of the festival the emperor enquired whether all had performed the duty of sacrificing. He was answered that Hipparchus and Philotheus had for three years constantly absented themselves from the public worship of the gods. Messengers coming to the house of Hipparchus found the seven assembled together. The emperor ordered that they should be chained, and kept in separate dungeons, without meat or drink, till the festival should be over.

The solemnity in honour of the gods being concluded, the emperor caused a tribunal to be erected in a meadow near the banks of the Euphrates and by his orders the confessors were brought before him. Upon their refusal to offer sacrifice, they were all stretched upon the rack and each received twenty stripes upon his back, and was then scourged with thongs upon the breast and belly. This being done they were carried back each to his own dungeon, with strict orders that no one should be allowed to see them and they should be furnished with just so much coarse bread as would keep them alive. In this condition they lay from the 15th of April to the 25th of June. Then they were again brought before the emperor, but looked more like carcases than living men. He told them that if they would comply he would have them carried to the palace and re-established in their dignities. They all prayed that he would not seek to draw them from Jesus Christ. The emperor then commanded that cords should be put across their mouths and bound round them and that they should be crucified.

Hipparchus died on the cross in a short time. James, Romanus and Lollianus expired the next day, being stabbed by the soldiers on their crosses. Philotheus, Habibus and Paragrus were taken down living and had huge nails driven into their heads.

11 DECEMBER

St. Damasus

POPE

A.D. 384

Pope Damasus is said to have been a Spaniard; which may be true of his extraction, but he seems to have been born at Rome. His father, either after the death of his wife or by her free consent, engaged himself in an ecclesiastical state and was successively reader, deacon, and priest of the parish Church of St. Laurence in Rome. Damasus served in the ministry in the same church.

Liberius died in 366, and Damasus, who was then sixty years old, was chosen Bishop of Rome. Soon after, Ursinus, who could not bear that St. Damasus should be preferred before him, got together a crowd of disorderly and seditious people and persuaded Paul, Bishop of Tivoli, to ordain him Bishop of Rome. Juventius, prefect of Rome, banished Ursinus, and Maximum, a magistrate, put several schismatics to the torture.

In 370, the Emperor Valentinian, to repress the scandalous conduct of ecclesiastics, who persuaded persons to bequeath legacies to the church in prejudice of their heirs, addressed a law of Damasus, forbidding the clergy of monks to frequent the houses of orphans and widows or to receive from them any gift, legacy or feoffment in trust. This edict Pope Damasus caused to be read in all the churches of Rome and he was very severe in putting the same in execution.

Arianism reigned in the East, though vigorously opposed by many pillars of orthodoxy. In the West it was confined to Milan and Pannonia. Utterly to extirpate it in that part of the world Pope Damasus in a council in Rome in 386 condemned Ursacius and Valens, famous Arian bishops in Pannonia, and in another in 370 Auxentius of Milan. The heresy of Apollinaris caused a greater breach, his name being first anathematized by Pope Damasus at Rome.

When St. Jerome accompanied Epiphanius and Paulinus to Rome, Damasus detained him near his person, employing him in quality of secretary. This pope, who was himself a very learned man and well skilled in the holy scriptures, encouraged St. Jerome in his studies.

St. Damasus rebuilt or repaired the church of St. Laurence where he had officiated after his father, and which to this day is called from St. Laurence, *in Damaso*. He likewise drained all the springs of the Vatican which ran over the bodies that were buried there, and he decorated the sepulchres of a great number of martyrs. In the few letters of this pope which we have out of the great number which he wrote, it appears that he was a man of genius and taste.

Having sat eighteen years, he died on the 10th of December, 384, being near fourscore years of age.

12 DECEMBER (21 AUGUST)

St. Jane Frances de Chantal

WIDOW AND ABBESS
A.D. 1641

The father of St. Jane de Chantal was Benignus Fremoit, one of the presidents of the parliament of Burgundy. President Fremiot was left a widower whilst his children were yet in their infancy; but he took such care of their education that no instructions were wanting for forming them in the practice of every religious duty. Jane, who at her confirmation was called Frances, was most tenderly beloved by her father, who gave her in marriage when she was twenty to the Baron de Chantal, then twenty-seven years old, an officer of distinction in the French army. The marriage was solemnized at Dijon and a few days after, she went with her husband to his seat at Bourbilly. She found a family which had not been much accustomed to regularity, which she made it her first care to establish.

The baron went out one day shooting; and his friends shot him in the thigh. He survived this accident nine days and expired in the arms of his disconsolate lady, who was left a widow at twenty-eight, with one little son and three daughters; besides which she had buried two children in their infancy. When the year of her mourning was expired her father sent for her to his house at Dijon. A year after this, she was obliged to go with her children to live with her father-in-law, the old Baron de Chantal, who was then seventy-five.

It happened in the year 1604 that St. Francis of Sales came to preach at Dijon, upon which occasion the devout widow made a visit to her father that she might have the opportunity of assisting at the sermons of that celebrated preacher. She began to entertain thoughts of renouncing the world. When she had disclosed this inclination to St. Francis he proposed to her divers religious Orders and mentioned his project of forming a new congregation of the Visitation of the Virgin Mary. She laid the foundation of her new institute at Annecy in 1610, the bishop having provided there a convent for that purpose. Two other devout women took the habit with her, and were joined soon after by ten others. St. Jane exhorted her nuns to complete in themselves by a spirit of prayer, the work which they began by humility, obedience and self-denial.

The affairs of her children and the foundation of many new convents obliged her often to leave Annecy. She governed her convent at Paris for three years from 1619 to 1622. In the following year the death of St. Francis was a grievous affliction to her. A pestilence raged violently two years at Annecy. The Duke and Duchess of Savoy endeavoured to engage our saint to provide for her safety by flight; but she could not be induced to abandon her flock and by her alms exceedingly alleviated the public calamity in that city. She died on the 13th of December, 1641.

13 DECEMBER

St. Lucy

VIRGIN AND MARTYR
A.D. 304

St. Lucy was born of wealty parents in the city of Syracuse and educated in the faith of Christ. She lost her father in her infancy, but Eutychia, her mother, took singular care to furnish her with sentiments of piety. She was yet very young when she offered to God the flower of her virginity. This vow, however, she kept a secret, and her mother, who was a stranger to it, pressed her to marry a young gentleman who was a pagan. The saint sought occasions to hinder this design from taking effect, and her mother was visited with a troublesome flux of blood under which she laboured four years without finding any remedy. At length she was persuaded by her daughter to go to Catana and offer up prayers to God for relief at the tomb of St. Agatha. St. Lucy accompanied her, and their prayers were successful. Hereupon our saint disclosed to her mother her desire of devoting herself to God in perpetual virginity and bestowing her fortune on the poor: and Eutychia, in gratitude, left her at full liberty to pursue her inclinations.

The young nobleman with whom the mother had treated about marrying her, came to understand this by the sale of her jewels and goods, and the distribution of the price among the poor, and in his rage, accused her before the governor as a Christian, the persecution of Diocletian then raging with the utmost fury. The judge commanded the holy virgin to be exposed to prostitution in a brothel-house; but god rendered her immovable, so that the guards were not able to carry her thither. He also made her an overmatch for the cruelty of her persecutors. After a long and glorious combat, she died in prison of the wounds she had received about the year 304.

Her festival was kept in England, till the change of religion, as a holy day of the second rank, in which no work but tillage or the like was allowed. St. Lucy is often painted with the balls of her eyes laid in a dish: perhaps her eyes were defaced or plucked out, though her present acts make no mention of any such circumstance. In many places her intercession is particularly implored for distempers of the eyes.

14 DECEMBER (24 NOVEMBER)

St. John

OF THE CROSS
A.D. 1591

St. John, by his family name called Yepes, was youngest child of Gonzales of Yepes and born at Fontibere, near Avila, in 1542. The death of his father left his mother destitute with three little children, whom she settled at Medina. John continued his studies in the college of the Jesuits, and at twenty-one years of age he took the religious habit among the Carmelite friars at Medina in 1563. When he arrived at Salamanca, to commence his higher studies, the austerities which he practised were excessive. It was his desire to be a lay brother, but this was refused him. In 1567 he was promoted to the priesthood.

St. Teresa was then busy in establishing her reformation of the Carmelites and heard of the virtue of brother John. She told him that she had received authority from the general to found two reformed houses of men, and that he should be the first instrument of so great a work. This was the beginning of the Barefooted Carmelite Friars. St. John, after tasting the first sweets of holy contemplation, found himself deprived of all sensible devotion. This spiritual dryness was followed by interior trouble of mind. He describes what a soul feels in this trial in his book *The Obscure Night*.

The convent in which St. Teresa had made her first profession at Avila had always opposed her reformation. Yet the Bishop of Avila thought it necessary that she should be made prioress there. She sent for St. John and appointed him the spiritual director of this house in 1576. The old friars looked upon this reformation as a rebellion against their Order and condemned St. John as an apostate. They sent soldiers who removed him to Toledo where he was locked up in a dark cell. He was released after nine months by the credit of St. Teresa. He had no sooner recovered his liberty but he was made superior of the convent of Calvary and, in 1579, founded that of Baeza. In 1588 he was chosen first definitor of the Order. God was pleased to finish his martyrdom by a second persecution from his own brethren. There were in the Order two fathers of great authority who declared themselves his enemies. One of them boasted that he had proofs to have him expelled the Order. This storm ceased when the informations were laid before the superiors, for they amounted to nothing which deserved any chastisement.

St. John, living in the practice of extreme austerities fell sick, and the provincial ordered him to go to Baeza or to Ubeda. The first had for prior a friend of the saint. The other was poor and the prior there was his enemy. The love of suffering made St. John prefer Ubeda. The unworthy prior treated him with the utmost inhumanity and locked him up in a little cell, though he later begged the saint's pardon. St. John died on the 14th of December 1591.

17 DECEMBER

St. Olympias
WIDOW
ABOUT THE YEAR 410

St. Olympias was born about the year 368, and left an orphan under the care of Procopius, who seems to have been her uncle; but it was her greatest happiness that she was brought up under the care of Theodosia, sister to St. Amphilochius, a most virtuous woman. Olympias was very young when she married Nebridius, treasurer of the Emperor Theodosius the Great; but he died within twenty days after his marriage.

Our saint was addressed by several of the most considerable men of the court and Theodosius was very pressing with her to accept for her husband Elpidius, a Spaniard and his near relation. She modestly declared her resolution of remaining single the rest of her days; the emperor continued to urge the affair, and after several decisive answers of the widow, put her whole fortune in the hands of the prefect of Constantinople, with orders to act as her guardian till she was thirty years old. At the instigation of the disappointed lover, the prefect ordered her from seeing the bishops or going to church, hoping thus to tire her into a compliance. She told the emperor that she was obliged to own his goodness in easing her of her heavy burden of managing her own money; and that the favour would be complete if he would order her whole fortune to be divided between the poor and the church. Theodosius restored to her the administration of her estate in 391. The use which she made of it was to consecrate the revenues to the purposes which religion and virtue prescribe. She embraced a life of penance and

prayer. Her dress was mean, her furniture poor and her charities without bounds.

The devil assailed her by many trials. Frequent severe sicknesses, most outrageous slanders and unjust persecution succeeded one another. Her virtue was the admiration of the whole church, as appears by the manner in which almost all the saints and great prelates of that age mention her. St. Amphilochius, St. Epiphanius, St. Peter of Sebaste and others maintained a correspondence with her. Nectarius, Archbishop, of Constantinople, created her deaconess to serve that church in certain functions of the ministry of which that sex is capable, as in preparing them for the altars, and the like. St. Chrysostom had not less respect for her and she was one of the last persons whom he took leave of when he went into banishment in 404. After St. Chrysostom's departure she had a share in the persecution in which all his friends were involved. Atticus dispersed and banished the whole community of nuns which she governed, for it seems, by what Palladius writes, that she was abbess or at least directress of a great monastery.

The other Palladius tells us that she died under her sufferings.

19 DECEMBER

St. Nemesion
MARTYR, AND OTHERS
A.D. 250

In the persecution of Decius, Nemesion, an Egyptian, was apprehended at Alexandria upon an indictment for theft. The servant of Christ easily cleared himself of that charge, but was immediately accused of being a Christian. Hereupon he was sent to the Augustal prefect of Egypt, and confessing his faith at his tribunal, he was ordered to be scourged and tormented doubly more grievously than the thieves; after which he was condemned to be burnt with the most criminal amongst the robbers and other malefactors, whereby he had the honour and happiness more perfectly to imitate the death of our divine Redeemer.

There stood at the same time near the prefect's tribunal four soldiers named Ammon, Zeno, Ptolemy and Ingenuus, and another person, whose name was Theophilus, who, being Christians, boldly encouraged a confessor who was hanging on the rack. They were soon taken notice of, and presented to the judge, who condemned them to be beheaded, but was himself astonished to see the joy with which they walked to the place of execution.

Heron, Ater, and Isidore, Egyptians, with Dioscorus, a youth only fifteen years old, were committed at Alexandria in the same persecution. First of all, the judge took the youth in hand, and began to entreat him with fair speeches; then he assailed him with various torments; but the generous youth neither would bow at his flatteries, nor could be terrified or broken by his threats of torments. The rest, after enduring the most cruel rending and disjointing of their limbs, were burnt alive. But the judge discharged Dioscorus on account of the tenderness of his years, saying he allowed him time to repent and consult his own advantage, and expressing that he was struck with admiration at the dazzling beauty of his countenance. In the Roman Martyrology, St. Nemesion is commemorated on the 19th of December, the rest of these martyrs on other days.

25 DECEMBER

The Nativity of Christ
OR CHRISTMAS DAY

All things were accomplished which, according to the ancient prophets, were to precede the coming of the Messiah when Jesus Christ, having taken human flesh, was born for the redemption of mankind.

A decree was issued by Augustus, and published all over the Roman empire, ordaining that all persons, with their estates and conditions, should be registered at certain places, according to their respective provinces, cities and families. The decree was given by the emperor for political views of state; but proceeded from an overruling order of providence that by this most public act it might be manifest to the whole world that Christ was descended of the house of David, and tribe of Juda. For those of his family were ordered to be registered at Bethlehem, a small town seven miles from Jerusalem.

The Blessed Virgin and St. Joseph, after a painful journey of at least four days in a mountainous country, arrived at Bethlehem. There they found the public inns already full; nor were they able to procure any lodgings in the town, everyone despising their poverty. Joseph and Mary, in this distress,

retired into a cave made on the side of a rock, which is called a stable because it served for that purpose. It is a common tradition that an ox and an ass were in it at that time. In this place the holy mother brought forth her divine Son, wrapped him in swaddling clothes and laid him in the manger.

God was pleased that his Son, though born on earth with so much secrecy, should be acknowledged by men. Who are they that are favoured with the honour of this call? These happy persons were certain shepherds. Whilst the proud were asleep in soft beds, an angel appeared to these humble poor men and said to them, 'Fear not: for behold I bring you good tidings of exceeding great joy, that shall be to all the people. For this day is born to you a Saviour, who is Christ the Lord, in the city of David.' They immediately hastened thither and found Mary, Joseph and the infant. Here they did homage to the Messiah, and then returned to their flocks, glorifying and praising God.

The popes on Christmas Day formerly said three masses, the first in the Liberian basilica, the second in the church of St. Anastasia, the third in the Vatican. This custom was universally imitated and is everywhere retained, though not of precept. That Christ was born on the 25th of December, Pope Benedict XIV proves by the authority of St. Chrysostom, St. Gregory of Nyssa, St. Austin, etc. He doubts not but the Greek church originally kept this festival on the same day; and he takes notice that among the principal feasts of the year it holds the next place after Easter and Whitsunday.

PLATE 86. THE NATIVITY, 25 DECEMBER. BRITISH LIBRARY, KINGS MS 9, F. 93V.

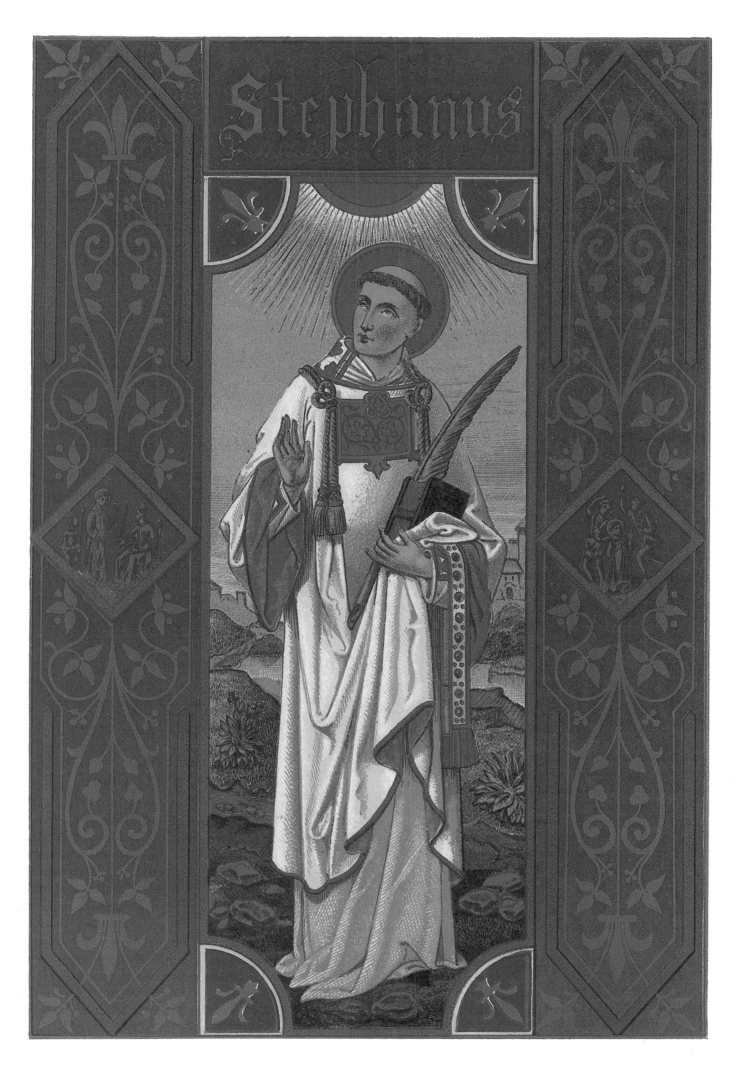

PLATE 87. ST. STEPHEN, 26 DECEMBER. BUTLER, *LIVES OF THE SAINTS*, TWO-VOLUME ILLUSTRATED 19TH-CENTURY EDITION.

26 DECEMBER

St. Stephen

THE FIRST MARTYR

FIRST CENTURY

That St. Stephen was a Jew is unquestionable, himself owning that relation. But whether he was of Hebrew extraction or of foreign parents incorporated and brought into that nation is uncertain. The name Stephen, which signifies a crown, is evidently Greek.

It is generally allowed that he was one of the seventy-two disciples of Our Lord, for immediately after the descent of the Holy Ghost we find him perfectly instructed in the law of the gospel. St. Stephen had the primacy and precedence among the deacons newly elected by the apostles and being filled with the Holy Ghost preached and pleased the cause of Christianity with undaunted courage. The successes of our holy deacons stirred up the malice and envy of the enemies of the gospel. The conspiracy was formed by the Libertines (or such as had been carried captives to Rome by Pompey, and has since obtained their freedom). At first they undertook to dispute with Stephen, but finding themselves unequal to the task they suborned false witnesses to charge him with blasphemy against Moses and against God. The indictment was laid against him in the Sanhedrim, and the saint was hauled thither.

After the charge was read, Caiphas, the high priest ordered him to make his defence. According to the licence given him he made his apology, but in such a manner as boldly to preach Jesus Christ in the Sanhedrim itself. He showed that Moses foretold a new law and the Messiah; that Solomon built the temple; but that the temple and the Mosaic law were temporary ministrations, and were to give place when God introduced more excellent institutions. This he had done by sending the Messiah; but as their fathers had persecuted and slain many of the prophets who foretold the Christ, so they had betrayed and murdered Him in person.

The saint, not heeding what was done below, had his eyes and heart fixed on higher things, and looking up steadfastly to the heavens, saw them open and beheld his divine Saviour ready to protect, receive and crown his servant. The Jews became more hardened and enraged by hearing the saint's declaration of this vision, and resolved upon his death without further process. In the fury of their blind zeal, they stayed not for a judicial sentence, nor for the warrant of the Roman governor, without which no one could at that time be legally put to death among them. But they with great clamour rushed upon him, furiously hauled him out of the city, and with a tempest of stones, satiated their rage against him. The holy martyr prayed, saying 'Lord Jesus, receive my spirit'. And falling on his knees, he cried out with a loud voice and the greatest earnestness, 'Lord, lay not this sin to their charge.' When he said this he had fell asleep in the Lord.

27 DECEMBER

St. John

APOSTLE AND EVANGELIST

FIRST CENTURY

St. John the Evangelist, who is styled 'the beloved disciple of Christ', was a Galilean, younger brother of St. James the great, with whom he was brought up to the trade of fishing. He is said to have been the youngest of all the apostles, probably about twenty-five when he was called; for he lived seventy years after the suffering of his Master.

After Christ's Ascension St. Peter and St. John were imprisoned, but released again with an order no more to preach, but no threats daunted their courage. They were sent to confirm the converts in Samaria. St. John was again apprehended by the Jews and scourged. When St. Paul went to Jerusalem in the fourteenth year after his conversion he addressed himself chiefly to Peter and John, who confirmed to him his mission. About that time St. John assisted at the council which the apostles held at Jerusalem in 51.

St. John seems to have remained chiefly at Jerusalem for a long time, though he sometimes preached abroad and took care of all the churches of Asia, which, St. Jerome says, he founded and governed. In the second general persecution in the year 95, St. John was apprehended by the proconsul of Asia, and sent to Rome, where he was miraculously preserved from death when thrown into a cauldron of boiling oil. The idolaters who pretended to account for such miracles by sorcery, blinded themselves to this evidence, and the tyrant Domitian banished St. John to the isle of Patmos, one of the Sporades. In this retirement the apostle was favoured with those heavenly visions which he has recorded in the book of the Revelations: they were manifested to him on a Sunday in the year 96. The first three chapters are a prophetic instruction to seven neighbouring churches of Asia Minor. The last three chapters celebrate the triumph of Christ. The intermediate chapters are variously expounded.

His exile was not of long continuance; for Domitian being slain in September 96, his successor recalled all those who he had banished. St. John returned to Ephesus where he was obliged to take upon him the government of that church, which he held till the reign of Trajan. The ancient fathers inform us that it was principally to confute blasphemies that St. John composed his gospel. Some think he wrote it in Patmos; but it is the more general opinion that he composed it after his return to Ephesus, about the year 98. This apostle also wrote three epistles.

St. John died in peace at Ephesus in the third year of Trajan (as seems to be gathered from Eusebius's chronicle), that is, the hundredth of the Christian era, the saint being then about ninety-four years old. He was buried on a mountain without the town. The dust of his tomb was carried away out of devotion and was famous for miracles.

PLATE 88. ST. JOHN, 27 DECEMBER. BODLEIAN LIBRARY, MS. ADD. A 185, F. 13.

28 DECEMBER

The Holy Innocents

Our Divine Redeemer was persecuted by the world as soon as he made his appearance in it. Herod, hearing from the magi who were come from distant countries to find and adore Christ that the Messiah was born, trembled lest he was come to take his temporal kingdom from him. The tyrant was disturbed beyond measure, and resolved to take away the life of this child. But God admonished the magi not to return to him. St. Joseph was likewise ordered by an angel to take the child and his mother and to fly into Egypt. It is an ancient tradition of the Greeks that at his entrance into Egypt all the idols of that kingdom fell to the ground, which literally verified the prediction of the prophet Isiah.

Herod, finding that he had been deluded by the magi, was transported with rage and anxious fears. To execute his scheme of killing the Messiah, he formed the bloody resolution of murdering all the male children in Bethlehem and the neigh-bouring territory which were not above two years of age. Soldiers were forthwith sent to execute these cruel orders, who, on a sudden, surrounded the town of Bethlehem, and massacred all the male children in that and the adjacent towns and villages. This more than brutish barbarity was accompanied with such shrieks of mothers and children that St. Matthew applies to it a prophecy of Jeremiah: 'A voice in Rama was heard, lamentation and great mourning: Rachel bewailing her children, and would not be comforted because they are not.' Rama is a village not far from this town, and the sepulchre of Rachel was in a field belonging to it. The slaughter also was probably extended into the neighbouring tribe of Benjamin, which descended from Rachel. The Ethiopians in their liturgy and the Greeks in their calendar count fourteen thousand children massacred on this occasion; but that number exceeds all bounds, nor is it confirmed by any authority of weight. These innocent victims were the flowers and the first fruits of Christ's martyrs, and triumphed over the world without having ever known it.

Herod lived not many days longer to enjoy the kingdom which he feared so much to lose. About the time of our Lord's nativity he fell sick. A fever violently burnt him within, and such an offensive smell exhaled from his body as shocked his best friends. He died five days after he had put his son Antipater to death.

PLATE 89. THE HOLY INNOCENTS, 28 DECEMBER. BRITISH LIBRARY, ADD. MS 54782, F. 139V.

29 DECEMBER

St. Thomas

MARTYR, ARCHBISHOP OF CANTERBURY
A.D. 1170

St. Thomas Becket was born in London in 1117. He pursued his studies in Oxford and Paris where he applied himself to the canon law. When he came back to London he was made secretary to the court of that city.

A strict intimacy had intervened between Theobald, who was advanced to the archbishopric of Canterbury in 1138, and our saint's father. Some persons therefore having recommended Thomas to that prelate he was invited to accept some post in his family. With the leave of the archbishop he went to Italy and studied a year at Bologna, then some time at Auxerre. After his return the archbishop ordained him deacon, and he was successively preferred to canonries at Lincoln and St. Paul's in London. The archbishop nominated him Archdeacon of Canterbury, sent him several times to Rome on important errands, and recommended him to the office of Lord-Chancellor of England, to which King Henry exalted him in 1157. Amidst the honours which he enjoyed, he always lived most humble, modest, charitable to the poor and perfectly chaste.

Theobald died in 1160. King Henry was then in Normandy with his chancellor, whom he immediately resolved to raise to that dignity. St. Thomas refused to acquiesce till the Cardinal of Pisa, legate from the holy see, overruled his scruples. The election was made in 1162, and the saint set out for Canterbury. St. Thomas first offended his majesty by resigning the office of chancellorship. But the source of mischief was an abuse by which the king usurped the revenues of vacant benefices, which injustice St. Thomas would not tolerate. A third debate was that the archbishop would not allow lay judges to summon ecclesiastical persons before their tribunals. The king told the archbishops that he would require of them an oath that they would maintain all the customs of the kingdom. Thomas understood that certain notorious injustices were called by the king 'customs' and refused that oath, but later complied in an assembly at Clarendon in 1164. He soon after repented. The king was extremely offended and declared all his goods confiscate. St. Thomas resolved to leave the kingdom and landed in Flanders in 1164.

It pleased God to inspire Henry with a desire of reconciliation, and having been seven years absent, the saint landed at Sandwich. The Archbishop of York accused St. Thomas to the king, who cried out that he wished to be rid of the one bishop who gave him more trouble than all the rest of his subjects. Four gentlemen, who had no other religion than to flatter their prince, conspired privately together to murder him. They went to Canterbury to the archbishop, who was then gone to church for it was the hour of vespers, entered sword in hand and stuck him down near the altar of St. Bennet. St. Thomas was martyred on the 29th of December in 1170.

PLATE 90. ST. THOMAS BECKET, 20 DECEMBER. BUTLER, *LIVES OF THE SAINTS*, TWO-VOLUME ILLUSTRATED 19TH-CENTURY EDITION.

31 DECEMBER

St. Sylvester

POPE

A.D. 335

St. Sylvester was a native of Rome, and son of Rufinus and Justa. His virtuous mother for his education in the maxims and practice of religion and in sacred literature, put him young into the hands of Charitius, or Carinus, a priest of great abilities. Being formed under an excellent master, he entered among the clergy of Rome, and was ordained priest by Pope Marcellinus, before the peace of the church was disturbed by Diocletian. His behaviour in those turbulent and dangerous times recommended him to the public esteem, and he saw the triumph of the cross by the victory which Constantine gained over Maxentius within sight of the city of Rome, on the 28th of October, 312.

Pope Melchiades dying in January 314, St. Sylvester was exalted to the pontificate, and the same year commissioned four legates, two priests and two deacons to represent him at the great council of the Western church held at Arles in August, in which the schism of the Donatists, which had then subsisted seven years, and the heresy of the Quartodecimans were condemned, and many important points of discipline regulated in twenty-two canons. These decisions were sent by the council before it broke up, with an honourable letter, to Pope Sylvester, and were confirmed by him, and published to the whole church. The general council of Nicaea was assembled against Arianism in 325. Socrates, Sozomen and Theodoret say that Pope Sylvester was not able to come to it in person on account of his great age, but that he sent his legates.

St. Sylvester greatly advanced religion by a punctual discharge of all the duties of his exalted station during the space of twenty-one years; and died on the 31st of December, 335. He was buried in the cemetery of Priscilla. St. Gregory the Great pronounced his ninth homily on the gospels on his festival, and in a church which was dedicated to God in his memory. Mention is made of an altar consecrated to God in his honour at Verona, about the year 500; and his name occurs in the ancient Martyrology called St. Jerome's. Pope Gregory IX, in 1227, made his festival general in the Latin church; the Greeks keep it on the 10th of January.

INDEX OF SAINTS

The following index contains the names of some of the principal saints of the Christian calendar, together with the dates of their lives, their patronages (if any) and the days on which their feasts are or were celebrated. Some of the major festivals are also included. Page numbers refer to entries in this volume.